THE ROCKY MOUNTAIN

Native Plant Primer

THE ROCKY MOUNTAIN Native Plant Primer

225 Plants for an Earth-Friendly Garden

BRYAN FISCHER
AND LAUREN SPRINGER

Timber Press
Portland, Oregon

Frontispiece: Native wildflowers and grasses mingle in Lauren Springer's dry prairie-inspired planting.
Opposite: Few things are as cheery as a sea of swaying coreopsis flowers.

All photos by the authors except for those listed on page 292.

Timber Press
Workman Publishing
Hachette Book Group, Inc.
1290 Avenue of the Americas
New York, New York 10104
timberpress.com

Timber Press is an imprint of Workman Publishing, a division of Hachette Book Group, Inc. The Timber Press name and logo are registered trademarks of Hachette Book Group, Inc.

Printed in Shenzhen, China (APO), on responsibly sourced paper
Text design by Mary Velgos based on a series design by Debbie Berne
Cover design by Sara Isasi based on a series design by Amy Sly

ISBN 978-1-64326-364-9
A catalog record for this book is available from the Library of Congress.

To my dad, Bill.

—Bryan

To my mom, who gifted me with her love of the natural world—a gift that never stops giving.

—Lauren

Contents

Introduction

If you've picked up this book, chances are you already know about the precipitous decline of insects, the perils facing migrating butterflies, the bulldozer fate of a wildflower field near your home, and the disheartening realities of a climate that is rapidly changing. You've probably also heard that including native plants in your garden offers many of the best resources for those native bees or that caterpillar, a new home for some of the same types of wildflowers from that field, and one of the homeowner's best tools for helping the natural world endure and maybe again flourish in this new geologic era: the Anthropocene, an era initiated and shaped by humans on the earth.

◀ A landslide of exuberant wildflowers celebrates the arrival of summer on a slope in the high country.

We, as horticulturists, plantspeople, and (perhaps most important) gardeners with a shared passion for nature and keen drive for observational learning, aren't interested in bringing the reader down with talk of what this world has lost. Rather, we've decided to focus this text on what the reader can do on their patch of land to make it a better place. Telling someone who is already interested in growing native plants why they should be growing native plants is, essentially, preaching to the choir. Instead, consider this book an empowering companion in the practice of gardening with native plants: one that can help you read between the lines of a black-and-white approach so frequently presented in pop and social medias and, just as importantly, guide you in understanding and applying valuable garden skills and concepts, all while providing insight as to which native plants may grow best in your home garden. We hope that not only our knowledge of these practices and plants, but also our joy and passion about them, kindles a similar fire in you or stokes flames already present. After all, we as gardeners aren't here to preach to any choir; we are here to join the chorus and make the world just a little better place in the process.

This book is based on our training, research, and—more than anything—experience and observations in the wild and in gardens we have designed and care for. Its scope is limited to our experiences. This ensures that all content we present is regionally relevant yet won't universally be true for all readers; not all plant-insect interactions, for example, are the same in all parts of the region; they often vary from one yard to the next. It is also important to note that we know about and can represent only a fraction of the varied important human uses, relationships, histories, and values of these plants, especially in relation to those of Indigenous peoples who have lived side-by-side with our region's flora for millennia. We as gardeners can tell our story, a very useful one to those wanting to garden with these plants, but it's only a small piece of the much bigger story between these plants, creatures, and people.

An indelible part of our region's identity, fall-glowing masses of aspen illuminate the Rockies with billowing, delicate-looking canopies that belie their tough nature.

What Is a Native Plant?

Before gardening with native plants, it's important to understand what makes a plant native. Much like the word "natural" in food marketing, the term does not have a set definition, and it's wise to consider a few different perspectives as opposed to taking any as absolute.

◂ Creamy yellow antelope bitterbrush rises through a cloud of blue mist penstemon just as spring gives way to summer.

Before Europeans renamed and colonized the Americas, plants here were, more or less, just plants. Calling any plant native would have been irrelevant, as relatively few—only ones that served as food, fiber, medicine, or had other cultural significances—had been moved around by humans. Plants rarely survived transcontinental journeys, unlike the many problematic weeds delivered in the last century or so. With the colonization of North America came a profound and widespread disturbance of natural habitats, fundamentally changing their suitability for plants already growing on the continent and the mobilization of plants here in new ways. For these reasons, among others, we define a native plant as a plant occurring within our region prior to European colonization.

Change as Constant

Crucial to this conversation, and easily overlooked with well-intentioned dogma focused on preservation, is the reality that change is here to stay. It's everywhere: seen in our fields and streams as introduced species, felt in our high country as more and widening mountain roads, and most pervasively experienced in our climate. Ongoing human-made changes to our climate are inevitable but remain uncertain in exact severity and impact. Regardless, a few broad concepts are worth keeping in mind when thinking about the phenomenon: precipitation patterns are changing while overall temperatures are climbing due to human-caused atmospheric modifications. Both variables—temperature and precipitation—are primary factors determining what plants grow best in any environment. Our native flora will have to adapt, move, or die due to anthropomorphic climate change, as they did in similar but slower shifts caused by the coming and going of ice ages. Studies have already shown plant communities climbing in elevation and latitude to remain in their preferred temperature bands as temperatures rise. It's possible that not all plants will climb fast enough or adapt quickly enough. And some, like those of the alpine biome, will literally run out of mountain to climb.

To complicate matters, this change—rapid warming—is also arriving on the heels of an Ice Age. As the period gradually developed, many plants we know today were forced south or to lower elevations, the impact of which can still be seen in plant range maps and recent plant-migration histories. Though the ponderosa pine is now the state tree of Montana, it returned to central Montana in just the last millenium after beginning the journey north from its glacial refugia in the Southwest around 13,000 years ago. If the ponderosa pine, a plant with the benefit of fast-moving birds to distribute its seeds throughout the Rockies, only just returned, what might that mean for plants without far-flying seed distributors? If this book could have been written two thousand years ago, would readers in Montana consider the ponderosa a native plant?

During its time restricted to the Southwest, the ponderosa pine would have grown shoulder-to-shoulder with a whole host of other species escaping glaciation's icy grip in the Rockies but also with species already present in the Southwest. There, the mixing of plants formed diverse, new plant communities we haven't seen since. In those communities, the ponderosa competed with some species but also created food and shelter for others. For this reason, we feel it isn't fair to a plant for us to assume that present-day ecosystem of origin is the only one in which a native plant has value: often, a species we know today has been a valuable member in several plant communities before settling into its current haunts. Though many convey a sense of permanence, plants and their communities aren't static. Many native species will go on to thrive in western communities they don't inhabit now, and a good number still will help form new communities, whether naturally occurring or in our gardens.

In recent years there has been increasing buzz surrounding growing the locally adapted forms of widespread native plants, called ecotypic seed or ecotypic plants. Historically, such plants are exquisitely adapted to local soils, climate, and precipitation patterns and bloom in sync with the arrival and habits of local animals and insects. That being said, some ecotypic seeds and plants may not be the best

The shrub steppe, sun, wind, and snow are reclaiming this once-thriving homestead in the Rockies.

adapted to your site—say, if your site has significant urban heat-island effect not historically present in the surrounding countryside, or if your site's soil has been gardened for decades or pulled up from the basement during construction. Similar mismatches may also hold true for some ecotypic seeds as climate change alters our environment.

We encourage readers to mull over what native means to them and to their landscape, as the term in plants is relative to both place and time. Some gardeners may wish to maintain a strict native-to-state or -site distinction, while others like Lauren and Bryan take a broader approach, including plants from across the plains, basins, and mountains of the interior West in their native plantings without dampening their enthusiasm for growing ecotypic plants. Ultimately, we encourage you to remember that a bluegrass lawn—a single Eurasian plant species—alongside a couple foundation plantings of shrubs is the baseline for the average suburban yard today. Almost any kind of native planting, whether native to your site, state, or the region, whether big or small, messy or tidy, is an impactful step in the right direction for plants and creatures alike.

An eagle takes flight from a stately narrowleaf cottonwood that has begun to transition toward its next phase in life: one defined by recession rather than growth, marked by the trunk splitting in two.

What to Know

The Big Picture: Defining the Rocky Mountain Region—Macroclimates and Hardiness Zones

It goes without saying that the Rocky Mountain region centers around the mountains lending the area its name. Using state boundaries, this book covers plants, landscapes, and concepts relevant from northern New Mexico and northern Arizona through Colorado, Utah, Wyoming, and on up through Montana and Idaho. That isn't the entire extent of this book, however: many of the largest population centers in these states are actually on plains and in large, lower-elevation basins between our mountains. And so, this book covers plants of and practices for not only the Rockies and Intermountain West but also the Great Plains; for many of our readers, they are inseparable.

◂ A lovely wild prairie matrix of annual gaillardia festooning a carpet of buffalo grass, accented by silvery threadleaf sage and handsome yucca.

This approach—including plants of the western two-thirds of the Dakotas, Nebraska, Kansas, Oklahoma, and the Texas Panhandle—also maximizes our ability as experts to help gardeners prepare for climate change. At present, much of the Rocky Mountain and High Plains region is forecast to grow warmer and slightly wetter than it is now, making the inclusion of plants from our region's southern margins particularly relevant to this book. Even with a net precipitation increase, higher temperatures will result in snowmelt occurring more quickly, making capture and use of irrigation water more difficult and keeping waterwise garden practices relevant for many years to come.

Biomes of the Region

As we've highlighted so far, native can mean many things, particularly in relation to scope of place and time. While using state and county boundaries to define what plants might be native is practical for a quick understanding, it isn't the most useful, as plants don't recognize these arbitrary human-made distinctions. Instead, they live in one or more of several broad communities that suit their adaptations. These biomes are shaped by natural forces and features, such as availability of water, intensity and duration of winter or summer, and physical features of the landscape, including mountain ranges and valleys. The sharp elevation changes in our region also result in biomes that change more abruptly than in much of North America, as well as higher plant diversity over a straight-line distance, giving native plant gardeners here the good fortune of a strikingly broad palette of plants to choose from.

Both of our gardens in the Fort Collins area, for example, were naturally dominated by shortgrass prairie prior to development. So, it's common that plants from prairies, be they from 60 miles away across the Wyoming border or 360 miles away from the plains of Kansas and Nebraska, grow most easily and provide more appropriate food and habitat for local critters than would a Colorado native plant from a very different biome, like the alpine, which may be only a 25-mile crow's-flight away. Such a plant, though a Colorado native, would languish in our summer heat, requiring quite a bit of supplemental water to compensate for lack of snowfall, and would struggle in our generally heavier soils. As a result, we both emphasize flora from the plains in our plantings. We also grow plenty of plants from elevation bands and biomes adjacent to ours, like pinyon-juniper, shrub steppe, and foothills communities, and can include plants from bands and biomes farther removed from ours with thoughtful use of microclimates and acceptance of a higher rate of failure.

In short, emphasizing plants from your garden's would-be biome—what would have been on your site before European colonization—but also from biomes similar to the current site will help you put together the right mix of natives. Since biomes typically blend with one another gradually, consider including plants from intergrading biomes—those with which yours blends—to significantly diversify your plant palette with site-appropriate plants. Many of us, like Lauren, live in places where ecosystems overlap and blend. She has naturally occurring species of plants and animals from both the plains and foothills biomes on her five acres at the edge of Fort Collins. She also extends the pollen and nectar season for insects and hummingbirds by planting late-blooming natives of late-summer and fall monsoonal areas in her spring-moisture location. Also, keep in mind that while the sunny places in your yard may be more like their original biome, shady places—in between tightly spaced houses or under large trees—may be more like a completely different biome. Since shade is rare on the plains, shrub steppe, and in pinyon-juniper biomes, gardeners with shady sites in those biomes may actually find that plants from another biome, such as the foothills or montane—where naturally occurring shade is common—grow best. With climate change at play, many of these zones are climbing in altitude and latitude, so growing some plants—especially long-lived plants such as trees, some grasses, and shrubs—from a bit farther "down the mountain" and/or farther south but that can handle your garden's current climate and winter lows will help hedge bets for a durable, regionally appropriate garden over coming decades.

Use the following guide for help determining to which of our region's life zones your garden might naturally default in the absence of human disturbance. The plant communities of this life zone sometimes pop up in vacant lots and appear in wild spaces around the edges of your community and, of course, the countryside around your home. In the plant-profiles section, we've noted from which life zones each featured plant originates so that you can use both to help you choose plants that may be a good fit for your site. Life zones in our high-elevation region develop relative to one another and begin at lower elevations moving north. For example, the alpine zone can occur as low as 6500 feet at our region's northern edge, while in the south it can start as high as 12,000 ft.

plains (including prairies and grasslands)

low elevations in our region

Example: Billings, Montana

The Great Plains or just "the Plains" are terms referring to the geologic feature that is the large expanse of relatively flat land in central North America. High Plains typically refers to the western half or so of this region, which rises in elevation as it approaches the Rockies. These terms are distinguished from "prairie," which references plants, not geology, in particular the grass-dominated plant communities of central North America. While arid grasslands also occur west of the Rockies, they are not generally considered prairie. We have designated all these biomes in plant profiles as "plains." The plains biome abuts and intergrades with foothills, shrub steppe, and pinyon-juniper biomes.

foothills

low to moderate elevations

Example: Golden, Colorado

A floristically diverse zone on the eastern slope of the Rockies, the foothills represent a blending of plains and montane plants mixed with a smattering of plant species found only in the foothills themselves. Dominant plant communities include ponderosa pine parklands, open meadows, and rich shrublands. This zone often receives more moisture than the plains and drains cold air better, resulting in protected pockets of relict plant communities, like patches of tallgrass prairie plants. The foothills biome intergrades with all other biomes except subalpine and alpine.

Perhaps more so on the plains than in any other biome, the horizon—broken only by occasional buttes and bluffs—creates a defining sense of scale and unique beauty.

In the foothills biome, grasses and wildflowers converge with shrubs and evergreen trees for a highly diverse and beautiful mingling of plant species.

pinyon-juniper woodlands

low to moderate elevations

Example: Santa Fe, New Mexico

Characterized by open woods of short, drought-adapted evergreens, pinyon-juniper woodlands occur on the eastern slope of the Rockies north to central Colorado, while on the western slope, they occur north into Idaho. A diversity of deciduous shrubs and shrubby trees grow between the often widely spaced evergreens, including a number of shrubby oaks seen more commonly in the Southwest. This zone intergrades with all zones except subalpine and alpine.

shrub steppe

low to moderate elevations

Example: Cody, Wyoming

High-elevation, arid shrublands occur in places too dry for grassland or forest, often between mountain ranges and in large, dry basins such as the Bighorn Basin of Wyoming. These locations can be among the chilliest in our region, enduring the settling of denser cold air from surrounding mountain ranges, and are known to experience high winds. The iconic "sagebrush sea" is emblematic of the shrub steppe, with each species of sagebrush exquisitely adapted to a specific soil depth or type in these areas. This zone intergrades with all zones except subalpine and alpine.

montane

moderate elevations

Example: Vail, Colorado

The montane biome contains the plant communities most folks think of when they hear "the Rockies," including pine parklands, lush meadows, and deciduous aspen woods. Soils are generally shallow, well-drained, and rocky on mountainsides, though deeper in valleys and basins. Snow holds through winter, and growing seasons in these places are short and cool. Grazing effects from elk and deer can be significant. The montane receives more precipitation than most of our region's zones and intergrades with all zones except plains and alpine.

Often underappreciated in the West, shrubs are a resilient group of plants forming the foundation of the shrub steppe biome, where they provide food and shelter for a host of other plants and animals.

Spectacular wildflower meadows with backdrops of grand peaks, such as this summer scene in South Park, Colorado, define much of the montane biome.

subalpine

high elevations

few human inhabitants

A transitional zone, the subalpine biome is a relatively small life zone that represents the highest elevation at which trees in our region can grow. Thanks to heavy and dependable winter snowfall, lush dense forests of tall, slender conifers dominate the lower portions of this region. Krummholz (German for bent/crooked wood) are stunted, shrublike evergreen trees shaped—as if bonsai—by relentless winds. These peter out at treeline, which defines the upper limit of this zone. The subalpine intergrades mostly with the montane and alpine zones.

alpine (above treeline)

highest elevations in our region

few human inhabitants

Above the krummholz, woody plants more than a few inches tall disappear. Buffeting, desiccating winds, exposure to extreme cold, and a severely short growing season, often combined with little in the way of reliable groundwater, result in communities comprised almost entirely of low-growing grasses, sedges, and wildflowers. Adapted to cool temperatures year-round, plants from the alpine are best suited for high-elevation gardens. Though often called tundra by locals, the alpine biome and tundra are not the same: though both occur above the range of trees (in latitude or altitude), alpine lacks permafrost, while tundra features growth-limiting permafrost. The alpine intergrades primarily with the subalpine zone.

watercourses, riparian habitats, and wetlands

all elevations

Although these are distinct habitats defined by access to water, they are lumped together in this book, as most plants from these areas thrive in similar garden conditions. These plants typically appreciate richer, moister soils than are common in our region. Many of these plants also provide excellent forage for large and small wildlife alike, remaining green and lush through summer's heat.

Cottonwoods line a canyon creek, creating a cool, shady oasis where wildlife can eat, drink, and rest.

Tolerant of periodic inundation, pale, watery blue iris flows like a river of its own alongside a swollen, meandering creek in this mountain parkland.

Hardiness Zones

Today, one of the first metrics used to determine if that cute flower or handsome sapling is a good fit for a garden is the hardiness zone listed on its tag at the nursery. For those who may not know, hardiness zones are numerical ratings given to plants by their tolerance for winter temperatures. Each number represents a 10-degree Fahrenheit range of average lows, and the numerical scale ranges from 1 (arctic conditions) to 13 (tropical conditions) and is often accompanied by a color-coded map. With the advent of the internet, this map can now also be searched by zip code, eliminating the eye-straining needed to guess one's zone using a four-inch-wide map of the entire country.

The United States Department of Agriculture creates this map by averaging the coldest temperature each winter for the last thirty years at each of many data-collection sites across the nation. Even accounting for updated technologies used to make the 2023 map that gives finer detail to each zone, especially in intensively variable regions like ours, the impact of a warming climate is easy to visualize. Grow zones defined by winter lows are steadily creeping north and higher in elevation.

We aren't highlighting this change for the sake of doom and gloom; great plants grow and will continue to grow in all these zones. Rather, it is important to understand how to use this changing gardening tool, including its limitations. That's because the hardiness zone system is one of the fastest ways to gain a general understanding for a plant's suitability for your site when shopping at the nursery, but it's only part of the picture for plant hardiness. Rate of temperature change (often faster here in the Interior West than in other places), duration of cold, and presence of other stressors, like drought, all impact a plant's ability to tolerate

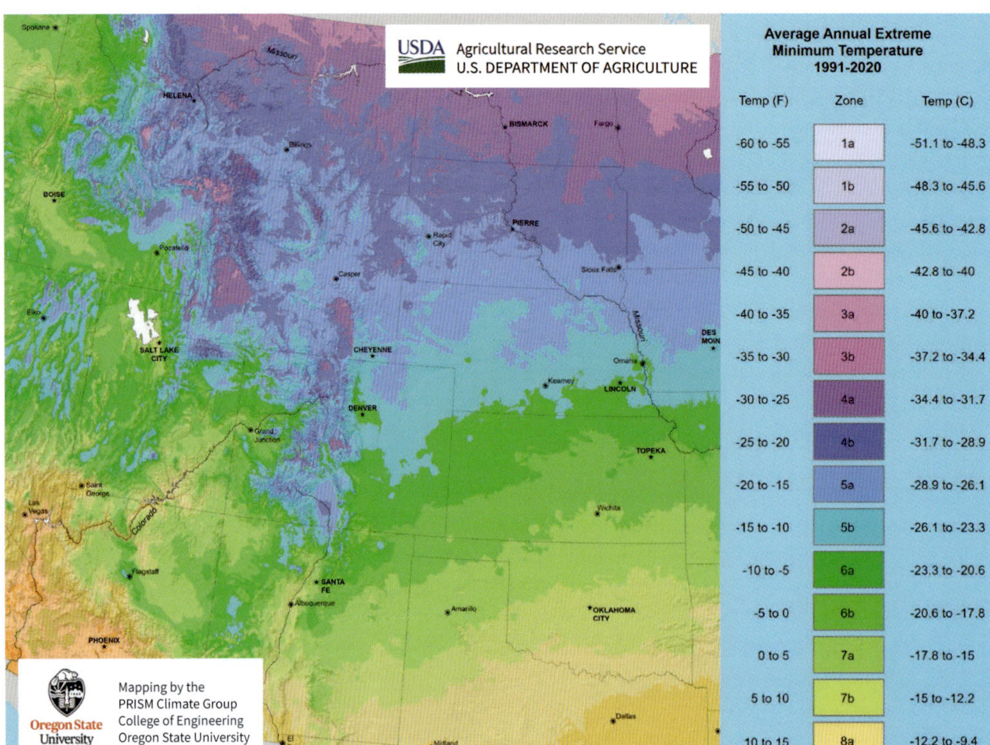

2023 USDA Plant Hardiness Zone Map

the reading on the thermometer. For these reasons, consider the hardiness zone map a guide and a useful starting point rather than the law when it comes to assessing how cold-hardy a given plant is. What's more, tolerance to winter cold is only one of several factors determining a plant's suitability for your landscape. The little picture—painted by summer heat, precipitation patterns and amounts, sun duration and intensity, soil type, and wind—impacts a plant's ability to succeed in a garden as well.

The Little Picture: Aspect and Microclimates

In the Rocky Mountain region, perhaps more so than in any other part of North America, a confluence of high elevation, intense solar radiation, and low humidity creates very distinct microclimates, even on the four sides of a house. A north side typically remains cooler, moister, and often windier in winter than other sides. A south side tends to be more protected from wind in winter and is the hottest and driest side year-round unless sheltered by mature shade trees. East is the most temperate, protected from harsh afternoon sun but still receiving the warming rays of the morning. West is wild with extreme fluctuations—some shade in the morning and then suddenly exposed to intense hot afternoon sunlight, and often buffeted by strong prevailing winds.

So, the four cardinal directions can make one small property feel as if it's in a baked New Mexican valley on the south side of the house and in the chilly Montana foothills on the north. You may be able to grow a healthy small glade of aspens, ferns, columbines, and wood lilies on the north side of the house and a thriving community of cacti, sage, paintbrush, and yuccas on the south.

The key to making the most of your microclimates is to be observant. Before making in-depth planting plans, watch sun and shadow patterns on your property over the four seasons, as those change a great deal. Pay attention to where snow tends to linger and where it melts off first, and if there are any seasonally moist or even wet areas. Out in the open, away from house, outbuildings, mature trees, masonry walls, or solid fences, the harsher effects of wind, dryness, and extreme heat or cold can intensify.

You can make use of or intentionally create even smaller microclimates on your property with slightly less pronounced effects than those caused by a house and other structures. Shrubs, boulders, slopes, and berms also have adjacent planting aspects with slightly different sun, temperature, and moisture levels. One of the simplest ways to learn about these special spots is to watch where, when, and what creatures do. Where do birds gather to shelter when the wind blows? Where does the dog lay on a hot summer afternoon? Where does the cat sunbathe on a cool spring morning? All these microclimates make for wonderfully diverse offerings to plants and creatures and a lot of fun for the gardener because they mean many plant options. And since our region is so varied in topography, climate, soil, and plant and animal communities, there are special native plants that have evolved to thrive in each microclimate you may have to offer.

Rocks protect snowball cacti from wind, while keeping the soil warmer in winter and cooler in summer, in the unwatered cactus area of the Undaunted Garden at The Gardens on Spring Creek in Fort Collins.

Soils

Most folks who grow up around gardeners, or as gardeners themselves, have the understanding that there are good soils—those with higher organic matter and higher fertility (dirt that looks like chocolate cake)—and bad soils—most everything else and including most soils in the West, ranging from heavy clays to thin sands. This notion stems from the fact that most of the people who passed this concept down did so with the understanding that soils were for growing crops more than for gardens, and regardless of whether one was to grow a crop or garden, a relatively small palette of plants was to comprise either. So, with a fixed plant palette, it made sense to modify the soil's characteristics to meet the needs of those plants.

Growing native plants presents a departure from a fixed plant palette into a whole new array of colors, forms, and botanical behaviors, all coevolved to thrive on native soils. Many of our native plants actually despise a so-called good soil and thrive only on a leaner, well-drained, mineral-influenced soil more reminiscent of their western haunts. So, throw out the notion of good and bad. Instead, approach your soil by understanding its texture (how big or small its particles are) and its organic-matter content (how much dead-plant material is already in the soil). We've indicated if a plant has a strong soil-type preference in its plant profile. With that information, you can modify your plant palette rather than your soil. So, say goodbye to the days of amending, fertilizing, and double-digging, and say hello to a whole new suite of garden denizens.

Determining the texture of your garden's soil isn't as daunting as it might first seem. With a bit of practice, a person can identify soil texture quickly and as accurately as is necessary for success with native plants. In most cases, understanding whether your garden's soil is fine-textured and dense (dominated by small, compaction-prone, poorly draining, nutritive clay particles) or coarse-textured and lighter (dominated by larger, well-draining, less nutritive silt or sand particles) suffices. One quick test is simply to water the garden deeply with a sprinkler. If the water pools during irrigation and soil then sticks to the shovel blade or comes out of a freshly dug hole in heavy clods, a fine-textured soil such as clay is likely. Seen occasionally on maps and in test results, loam soils have relatively equal particles of sand, silt, and clay, and so have physical properties in between fine- and coarse-textured soils. In addition, soils can receive sub-designations, like clayey-loam or silty-sand. In that case, the second soil type listed is the main soil texture but is influenced by the first. Clay particles have a disproportionately large impact on soil properties, so clayey anything can behave a bit like clay. If still unsure, consider sending a sample to your local land-grant university, or easiest of all, visit the fantastic online tool known as the Web Soil Survey, created by the United States Department of Agriculture's Natural Resources Conservation Service.

Due to their tendency to compact, clay soils shouldn't be worked in when wet. Bryan, who gardens on a clayey soil, irrigates the day or two before his garden chores, allowing time for water to move gradually through the soil's profile. That way, his soil is not so dry as to be tough digging or weeding, but not so wet as to clod or stick to tools or compact from being stepped on. Silty and sandy soils hold less water and so need more frequent irrigation, especially for plants not yet established, but open up a whole new plant palette. Lauren, who gardens on a silty property, is able to grow a good number of plants, such as bush morning-glory (*Ipomoea leptophylla*), that would rot in Bryan's heavier soil.

Mountain gardeners may find themselves on very thin soils that don't quite fit into any of these groups. Such soils are generally described as young, or gritty, and almost look or feel like digging in gravel with a modest amount of soil mixed in. Frequently, these soils are less than eight inches deep with bedrock right below. Along with soils low in organic matter, it is quite common to hear these soils referred to as ***mineral*** or ***lean*** in contrast to those with deeper profiles and more organic matter, called ***organic*** or ***rich***. The truth is that soils with significant amounts of organic matter are rare in the West, as they develop where generous precipitation and soil moisture support large amounts of plant growth and decomposition. Adding organic matter is an endless effort in perennial and shrub gardens, since it is constantly broken down by soil microbes and creates disturbance to the microorganism biome with feast and famine cycles. And, since most of our region's plants actually prefer leaner soils with less organic matter, it won't be in the best interest of your native plant garden anyway. The natives that enjoy richer soils come from environments with abundant surface or subsurface water—watercourse edges, mountain meadows, and wetlands—and comprise a small minority of our horticultural plant palette. Save your time, money, and energy for other garden-related pursuits.

In rare cases of extremely lean, thin soils, such as exceptionally sandy or gritty soils, light soil amendment with low-salt compost or undecomposed organic matter, such as dried leaves or alfalfa pellets, can help. This is also true for compacted soils that have sat barren, as organic matter jump-starts beneficial soil microbe activity. Such microbes provide many benefits to soil structure and plants alike, including making mineral nutrients bioavailable. Less is always more, as too much of any organic amendment will cause problems in most native gardens, ranging from salt damage to excessive, less-hardy soft growth. A loose scattering of alfalfa pellets, one inch of compost, or a few inches of

Defying the notion that flowery plants like rich soils, blue mist penstemon grows and blooms with abandon on nothing more than decomposing foothills granite.

an organic matter dug or tilled as deep as you can manage at the outset of plantings should do the job.

Since many regional soils and groundwater already have excessive salts, amending with salty compost or manure quickly does more harm than good. High salt levels are evident as a white or brown-white crust on soil surfaces, stunted plant growth, leafburn, and poor soil structure. If high salts are suspected, consider a soil test through your nearest land-grant university. University extension agents are available online or by phone to interpret and discuss test results and provide management recommendations. In this case it's usually most practical to tailor the plant palette to the existing salt levels in your garden, though flushing of salts is sometimes appropriate.

Soils around homes, especially newer homes, are often just the subsoil pulled from excavation for the basement, crawlspace, or foundation, not the native soil plants are adapted to grow in. Such soils are another exception where a one-time application of organic matter before planting begins can be beneficial, but resist the urge to do more. As with compacted, barren soils, a one-time amendment helps to loosen soil structure and jump-start microbial activity. A subsoil brought to the surface can often be spotted by its color and texture difference when compared to soil farther out in the yard; in our area, such soils are often a paler color and pack densely, leaving almost unbreakable, fist-sized chunks on the surface after being turned over, while soil in the yard is darker and easier to work.

Like soil texture, soil pH represents a spectrum. It can range from strongly acid to strongly alkaline, with true neutral (pure water) measuring 7. You can make general guesses as to whether your soil pH may be acid, alkaline, or relatively neutral by observing precipitation and plant patterns as well as bedrock. Higher-precipitation regions, like high-mountain areas with heavy winter snowfall, trend toward acidity, while lower-precipitation areas trend toward alkalinity. Granite predisposes a soil toward slight acidity, while many sedimentary rocks (like limestone and mudstone) as parent materials do the opposite. Few of our region's native plants have strong soil pH preferences.

Modifying soil texture is prohibitively costly in terms of labor, amount of materials, and dollar investment. This is also true for lowering the pH of many alkaline soils, which often have extraordinary ability to buffer their pH back up to original levels after being acidified. The goal in understanding your soil is not to change it, but rather to tailor your plant palette to the soil.

Sunlight

This region's many sunny days and intense sunlight are among the main draws for people visiting or moving here. Our higher elevation receives more days of sunshine and more intense solar radiation than most parts of the country. Many plants native here have evolved sun protection in the form of felt, hairs, spines, or wax that either shade from or reflect the bright sunlight. Much like a human being's darkened skin, plants also concentrate pigments as protection, giving many Rocky Mountain flowers a deeper, richer color than when grown where sunlight is less intense.

Full sun or all-day sun here is much stronger than full sun at lower elevations and/or in regions with more cloudy days. Half-day sun in the afternoon blasts plants with hours of the most intense solar radiation of the day, so a native plant for the west side of a structure or a west-facing slope ideally is a species that grows in full sun in the wild. West-side plants sited close to a structure are most affected by the morning shade and tend to grow toward or lean westward, so keep this in mind and choose lower-growing plants for those spots if you don't want that leaning to look so obvious. Part sun or light shade describes the light plants receive growing in the dappled shade of an open forest or tree grove, at woodland's edge, or on north- or east-facing slopes open to the sky but with no direct sun in the afternoon. Shade falls where no direct light comes through and where few of our region's native plant species thrive and can be found beneath evergreen trees, low eaves, or near the north side of a tall structure.

Inspired by the nearly treeless plains and shrub steppe, Bryan Fischer's sunny Prairie Garden at The Gardens on Spring Creek emulates the ecosystem's textured, flowing beauty in a layered matrix planting.

Additionally, our region features a huge spread of elevations and latitudes from northern Arizona to the Canadian Rockies, making for a massive range of seasonal disparities in both light intensity and day length. To further impact and complicate sunlight matters, higher elevations in the mountains generally have more cloud cover, receive more moisture in the form of snow and daily and/or seasonal rains, and often receive fewer hours of sunlight depending on how close, high, and in what direction the slopes directly facing and potentially blocking lower sun rays to the location are. At lower elevations, lower latitudes, on south- and west-facing slopes, and on flatter, open terrain, sunlight brings higher temperatures and depletes the soil of moisture more quickly during the growing season.

Sunlight can cause sunburn, or ***sunscald*** as it's called in plants; it's mostly an issue for those that are young or newly planted. Ideally, plants should be slowly acclimated to the intensity and duration of sunlight they'll receive on-site for at least a week or two before they are planted in the ground. To help new plantings that didn't receive that treatment, shade them a bit for a few weeks in the ground. In the case of small transplants, one of the simplest ways to do this is to place the pot they were grown in on the southwest side of the plant for a few weeks and put some mulch in it to keep the pot upright and prevent from blowing away. This also marks the plant so it can be easily found for hand-watering while it establishes. During winter, the bark on some young trees can also scald or worse, crack, thanks to the lower angle of the sun directly hitting the dormant, drier, less pliable plant tissues and due to expanding and contracting of those tissues with the more extreme temperature differential of warm daytime sunlight and cold nights. Wrapping young tree trunks, especially those with smooth bark, with paper wrap or white tubular plastic covers during winter for their first few years in the ground may help prevent this deep and often permanent damage, as does keeping the plants well-hydrated with periodic watering in dry winters. Some evergreens also suffer sunscald on their leaves/needles in winter; here again, keeping them hydrated in dry, windy winters with monthly deep watering when possible minimizes burned foliage. Should there be damage, new foliage will expand in spring and old, disfigured, and discolored leaves will become less noticeable and drop off in time.

Sunscald obviously is possible and probable when a plant that evolved in some shade is mistakenly planted in an overly sunny site. Time, then, to move it to where it belongs. But harsh sunlight can also harm sun-loving plants native to montane, subalpine, or alpine regions when planted in full sun at lower elevations; often for these plants, it's the extra heat that is problematic. These plants fare best when sited in part-sun conditions in those areas and will need less water in less sun, as well.

Because sunlight is so multifaceted and complicated in our region, it's important to learn what kind of sunlight a Rocky Mountain plant receives in its native haunts in order to make the best choices for its placement in a planting, and in each plant profile we use this information to suggest the best types of sunlight.

Wind

Wind is one of the defining environmental features affecting plants in this region. Strong, persistent winds buffet tender plants and sap moisture from delicate leaves, limiting the use of many traditional European and East Asian plants as well as eastern and western North American woodlanders, except in sheltered spots and built-up urban areas.

Prevailing winds vary in direction and by season and differ greatly within the Rocky Mountain region. Some parts of the southern Rockies have strong desiccating spring winds, making planting a challenge during that season. With this situation and that region's more dependable late-summer and fall monsoonal rains, fall planting is often a better choice. On the plains, the harshest winds often occur in winter and can cause a lot of foliar and branch-tip burn, damaging some plants with evergreen leaves and/or aboveground stems and branches, especially when those winds are coupled with extremely low temperatures, as happens during a polar-vortex event.

Cushion phlox and sagebrush make a good team: sage shades and cools phlox's tops while phlox does similar for sage's roots, helping each other endure a harsh and windswept climate.

The most important strategy is once again to observe. Once you figure out from where and when strong winds come to your site, you can find and/or create sheltered spots for your most vulnerable plants or choose plants that can handle the wind. Microclimates are key, both discovering those you already have on a site and perhaps creating some new ones. You may also adjust the schedule of planting management activities to avoid times when winds tend to be the worst. Both Bryan and Lauren live along the northern Front Range in Colorado and often end up doing spring cut-back either in February or April, because March winds here are frequently so strong that they'd be chasing the cut-back duff tumbling a mile down the road.

Moisture Inputs

Knowing how much and when moisture falls from the sky to the ground—whether rain or snow—is vital to understanding what plants may need in terms of additional water, if any. Two great tools for measurement are a simple rain gauge and local online precipitation reports. In our region, with limited natural-water sources and more and more people living here who need water for their everyday lives, choosing plants that thrive with little moisture input not only makes sense but is becoming a community-minded necessity.

Many native plants need no additional irrigation once established, but a good number benefit from a bit of extra water delivered during drought-like periods or at a time of the year when they are accustomed to receiving moisture in their localized native haunts. Lauren only waters her cactus plantings when there is no late-summer monsoonal rainfall at all in July, August, and September, which is when many of those cacti are accustomed to receiving most of their

Silver prairie sage, yellow coneflower, and Apache plume make a sweet, water-thrifty vignette in the heat of midsummer.

In a sloped, unirrigated, south-facing garden, lush-looking lanceleaf chiming bells bloom at the base of a purple-padded pricklypear in early spring.

annual moisture in the wild in the southwestern parts of our region.

A few of our natives aren't truly water-thrifty, such as most of our native deciduous trees that naturally grow along watercourses and need more regular irrigation when planted elsewhere. Many of the needled evergreens native to the higher elevations on moist slopes, in ravines, and in draws have similar higher water needs in a landscape or garden planting.

Sunlight and wind both affect the moisture needs of plants. More wind and more sun, and the same plant needs more water. So, siting a plant in a sheltered spot is a way to conserve moisture. And of course, choosing plants that are native to sunny, dry locations when you have a sunny and dry site is the most effective way to keep moisture needs low. Matching plants' needs with your site's characteristics is the golden rule to planting success.

Sometimes the soil and lay of the land of the site can be modified to increase (or, less commonly, decrease if poor drainage is an issue) moisture retention. By moving the soil around just a bit, creating a few slightly lower and higher areas—all that's needed is a few inches in grade change—extra dry-loving plants will thrive perched on the slopes or atop the higher spots, and plants that want more moisture will thrive nestled in the lower areas where moisture tends to linger a bit longer. Minimally, if your lot has been graded to divert water off it, as is commonly the practice when new neighborhoods are developed, making a few shallow swales and low berms can divert, direct, and slow water movement, allowing more absorption and tempering soil erosion. This will also keep it from running off onto streets and into culverts, picking up contaminants and then polluting waterways in the process. Rain barrels, gutter extensions, and diverters are other simple ways to make the most of the scarce treasure that is our region's weather-delivered moisture.

All plants need more moisture during establishment—right after being planted, before their roots have grown out into the soil and are able to access what's available there. Timing planting with seasons or days with higher probability of natural precipitation is ideal but not always possible, so it's important to always have a water source available during the establishment period, whether it's as generous as a temporary or permanent irrigation system or just a hose-end or a few watering cans that can be filled and carried from the house.

Planting with Wildfire in Mind

With population growth and increasing temperatures, prolonged heat waves, and more common and often extenuated drought periods, people living in our region now face the more regular occurrence of wildfires. Recently, some of the most destructive regional fires have occurred not in the traditionally-deemed-more-vulnerable wooded foothills and mountain areas, but in towns and neighborhoods in grassy and shrubby areas. And these days wildfires are caused ever more frequently by human beings, either directly by careless camping use of stoves and fire, smoking, or driving vehicles on dormant grass, or more indirectly by downed live powerlines. For all these reasons, we are going to devote some extra space here to plant selection and garden management with wildfire front-of-mind. It's worth noting that this section emphasizes wildfires as they relate to home gardens rather than buildings.

In the Rocky Mountain west, vulnerability to ignition by fire is one of the few applications where native plants aren't always better suited than exotics, as some natives have adapted to naturally caused fires but aren't necessarily less flammable. These have developed the ability to come back either from roots or by repopulating a burned area with fire-resistant seeds, but the plants themselves often ignite and burn quickly and easily. Many native shrubs,

Though often seen in a negative light, fire helps cleanse and refresh overgrown, stagnant plant communities. The years following a healthy burn can be among the most floriferous, verdant, and diverse in a forest community's life trajectory.

including favorites such as mountain mahogany, fernbush, Apache plume, rabbitbrush, and sage, are very flammable. All our native conifers and larger grasses are among the most combustible and dangerous choices to plant near a structure in wildfire-prone sites.

If you live in or adjacent to a wild or unmanaged area, even a field of pasture grasses that isn't mowed when dormant, it's important to consider finding a balance between best practices for water conservation, plant choices, and planting management that supports wildlife and insects, while keeping your home area as resilient and defensible against fire as possible. You can begin to accomplish this by choosing low-water-need plants that are not very flammable; ensuring that they are healthy and not drought-stressed; by removing dead-plant material as soon as the plant goes dormant; and by using gravel, rock, sand, or leaving soil bare where mulch may be wanted instead of the common mulches of pine needles, bark, or wood chips. Avoid rubber and synthetic mulches, which are among the most flammable of all options and can create highly toxic fumes while burning. These relatively simple changes will help you make good progress toward defending your home. But there's more that can and should be done.

Fortunately, simple mitigation practices related to plants and plantings have been developed from observation and research, such as implementing a series of three protective planting zones around your building. Consult the following table to begin a list of least-flammable native plants, and use those in zones closer to your building—plants vary greatly in their resistance to fire, how quickly and how hot they burn when they do ignite, and whether they are capable of spreading fire over distances with windblown or exploding embers. Practice ongoing proactive management of plantings through the seasons and years and, in so doing, be sure to use gas and electric power tools thoughtfully; even they can spark a fire if conditions are just right.

Zoning your property for defensible space in case of fire is paramount, with plants and plant spacing appropriate to each of three zones. The first zone is simple—the first five feet out from your structure should have no plants whatsoever and consist of only entirely nonflammable materials (including garden ornaments and fences). Zone two—five to thirty feet from the house—is the most complex, because we tend to want this area to be beautiful and enjoyable. Here you want to grow low-combustible, mostly shorter plants, which include many of our native wildflowers that remain less than a foot tall, groundcovers, and cacti and succulents. Short native grasses can also be included, ideally planted as accents and not in a mass or lawn unless it's the ultra-low-growing buffalo grass. Low-flammability deciduous shrubs and taller wildflowers can be included as accents, but not in large, dense groupings. A few widely spaced deciduous trees—something many of us want and need for shade in our sunny, often hot summers—are also possible.

Another important thing to do in zone two is to keep any plants taller than a few inches away from the bases of shrubs so they don't serve as ignition ladders. Use paths and patios made of sand, compacted soil, gravel, flagstone, concrete, brick, or other nonflammable materials not only for walking and places to be, but also to separate the planting spaces, creating firebreaks. The most effective firebreak is five feet wide or more. Rock and crevice gardens and accent boulders can also serve both aesthetics and safety.

The last zone is thirty to one hundred feet from the house. Here you can plant deciduous trees and more safely leave, if they are already present, a few well-spaced conifers if desired—ideally ones you can remove the bottom branches from, such as ponderosa pine. This is known as ***limbing-up*** and keeps the lowest branches much higher off the ground so they can't ignite as easily. Keep grasses mowed when they're not actively growing, and cut back tall wildflowers to eight inches or less when they go dormant. Prune out and remove any deadwood and accumulated dried foliage within and under shrubs. Keep the bases of trees, especially conifers, free of any debris and of plants taller than a few inches so there isn't a ladder-effect for fire to get into the trees. Last but not least, whether you use a hose to water plants or not, it's a good idea to have a hundred-foot-long one available, coiled up by each outdoor spigot.

Fire-Resistant Native Plants for Fire-Defensible Space

(not all-inclusive; these plants have been evaluated, but there are probably many more)

wildflowers, succulents, fiber plants

* = low-growing

yarrow *Achillea*
*pussytoes *Antennaria*
columbine *Aquilegia*
milkweed *Asclepias*
*cacti—all genera and species
*winecup *Callirhoe involucrata*
*roundleaf harebell *Campanula rotundifolia*
larkspur *Delphinium*
coneflower *Echinacea*
*hummingbird trumpet *Epilobium canum*
(*some) fleabane *Erigeron*
*buckwheat *Eriogonum*
*prairie smoke *Geum triflorum*
*blanketflower *Gaillardia aristata*
wild iris *Iris missouriensis*
gayfeather *Liatris*
wild blue flax *Linum lewisii*
lupine *Lupinus*
desert four o'clock *Mirabilis multiflora*
*evening primrose *Oenothera*
*sundrops *Oenothera*
(*some) beardtongue *Penstemon*
*phlox
(*some) creeping globemallow *Sphaeralcea coccinea*
yucca

shrubs

serviceberry *Amelanchier*
manzanita *Arctostaphylos*
grapeholly *Berberis*
redroot *Ceanothus*
red-twig dogwood *Cornus sericea*
rockspray *Holodiscus*
mock orange *Philadelphus*
sand cherry, chokecherry, American plum *Prunus*
Smith's buckthorn *Rhamnus smithii*
currant *Ribes*
willow *Salix*
snowberry *Symphoricarpos* spp.

trees

maple *Acer*
alder *Alnus*
birch *Betula*
hackberry *Celtis*
honey locust *Gleditsia triacanthos*
aspen, cottonwood *Populus*
oak *Quercus*
willow *Salix*

Getting Started

A few of you reading this book may be staring at a bare patch of ground in front of or behind your newly built home, but the majority of you are working with an existing planting of some sort, even if only a lawn. This present landscape needs to be addressed and parts of it incorporated and/or removed to create and install the desired planting. Along the lines of the previous subject of wildfire, Lauren wishes she had known more and integrated better fire-mitigation plantings and design before she began her present home plantings eight years ago. Anyone planning to plant in a fire-prone area should think about the three fire-defensible zones and remove existing plants accordingly before making further plans. This may be the hardest thing of all to do, way harder than planning and planting, as it can mean removing a beautiful mature pine or spruce that shelters many creatures but is way too close to the house, and cutting down foundation plantings that soften the building's appearance and may be hiding some unattractive part of the structure. Such removals are emotional, physically challenging, and potentially dangerous if you do them yourself, and they're expensive if you hire experienced help, which in the case of good-sized mature trees we highly recommend—professional removal is the wise choice.

◀ Inspired by the diversity of natural shrub steppe and chaparral plant communities, Lauren planted her property's perimeter to host and provide for creatures great and small.

It's important to determine what plants you have on your property, either with the help of an experienced gardener friend, a professional, or one of the several plant-identification apps or extension service guides available. Most aggressively spreading plants, exotic or native, should be considered unfriendly to the goal of creating diverse, pollinator- and wildlife-friendly native plantings unless you have a very large piece of land to work with. Perennial weeds, those that return for many years from their long-lived roots and that frequently can spread slowly by underground runners, often require some chemical intervention. Most noxious weeds and especially aggressive invaders such as Canada thistle, smooth brome grass, bindweed, leafy spurge, and spreading bellflower fall into this category. If there are only small bits of these plants on-site, tenacious deep digging and ongoing removal of new sprouts for a year or two can starve out the weeds.

Short-lived interlopers that have been on the site reseeding for some time can be handled in a couple different ways. They can be encouraged to sprout in spring by raking over the soil and exposing some of the seed and watering it, and then hoeing off the seedlings as they come up. This greatly reduces the seed bank—the collection of seeds built up in the soil, waiting for an opportunity to germinate. Then plant and apply mulch immediately after to prevent much further germination and be dogged about pulling any stragglers. Conversely, you can pass on encouraging germination of the weed seed bank, plant, and then mulch the entire area more deeply with three to four inches of gravel. This must be done when you can effectively bury any annual and biennial weeds presently growing, so typically quite early in spring, especially if your main weeds are cool-season germinators and growers, such as mustards and cheat grass. Either method has its pros and cons. The latter with deeper mulch is simpler but requires more gravel to buy and spread. It not only smothers existing annual and biennial weeds and keeps the seed bank from germinating, but also prevents potential blown-in weed seed from growing. Unfortunately, at the same time it also precludes any desired future self-sowing by plants you've planted, and it does little to keep existing perennial weeds from resprouting and spreading.

Among the most tenacious perennial plants that many people want less of are creeping turfgrasses used as traditional lawns, in our region most commonly Kentucky bluegrass. It's hard to keep a lawn of this sort from growing back into areas you want for other plants without deeply set edging or another hardscape feature. To keep Kentucky bluegrass green and attractive throughout the season requires a lot more moisture than most of our natives ever do, and its bright green color jars with the more muted grays and sage-greens of native plants. We enthusiastically recommend that you limit these kinds of turf areas to play areas for children and pets, if you need them; our native turf grasses, such as buffalo grass, don't tolerate high levels of traffic nearly as well as bluegrass. Otherwise, if you want the tranquil, low-profile look of a lawn in some areas, and/or would like to have such a planting as part of a fire-mitigating landscape, consider planting low-growing native grasses.

To kill off parts or all of a lawn, you can solarize it with clear plastic left on through the heat of summer; smother it for two full growing seasons with tarps, cardboard, or black plastic; or spray it with a one-time application of herbicide. Since bluegrass lawns can go dormant during dry times, browning and appearing dead while actually sitting dormant, withholding water is not a reliable turf-removal method. A browned, dormant lawn will resume green growth with precipitation or irrigation and will quickly grow into and outcompete the roots of freshly planted perennials, grasses, trees, and shrubs. If you happen to have very deep soil or sandy soil that falls off the roots of the turf when dug, you can consider using a sod cutter. The latter can otherwise be a problematic method in the long run, because you'll have removed the best and most biologically active top inches of soil along with the sod. Such topsoil is hard to come by in much of our region. You can turn the cut sod strips upside down, pile them up and wait a couple years for them to die off and compost and then use what's left, but the area you took the turf from has literally been strip-mined. The other options are better and roughly equivalent in that all three create some disruption to the soil fauna, whether from intense heat and lack of moisture and oxygen (solarizing); lack of sunlight, moisture, and oxygen (smothering); or chemical interference (spraying). These sod-removal options are all one-time events, and the soil fauna will recuperate once air, water, sunlight, the roots of new plants, and perhaps some alfalfa pellets are dug into the planting to jump-start the renewal process. A windy site usually precludes smothering and solarizing because—short of laying out large, very heavy pieces of plywood—it is darn near impossible to keep the smothering/solarizing device in place. Lauren managed to use tarps in smaller areas on her windblown site because she happened to have quite a few old, long 4-×-4-inch posts that she was able to lay along the tarps' edges and then threw some concrete blocks and large cobbles randomly in the middle of the tarps.

In the next section we'll dive into design, so we'll stop here with a suggestion: if you have a lot of tree, shrub, and lawn removal, don't try to redo your entire property in one season. Have plans that integrate all your prospective areas, but prioritize. Removing unwanted plants is probably the

Formerly only aggressive exotic grasses, Lauren's garden now features mainly native plants, including many species that would have been native to the site prior to pasture-grass seeding decades ago.

hardest work you'll do, and it's not fun hard work. It comes with a lot of negativity. You're killing plants and then you'll probably have some subsequent weed battles as well. It's easier on both body and soul to bite off one area at a time, except perhaps in the case of tree removal. With the latter you'll probably have professional help, and it's a lot less expensive to bring the team and equipment in once than to ask them to come several times.

While you're plotting plant removal and rethinking areas, also consider any changes you may want to make to your hardscape and/or grade—paths, patios, walls, driveway, and such. Would you like to create a more permeable version of what you have, to allow water to stay on your property and soak down into the soil? Do you want to create more paths for enjoyment and/or as firebreaks? Maybe a new gathering space? Some or all of the demolished materials from removal of existing hardscape can be repurposed as new garden walls or rock gardens. In most parts of our region, should you want to add a new hardscape item of some sort from materials not on-site, gravel and stone are available and at prices lower than in other regions of the country. Often local online listings advertise free or inexpensive rock offered by people who are making changes to their property and no longer want their rock. We love rock of many kinds and its myriad uses in native waterwise planting design. It looks right here; these are the Rocky Mountains, after all.

Sourcing Plants and Seeds; Growing Native Plants from Seed

Native plants have never been easy to find in our regional nursery trade. In recent years, the contraction of specialty, family, and small nurseries across the region has only exacerbated this issue. If you have a nursery nearby offering native plants and the means to do so, support them. Many of us don't have great local nurseries nearby, which leaves us seeking other options, especially given the poor ethics of wild-collecting plants.

Cheap to buy, transport, and store, seeds have become one of our preferred means for acquiring new plants. They can be purchased online, found in seed exchanges, or be collected in the wild. If wild collecting is of interest, only collect from private land with permission or be prepared to understand public land-collection requirements—most require a permit and have stipulations for seed use. Either way, collect just a small percentage of available seed to ensure wild populations can continue to maintain their numbers while feeding wildlife. Despite the challenges, wild-collected seeds are powerful tools in the face of climate change, containing valuable genetic diversity and traits not widely present in horticulture. The genetic diversity provided by growing from seed makes this exercise a delightful study in plant form, foliage and flower-color variations, and more.

Once you have seeds in-hand, the vast majority of native plants can be grown using at most two simple seed treatments: cold-moist stratification and hot-water scarification. Both treatments mimic a natural process the seed has adapted to take as a germination cue. If a seed needs either of these treatments, it's indicated in its plant profile. Most seeds can be grown with one treatment, and many can be grown without either.

The most commonly required treatment, cold-moist stratification, is simply sowing the seed and then exposing the sown seed to a cool, moist period (typically three to four months long). This treatment signals to the seed that spring has arrived, moisture is available, and it is a good time to begin growing. Seeds that don't require this treatment are unharmed by it; Lauren has grown most of her seeds this way for years, sowing all her seeds around New Year's. This allows her more time in the garden come spring rather than in the nursery sowing a second batch of seeds that don't require cold-moist stratification.

To cold-moist stratify seeds, create a seed-starting potting mix of two parts quality potting mix and one to two parts coarse sand. Plants from drier ecosystems, such as deserts, shrub steppes, dry prairies, and pinyon-juniper communities, appreciate the higher proportions of sand, while most other natives are fine with less—sometimes none—in the mix. Ensure the sand and potting mix are well combined, then fill pots (we prefer four-inch short pots), leaving half an inch or so of head space. Sow seeds directly on top of this mix, tamping them gently with the back of your hand, and cover them lightly with a thin layer of smaller pea gravel, coarse sand, or chicken grit (not oyster shell). Set your pots in a shallow basin of tepid water to hydrate the pot's soil mix from the bottom without disturbing your seeds, and then set them outside in winter shade. If kept moist over winter—even piling snow on them does the job just fine—they can be moved to a location with morning sun in mid-spring and will begin to germinate. This treatment should be started by New Year's Day to ensure seeds get three months or more of cool, moist chilling.

Depending on the seedlings' size before summer heat hits, these plants can then be potted up or directly transplanted into the garden. In recent years, Bryan has modified this method to sow seed into deep plug trays that he can thin to a single seedling per cell after germination. This way, he doesn't have to pot up and can transplant the resulting plant directly into his gardens, minimizing labor.

One alternative method of cold-moist stratification that Bryan has found quite useful for seeds that can be finnicky about their stratification needs (those needing an especially long stratification or those especially sensitive to drying during stratification) is simply to complete stratification in the fridge. This method is also a nice work-around if seeds arrive too late in winter to be cold-stratified outdoors. Seedlings are mixed with a small handful of moistened—not wet—vermiculite (available at garden centers), then placed, with their labels, in a closed baggie in the crisper drawer. Once stratification needs are met (usually three to four months), simply dump the contents of the baggie onto potting mix in a seedling pot, stick the label on the pot, and grow the seeds as you would any others. It's worth noting that true stratification in any style must be cool and moist, as storing seeds dry in the fridge does not achieve stratification, nor does putting them in the freezer.

A simple way to grow plants is to sow seed around New Year's and put the seed pots out on the colder, damper north side of a structure for winter, giving the seed cold-moist stratification to aid germination. The box frame and wire top keep rabbits and cats out.

Hot-water scarification is required by fewer seeds than is stratification, though it is still a regular treatment for the germination of seeds with thick or hard seed coats, like many native members of the pea family. To scarify seeds for planting, bring water to a boil in a pot or electric kettle while unpackaging and pouring seeds into a heat-tolerant vessel. Once the water boils, let it rest for a minute, then simply pour it an inch or so deep over the seeds. Allow seeds to soak until they sink. Then, sow them twice as deep as they are wide into a well-drained potting mix. If seeds are still floating after soaking for a few hours to a day, they are usually not viable. Seeds that need hot-water scarification typically don't require stratification—with a few exceptions, notably many native mallow family members, which often need both.

Seeds that need no pretreatment can generally be sown on the surface of your potting mix and covered lightly with gravel, coarse sand, perlite, or vermiculite. A small percentage of seeds—many in the aster or daisy family—require light for germination. These must still be covered in our region to avoid excessive drying; just cover them more thinly and avoid using sand as a covering.

Seeds of some short-lived plants are best sown directly on-site. Simply rough up a spot of bare ground and scatter and rake or carefully sow these seeds before covering them very lightly. Since a seedbed shouldn't dry out until seedlings have several sets of leaves, you may need to water every day if you end up direct-sowing seeds in late spring or summer, when wind and sun dry out the soil particularly fast. Sowing seeds before a winter snow is ideal, as the snow helps stick the seeds to the soil and slowly releases moisture to them with spring thaw.

A Note on Cultivars

Cultivars—selections of plants reproduced from parts of the plant other than the seed—have become the subject of an increasingly negative narrative in recent years. This is particularly in relation to doubled-flower cultivars. For those who don't know, a doubled flower is one that displays extra rows of petals that obscure the stamens, pistils, and nectaries of a flower. Single flowers, on the other hand, display a single row of petals—these petals may still overlap one another on their edges—that do not obscure the flowers' reproductive parts. Single flowers are the norm for plant species in the wild. Doubled flowers have become popular for their lush visual appeal but can be problematic for pollinators; in many cases not only do these petals obscure the flowers' nectar and pollen, but they also restrict access to them. The extra petals themselves are derived from reproductive parts that advertise but no longer offer pollen and nectar.

Unfortunately, this has led to a general sense in some circles that any plant modified from its wild state is less suitable for use in native plant gardens, and that's a shame. Called ***cultivars***—a portmanteau of "cultivated" and "variety"—these plants aren't only modified for the purpose of doubling their petals. Often, cultivars are grown for more practical reasons. Santa Fe phlox (*Phlox nana*), for example, was once considered to be a nonviable plant for commercial production despite its abundant, season-long bloom of nectar-rich, fragrant pink flowers. That's because the little creeping phlox was almost impossible to propagate for sale in the nursery industry due to seeds that self-eject when ripe, making collection nightmarish, and an intolerance for division or rooting from cuttings. The late David Salman, founder of High Country Gardens, was smitten by and set on selling the little native plant. Over time, David screened a multitude of Santa Fe phlox plants for their ability to root from cuttings, eventually finding one individual that would root reliably in his production greenhouses: 'Perfect Pink' Santa Fe phlox was found, opening up a new native plant species to the western market by mail-order. Surely, this has been as beneficial for pollinating insects as for us gardeners, who previously had no access to the plant.

Cultivars have been selected for all manner of attributes, and many have useful applications for western landscapes, ranging from slower growth on overly vigorous or large-growing species to clay tolerance in otherwise clay-intolerant species and longer periods of bloom than the wild type. So, don't assume that because a plant is listed as a cultivar, or even a variety, that it offers less to the invertebrates, birds, and mammals of your garden. Take the time to understand what that cultivar was selected for and whether those traits may be beneficial in your planting or not.

One notable challenge of cultivars is that each individual is genetically identical to all other individuals of that cultivar. As a result, such plants are then uniformly susceptible to the same pathogens and environmental stressors. So, when possible, we advocate for liberal use of seed-grown plants in addition to the thoughtful use of cultivars. Seed-grown plants offer superior genetic diversity, not only due to their population of origin, but also due to genetic recombination, giving seed-grown gardens more diverse plants. This diversity reduces the chances of one disease, weather event, or other variable having equal impact on each plant type in the garden and offers opportunity for the garden environment and the gardener to select against poorly performing individuals in the garden, strengthening the garden's attunement to the local climate and soils.

Planting Design

Gardens are to plants what cuisine is to food, poetry is to words, and music is to sound—we make them for joy and pleasure, not just out of necessity. Flowers and fruits attract creatures in order to be pollinated, eaten, and spread. Their distinct shapes, colors, sizes, smells, and tastes have evolved for specific creature clients. How fortuitous that they also attract humans with the same sensory beauty! We aim to celebrate both kinds of attractions for the best outcome, helping the reader balance both beauty and web-of-life function in their plantings.

In natural plant communities there's an ongoing process that occurs over time. The plant community that takes the longest to develop—sometimes centuries but typically decades—is called a climax plant community. The youngest, most disturbed, and vulnerable to weed invasion is called a pioneer plant community. Some areas in the wild stay in the pioneer state because they are continually being disturbed—for example a steep mountainside that experiences regular rockslides and avalanches, the bank of a river or creek that varies greatly in how much water it carries every few years, or an area of grassland that is heavily trafficked and grazed by native herbivores. The sites that most of us have the opportunity or desire to plant are usually already disturbed by human, livestock, and/or vehicular traffic, by grade changes and building, or by agriculture or logging—whether recent or decades-old. So, we usually start at or near the pioneer phase on our properties.

Including plants from the dominant climax plant community of the area—planting shrubs in a steppe or chaparral part of our region, grasses and wildflowers in an area where prairie or alpine meadows dominate, trees and/or woodland clearing plants in a partially forested area—will attract and support the creatures that are residents of that local, natural plant community. It also adds resilience and stability to your landscape's plant community while looking harmonious and related to the site and the region—because it is. This is what is often meant by that special, much desired but often elusive "sense of place."

We're not going to offer a step-by-step design tutorial, as we think there are few if any absolutes in design. By choosing plants that will thrive on your specific site and in your area's climate and that will give back to the web of life of this region, you're already on the right track. Secondly, but no less important, is that the plants (and the creatures they help support) appeal to you. A planting will not be loved, enjoyed, or tended by a person who is allergic to any species in the planting or to certain insect bites, or who finds certain plants truly unsightly.

Native Shrubs and Trees That Provide Fruit for Birds

thinleaf alder (*Alnus incana* ssp. *tenuifolia*)
western serviceberry (*Amelanchier alnifolia*)
manzanita (*Arctostaphylos*)
grapeholly, desert holly (*Berberis*)
hackberry (*Celtis*)
red-twig dogwood (*Cornus sericea*)
silverberry (*Elaeagnus commutata*)
desert olive (*Forestiera pubescens* var. *pubescens*)
juniper (*Juniperus*)
spruce (*Picea*)
pine (*Pinus*)
plum, cherry (*Prunus*)
Douglas fir (*Pseudotsuga menziesii*)
Smith's buckthorn (*Rhamnus smithii*)
sumac (*Rhus*)
currant (*Ribes*)
boulder raspberry (*Rubus deliciosus*)
elderberry (*Sambucus*)
silver buffaloberry (*Shepherdia argentea*)
snowberry (*Symphoricarpos* spp.)

In many parts of our region, creating some groupings and groves, perimeter and screening plantings, or hedgerows of both deciduous and evergreen trees and shrubs—and planting native bunchgrasses and wildflowers in a sunny, open panel instead of all lawn—offers diverse plants and habitats to suit a wide range of wildlife as well as being visually interesting and appealing. If you have room and your site, soil, and climate allow, include several distinct types of plantings—some shrubby, some woodland-like, and some open and prairie, steppe, or desert-like. These create contrasts and edges of open versus dense, short versus tall, and drier versus more lush that attract and support a huge diversity of creatures in all phases of their lives.

Layering plantings of several species that like the same conditions, are neighborly (meaning they don't overrun one another), and that look good together is a basic cornerstone of healthy, habitat-rich, and beautiful design. Be sure to consider plant textures and how they combine and contrast, as well as year-round interest. Flower colors are the dessert, offering seasonal excitement, while texture and form are the main course, holding the design together throughout the seasons. It can help to take black-and-white photos of plantings in the wild and in gardens. Without all the colors, you'll notice

Long-lived Plants for Varied Pollinators

early bloomers

trees

desert olive *Forestiera pubescens* var. *pubescens*

shrubs

western serviceberry *Amelanchier alnifolia*
hardy manzanita *Arctostaphylos ×coloradensis*
Oregon grapeholly *Berberis aquifolium*
desert holly *Berberis fremontii*
American plum *Prunus americana*
sand cherry *Prunus pumila* var. *besseyi*
Smith's buckthorn *Rhamnus smithii*
threeleaf sumac *Rhus trilobata*
golden currant *Ribes aureum*
wax currant *Ribes cereum*

wildflowers

kinnikinnick *Arctostaphylos uva-ursi*
creeping grapeholly *Berberis repens*
sugarbowls *Clematis hirsutissima*
cutleaf daisy *Erigeron compositus*
prairie smoke *Geum triflorum*
sandlily *Leucocrinum montanum*
lanceleaf chiming bells *Mertensia lanceolata*
white locoweed *Oxytropis sericea*
marsh phlox *Phlox kelseyi*
Rocky Mountain phlox *Phlox multiflora*
American pasqueflower *Pulsatilla nuttalliana*
plains gold banner *Thermopsis rhombifolia*

cacti

green-flowered hedgehog *Echinocereus viridiflorus*
snowball cactus *Pediocactus simpsonii*

long bloomers

trees

desert willow *Chilopsis linearis*

shrubs

fernbush *Chamaebatiaria millefolium*
shrubby potentilla *Dasiphora fruticosa*
Apache plume *Fallugia paradoxa*

and understand the roles of textures and forms—bold, fine, upright and strong, low and lacy, pale or dark, shiny or dull.

It's helpful to plant wildflowers in clusters and sweeps. This not only creates a feeling of unity, cohesion, abundance, and serenity, but also helps birds and insects find potential floral and seed food sources more easily from a distance while flying. Provide as long a season of bloom as possible, incorporating long-bloomers as well as plants with flowers on the very front and back ends of the growing season. Early-blooming plants are crucial to adult insects emerging hungry from their winter protection spots to feed or mate. The young hatchlings or larvae then go on to feed bird broods; the young of most birds, even seed-eating species, eat mountains of insect larvae, especially caterpillars. Late-season bloomers and seeds offer food that helps creatures store energy for migration, hibernation, and winter survival. And don't forget to include some night bloomers, especially if you live in the drier and hotter parts of the region, where numerous pollinator species forage at dusk and during the night to avoid the heat stress of the day.

Create safe havens and protected spots for wildlife to rear young. Trees and shrubs offer shade from hot sun, cover from predators (dense and/or thorny species in particular),

wildflowers

western yarrow *Achillea millefolium*
swamp milkweed *Asclepias incarnata*
butterfly milkweed *Asclepias tuberosa*
winecup *Callirhoe involucrata*
roundleaf harebell *Campanula rotundifolia*
Scott's clematis *Clematis scottii*
narrowleaf coneflower *Echinacea angustifolia*
hummingbird trumpet *Epilobium canum* ssp. *garrettii*
showy fleabane *Erigeron speciosus*
crispleaf buckwheat *Eriogonum corymbosum*
sulfur flower *Eriogonum umbellatum*
blanketflower *Gaillardia aristata*
desert four o'clock *Mirabilis multiflora*
horsemint *Monarda fistulosa* var. *menthifolia*
tufted evening primrose *Oenothera cespitosa*
Hartweg's sundrops *Oenothera hartwegii*
narrowleaf evening primrose *Oenothera macrocarpa* ssp. *fremontii*
silverleaf primrose *Oenothera macrocarpa* ssp. *incana*
Santa Fe phlox *Phlox nana*
four-nerve daisy *Tetraneuris scaposa*
western spiderwort *Tradescantia occidentalis*

late bloomers

shrubs

rabbitbrush *Ericameria nauseosa*

wildflowers

pearly everlasting *Anaphalis margaritacea*
Parry's gentian *Gentiana parryi*
broomweed *Gutierrezia sarothrae*
Maximilian sunflower *Helianthus maximiliani*
azure sage *Salvia azurea*
broom ragwort *Senecio spartioides*
stiff goldenrod *Solidago rigida*
white heath aster *Symphyotrichum ericoides*
smooth blue aster *Symphyotrichum laeve*
aromatic aster *Symphyotrichum oblongifolium*
western ironweed *Vernonia fasciculata*
cutleaf goldenaster *Xanthisma spinulosum*
Rocky Mountain zinnia *Zinnia grandiflora*

Hawk moths, also called sphinx or hummingbird moths, start out as huge caterpillars that feed voraciously on equally oversized desert four o'clock, the nectar of which the adult moths consume later.

Though understated during the first half of the growing season, Bryan's prairie garden grows more active and vibrant as days grow hot. Then, like a bonfire running out of fuel, the garden concludes its season by reveling in glowing yellows and ember-like oranges just before the dark, chilly onset of winter.

and shelter from wind and severe weather. If your site is too exposed or too dry to plant trees, use trellis and pergola spaces, semi-enclosed patios, and shrub thickets to fill the same roles. Be sure to offer water if possible, even just a couple bowls: one larger and with a couple rocks peeking out of it for bird perching, drinking, and bathing, and the other more shallow and filled with pebbles or marbles to provide easy access for insects to crawl on and sip water from without drowning. If you have the inclination, observe and spend time in the myriad wild places of our region: there you'll find some of the best design inspiration not only for plant choices but also for combinations and overall plant communities.

Beyond these guidelines, there's very little that can or should be offered as design rules. Our tastes are as diverse as the plants we plant. Lauren has been a designer of both public and private plantings for more than thirty years. She sums up the diverse plantings—wild and human-made—that she finds compelling in the following general descriptions: Wonderful outdoor spaces are immersive and inviting, filled with surprise and delight, with paths to explore through and places to linger. Plants chosen are extra special when they embrace and celebrate our region's seasons with their own dynamic changes and play with everchanging light. Nonliving materials that reflect the region and the person who is steward of the space give authenticity. Lauren likes to see both unity and contrast, drama and serenity, close-up and bigger-picture experiences, and the ephemeral and changeable alongside the constant and stalwart.

Lauren also often asks her clients to choose some favorite species and then incorporates more of them as signature plants in their gardens. Sometimes these form combinations that are repeated throughout the planting space, creating unifying vignettes or themes. These favorites can be from fond memories or can emerge over a few years, as plants that do best on the site and bring the client the most joy reveal themselves over time. In the past eight years of living on her five acres, she has added a dozen more golden currants for hummingbirds and bumblebees along with many additional seedling pasqueflowers, sugarbowls, and phloxes for spring enjoyment. For summer and fall, she's

Lauren's homestead combines a rugged property and evocative native plantings with places to enjoy relaxing outside. The stone patio doubles as a firebreak.

added dozens more gayfeather, aromatic aster, and hummingbird trumpet. For winter and year-round form and shelter, more limber and pinyon pines. And in large swaths of her property formerly filled with the invasive grass smooth brome, she's seeded fringed sage with paintbrush and mingled in plugs of several hundred muhly grasses, both ruby muhly and her hardy form of deer muhly. All because they delight in growing on her site, add diversity, food, and habitat for creatures, and delight her.

Soil Preparation and Upkeep

Soil preparation in native plant gardens remains one of the best-intentioned but most misguided aspects of garden-making. Since many of us learned to garden from our families, who employ practices passed down generationally from locales with greater precipitation and deeper soils (like northern and central Europe, the Midwest, or the East Coast), there historically has been a narrative about building good soil. In such a narrative, this desired soil is usually rich, moisture-retentive, and amenable to growing food crops and ornamental plants originating from moist, temperate climates quite unlike ours.

The thing is that in the Rockies and on the Plains, we aren't growing in such a climate, and our plants aren't adapted to those so-called good soils. Often, this well-intentioned preparation—like adding compost or fertilizer before planting—spells trouble for our natives, which do best in our unamended native soils. Successfully growing our region's native plants means embracing a paradigm shift away from modifying soil toward adjusting the palette of plants grown—something you've already done by picking up this book. We are confident that many plants profiled in this text are already adapted to the soil you have, and with 225 in this book to choose from, you're bound to find some that are good fits for your space.

When making brand new gardens, we as horticulturists rarely fertilize at all. If we do, it is with a one-time application of a slow-release nitrogen source to help speed new-transplant establishment, as that is a primary limiting nutrient in many of our region's soils. Lauren prefers alfalfa pellets spread across the garden, while Bryan uses a small amount of blood meal incorporated into each planting hole.

To minimize damage to soil structure, till only if a soil is so compacted it cannot be reasonably planted, and don't attempt to modify your garden's soil texture by amending with inorganic amendments unless so counseled by an expert. In the case of inorganic amendments, like sand, such actions cannot be reversed on the home scale.

Planting

Surprisingly, the foundational practice of planting is one that has enjoyed some of the most innovation in our field in recent years. Historically, plants were placed into large holes amended generously with organic matter, such as compost, and the hole was backfilled. The problem with this approach is that the plant's roots often fail to leave the amended hole and don't infiltrate the native soil around them, leaving transplants more vulnerable to drought, stunted, and less physically stable. More recent evidence suggests that not only does planting without amendment provide superior long-term results, but that removing potting mix from the plant's root ball can, too.

To prepare a transplant for the garden, begin by ensuring the plant's root ball is well-hydrated. Lauren simply carries a bucket of water as she works, dropping the whole plant, pot and all, inside to soak for a few minutes. Whether soaking your transplants or not, prepare a planting hole the same depth as your transplant's pot but about two to three times the pot's width. If recent weather has been dry, Bryan compensates by filling the planting hole with water at least once to ensure that dehydrated soils will not wick moisture away from the sensitive transplant. That transplant can then be removed from the water bucket and its pot; flip it upside down, threading your fingers over its potting mix and around its stem, and ease the pot up and down to slip the plant's root ball out of the container. You may need to squeeze the sides of the pot or rip overgrown roots off the bottom of the pot to help the plant out of the container.

Holding its stem at the crown (where shoots meet roots), carefully but sharply knock the root ball two or three times against the inside of another bucket to knock any loose media free, or crumble the root ball with your hands and gently shake any loose media free. This constitutes a reduced-media planting and offers superior results in our drought-prone climate, ensuring faster root contact with native soils. If no potting mix is shed and a dense network of roots is visible, your plant is rootbound. Make a vertical cut up one side of the root ball with a garden knife or pruners and gently peel the cut side open.

The plant can then be lowered into the planting hole and backfilled gently with soil, bringing the plant's crown to just aboveground. Ensure any remaining potting mix is below a layer of mulch or soil, as it will wick moisture from the root ball if exposed to air. If the transplant has stretched out, leggy new growth or is in bud or bloom, cut back the flowering stems and shorten the leggy shoots by a third to half. Lauren goes so far as to cut the foliage of all grasses back by half. This helps balance top-to-root ratio, since the transplant will no longer be receiving the nursery-style coddling it did while growing in a pot. Doing so also ensures the transplant diverts energy from bloom to rooting.

In the case of larger transplants, a gentle stream of hose water applied to the planting hole from start to finish helps ensure that soil settles around the plant. Bryan prefers to use this tactic, called mucking-in, for planting woody plants and bareroot plants; it reduces the need for staking, helps evenly disperse roots and soil in the planting hole, and reduces air bubbles. Deeply watering right after transplant is crucial for soil settling and plant-stress management.

In subsequent days, water routinely—this could be every day in hot and dry periods—to keep the remaining planting media on the root ball from drying out until the transplant begins to root into surrounding soil, which can take two or three weeks. As time goes by, reduce watering in frequency and increase in depth; by the one-month mark, most transplants can be watered twice weekly but more deeply, and by two months most transplants do well watered once weekly, except during extreme heat. New sprigs of growth indicate you may taper watering to the next step. In the case of shrubs and trees, supplemental watering may be necessary for a few years; expect a tree to need one year of extra help for each inch the trunk is wide.

Avoiding extreme heat and cold during the first few weeks of establishment dictates the ideal transplant season for most gardens: those that experience extreme heat in summer, like lower-elevation and southern areas in our region, typically transplant best in spring and fall, while those in cooler, mountain communities can transplant into midsummer. Fall planting is often the best time for those in the Front Range and plains, Wasatch Front, and Treasure Valley areas, as the air is cool while soils are warm and plants seek to produce roots, not shoots. This is not advisable in mountain communities, where plants may not have time to store enough food to survive a long and snowy winter.

Mulches

Mulches are spreadable materials applied on top of your soil, one to four inches deep. They can be organic (like leaves, dried plant debris, bark mulch, or wood-chip mulch) or inorganic (pea gravel, rock chip, or synthetic mulch). Differing from amendments in that they remain untilled and on the soil surface, mulches drastically reduce germination of annual and perennial weeds, increase soil-moisture retention, moderate soil-temperature changes (keeping them more even for favorable root growth), and protect soils from erosion and other losses.

Organic mulches gradually break down and feed soils with organic matter and a slow release of nutrients, but they must be reapplied periodically. They are frequently used for tree rings and shrub borders and can often be acquired for free. Don't till mulches into your soil, especially wood-chip mulch, which binds nutrients and increases pathogens if it is in rather than on your soil. Inorganic mulches don't break down and tend to keep plant crowns drier and slightly warmer—making them ideal for plants adapted to hotter and drier regions that can be rot-prone in garden settings—and so are more often used for waterwise gardens. And, while these general rules hold true for much of our region, they are not law; in some places, like Boise, Idaho, nearly all plants grow well in quality arborist chips, while in others—especially the High Plains—persistent, strong winds turn organic mulches into transient visitors. There, experienced gardeners stick to gravel mulches or plant densely, foregoing mulches entirely; though certainly helpful, mulches are optional. After all, the majority of our region's native plants grow without mulch in nature, and many animals, especially some native bees and insects, rely on undisturbed, bare soil for ground-nesting. In most cases, mimicking existing soil coverings in wild places near your property—be they gravel-like, exposed or gritty soils, or richer mats of pine needles or leaves—will get you in the ballpark of what is appropriate for your space, especially after some trial and error.

Serving as mulches in the wild, stones of many sizes help plants take hold and grow on this otherwise hot, dry, steep slope. The rocks and gravel slow moisture evaporation from the soil, hold the soil in place, and moderate its temperature both in summer and winter.

In the case of Lauren's gardens, she often prefers to plant densely and mulch in rings around each plant, ensuring the ring is about 30 percent larger than each plant's canopy. This minimizes how much gravel mulch she must buy and spread while ensuring her new transplants receive the benefits of a root-insulating mulch. It also leaves plenty of exposed soil for her favorites, the bumblebees. Bryan takes a similarly labor-saving approach in his meadow gardens, chopping standing plant material into sections with a hedge trimmer and letting it fall to the ground as mulch around the time the garden breaks dormancy.

Considering that each mulch has its own strengths and weaknesses that interact with each site, there is no best mulch—even living groundcovers can serve as mulches. There are, however, a few mulches that could be called the worst. Chief among these is shredded rubber—also known as synthetic mulch—which is likely the most flammable mulch available. Plastic sheeting and woven-weed barriers don't deliver the weed-suppression they promise as the years go by, and they impede air and water exchange with soils. Among organic mulches, bark mulch—not the same as wood-chip or arborist mulch—and cardboard are worth avoiding; bark releases waxy substances that coat soils, reducing water infiltration, and preliminary testing indicates that some cardboard batches contain mentionable levels of so-called forever chemicals, such as PCBs.

Watering

It isn't a stretch to say that water is poised to be to the twenty-first century what oil was to the last: a precious commodity, the presence or absence of which profoundly impacts quality of life. In the American West, where so many gardeners rely on water from a tap (served by seasonal precipitation as rain and snow or by dwindling groundwater reserves), irrigation remains front-of-mind. Many native plants grow well without any irrigation once established, but after planting, even cacti need additional water in order to establish and grow an adequate root system to support them long term.

What's more, as lifelong tenders of both professional and personal plantings, Bryan and Lauren both feel it is good to have the option to irrigate during drought. Leaving one's plantings to their own devices come what may is harsh and foolhardy in terms of potential loss of time and financial investment, never mind the emotional aspect of watching plants suffer and succumb when perhaps just one deep watering could have spared them.

The most efficient way to deliver water to your garden is by drip irrigation, which delivers 85 percent or more of irrigation water directly to the soil. Such systems require irrigation clocks, wiring, plumbing, and appropriate pressure-regulating and backflow-prevention devices, which can be pricey, but if you are transitioning a lawn to a garden, these may already be in place and can be adapted for a drip system. Both Lauren and Bryan, who are routinely tweaking planting designs and broadcasting seeds in manners not amenable to a drip system, appreciate the simplicity and utility of the less-efficient (but cheap and long-lived) hose-end, cast-iron sprinkler (with efficiency from 50 to 70 percent). Otherwise, rotary sprinklers offer superior reach and soaker hoses make mobile and budget-friendly fill-ins for drip systems.

Regardless of how you apply water, irrigating regularly with a hose-end water wand after planting, then deeply and much less frequently with drip, a soaker hose, or a sprinkler for established plants will result in superior plant health and a lower water bill. Bryan waters his established plantings only as needed and does so by soaking each area until he sees puddling, moving the hose to a new location before returning it to the original location for another soaking. That way, the soil profile is soaked more deeply than with a single application, helping his plants grow plunging roots that are less susceptible to winter kill and can tap into deeper soil moisture provided by his efforts and spring snowmelt alike. Lauren measured what her hose-end sprinklers deliver by setting out a dozen empty cat-food cans and learned she can put down one inch of water in an hour. By pushing a screwdriver into her soil before and after watering, she learned that an inch of water moistens her porous, silty, cobbly soil to a depth of eight inches or more.

In David Salman's garden, claret cup cactus and yucca make a stunning native planting that needs no extra irrigation.

Gardens without winter snow-cover benefit from winter watering, especially those with woody plants and plants that are not yet established. Do so with a hose-end sprinkler or soaker hose at least once monthly, on days when temperatures are routinely above 45 degrees Fahrenheit and soils are not frozen. Be sure to unhook your hose from the spigot afterward, too.

Weeding

In gardens, weeds are simply plants out of place. These can be native or nonnative and benign or aggressive; much of what is or isn't a weed comes down to personal opinion. Ironically, "weeds" sometimes wind up being plants the gardener actually added to the site. Usually, a plant earns the status of weed once it interferes with the planting in some functional or aesthetic way. Most often, this is due to aggressive tendencies or aesthetic clashes. Aggressive weeds in our region typically spread by seed or by runners—shoots at or below the soil surface—or are capable of growing in a manner that smothers desirable plants.

Just like garden plants, weeds can be short-lived or long-lived. Short-lived weeds are best managed by preventing seed set to ensure they cannot reappear next year. This can be done by hand pulling, or in the case of large problem areas, mowing. When done consistently, these methods ensure that fewer seeds remain in the soil to germinate each spring. The collection of weed seeds in a soil is referred to as the soil's seed bank. It's important to note that any kind of disturbance, including ground clearing, tilling, and planting, creates opportunities for seeds in the garden's seed bank to germinate when bare ground is exposed. So, aim to minimize disturbance when performing routine chores around the garden and consider employing a mulch—living, inorganic, or organic—if your weed seed bank proves significant.

Long-lived weeds can be managed mechanically, but doing so takes commitment and consistency; pulling or cutting on a regular interval to prevent significant shoot development is key, as is preventing flowering and seeding. Particularly entrenched specimens, whose roots or rhizomes may be well out of the reach of even a tenacious gardener, typically require a chemical intervention. If you're unsure of the best way to approach a weed problem, consider reaching out to your county Extension agent or weed-district representative. Although horticultural vinegars appeal in concept, they should be avoided; killing only short-lived weeds and the foliage of long-lived weeds, they miss deep roots and rhizomes even more than hand tools do. Much more concentrated than vinegars intended for home use, weeding vinegars can cause skin injury and blindness if spilled or sprayed onto a person. We'll take the weeds.

Hand tools and sharp weed-identification skills, especially at seedling stages when weeds are most easily managed, remain the best approach. Bryan prefers the hori hori, also known as a soil knife, a tool halfway between trowel and knife that he found to be so effective it fundamentally changed how he felt about the chore of weeding. Lauren, with her arthritic hands, prefers the long and slender dandelion digger (also called an asparagus knife), which allows her to get to and extract sinewy and deep roots with less gripping force thanks to more leverage. For large patches of weeds, especially young weeds in pea gravel or similar mulches, or for weeding large spaces, a hula hoe (also called *stirrup hoe* or *scuffle hoe*) is just the ticket; Bryan has found he can weed his half-acre prairie garden in a few hours with just a hula hoe and a bad attitude. Regardless, both authors have found that—aside from mulching—planting densely and reducing soil disturbance in new gardens remain the easiest ways to reduce weeding in the long run.

Occasionally, a plant—usually an introduced plant—becomes so aggressive or damaging to a region's agriculture or environment that it is classified as noxious by the state, even at times incurring management obligations for anyone on whose property it appears. Many of these weeds, such as bindweed, Canada thistle, bouncing bet, and leafy spurge, are our worst garden weeds and are capable of outcompeting our native plants. Take action as soon as you identify them to minimize their burden on your garden.

Volunteers help edit and weed the steppe-like shortgrass portion of the young Prairie Garden at the Gardens on Spring Creek.

Garden Pests and Pathogens

Pathogens—organisms that cause diseases—are a part of life. Expect to see them occasionally in your garden, and know pathogens occur but rarely kill native plants. Generally, it's not worth worrying about a pathogen until you've seen it impact the plant for two years or more, since disease development requires not only the right host plant and disease, but also just the right environmental conditions, and each season is different. If a disease has become a repeat problem, simply finding a new, suitable home for the plant is often the best course of action. If the plant is too far gone, this home could be the trash—never the compost. And moving on, finding a plant better suited for the particular spot will often correct the issue in the long run. Most diseases are opportunistic on native plants, taking hold when the individual is already stressed by something else, like an unsuitable environment. Disorders—problems with plant growth caused by environmental factors—can often be corrected by changing something about the plant's environment, such as the type of mulch used, or by moving the plant to a more suitable home, same as when managing pathogens.

Pests are far more common than diseases in native plantings, though they aren't necessarily issues either. Many insects that have traditionally been considered garden pests, like aphids and caterpillars, are important parts of healthy ecosystems. Robust, well-sited garden plants do a good job of managing such critters from the inside out with their own defenses until natural predators or natural seasonal changes to the environment suppress populations. In the case of severe aphid or other soft-bodied insect infestations, a sharp jet of water directly from the garden hose at the infested shoots can do wonders, and a single treatment will usually tide plants over until beneficial insects arrive. Grasshoppers, highly mobile and hard-bodied, are another matter and among the most frustrating pests to manage. Gardeners with large properties can take advantage of a few noisy but effective Guinea fowl, but regardless, it's always best to reduce plant stress by keeping plantings properly watered, as grasshoppers can detect and preferentially feed on stressed plants.

Rodents can damage plants by feeding on roots and crowns, usually in gardens with lots of shelter for them from predators or those with sustained snow cover. If they prove problematic—as snow melts, channels appear in mulches and on the soil surface where plants disappear—consider cutting the garden back in fall in future years to make the place less appealing to them. Larger mammals, such as browsing deer, moose, or elk, can be particularly challenging and are best excluded with a pricey, twelve-foot wildlife fence. Simpler is to choose plants that are less appealing to the animals. This will likely require trial and error, as the animals' tastes vary by individual, season, location, and forage scarcity, though smelly plants, hairy plants, and plants with thorns are generally least appealing. In places that routinely host large mammals in rut, woody plants need to be caged at planting; an unprotected sapling makes a poor competitor against a romantically frustrated 700-pound elk. Cages can be removed as woody plants mature to a height where most tender tissues are out of the animals' reach.

Managing Plantings

We've named this section ***managing*** rather than ***maintaining***. Maintenance has a static feel, one of keeping things as they are or were. Plantings are rarely if ever static. Plants have their natural life cycles: some long, some short, some made shorter by forces outside our control. As most folks who live in our region know, our weather is among the least predictable in the entire country. Climate and weather impact how plants perform annually, seasonally, and even daily. The plantings we create also have their own interactions with each other and with the creatures that coexist with them. Rabbits or deer may determine what you can and can't grow, as may Japanese beetles or grasshoppers in some regions. Certain plants may become overly successful to the detriment of other plants. The planter/tender affects the planting by how much or little they intervene and in what ways. You may like an unexpected effect or decide to remove the opportunistic plant, make peace with doing some regular refereeing or remain impartial and just let things run their course, whatever that may be.

Contrary to popular belief, a planting made mostly or entirely of natives doesn't necessarily need less tending, just a different sort. While it's true that most native plants generally require less input in terms of water, fertilizer, and soil amendments than many (but not all) exotics, when it comes to weeds, deadheading, cutting back, and replanting, it's the site along with the life cycle and growth habit of a plant, not its provenance, that determines how much care a plant needs. It's also true that natives can be widely adaptable or very specific about their needs, just like nonnatives. Poorly adapted plants of any provenance need more input of soil amendments, water, fertilizer, and such, and often still don't thrive. In our region we have such varied elevations, soil types, and precipitation patterns that if you've read this far, you are already aware how important it is to know much more about a plant than just whether it's native to the region in order to choose the best plants for your particular situation.

Once you know what a particular plant wants and what it does when it is thriving, you know what to offer it in terms of sunlight, soil, space, and moisture. This book will help with that and also with what to expect from a plant in terms of looks, life cycle, and lifespan. Though all four are beloved and garden-adaptable Rocky Mountain wildflowers, a columbine or a penstemon won't usually live as long as plains gayfeather or sugarbowls, and they have different seasonalities and site and soil preferences. But some things are harder to predict. Some plants known to self-sow may reseed in one site and not in another. Gardening is not an exact science. The best gardeners have had lots of experience and learned from it, have not been afraid to try and to fail, have good intuition gained from keen observation of places and plants in the wild and in cultivation, and trust their gut feelings. For example, it's easier to guess when it's best to move or divide a plant, if at all, if you know when it grows most actively and what kind of root system it has, and whether it's long- or short-lived. In much of our region, many plants are at their most active in spring after snowmelt has charged the soil with ample moisture, but in areas such as the mountain southwest that receive late-summer and fall monsoonal rains and that have hot, dry, windy springs, some plants actually do their most active growth in late summer and fall. Plants that have a shorter life cycle generally don't divide or move well unless they are quite young. Plants with carrot-like taproots don't divide well and often don't move well either, except when they are small seedlings, whereas those with threadlike, fibrous root systems can be divided at almost any age or size if their crowns—where the stems and leaves meet the roots—can easily be teased or split into sections.

Deadheading—removing spent flowers and often also the flowering stems, at least down to the next leaf on the stem—is a tenet of traditional gardening because it can make a planting look fresher and tidier, it often pushes fresh leaf growth, and sometimes also promotes new bloom. However, allowing a flower to form seed offers the possibility for reseeding, collecting seed, and growing more of the plants yourself. What's more, many species' seeds also feed creatures. And allowing flowers to ripen seeds biologically signals to the plant that its bloom season is nearly ended and it's time to get ready for the next phase, whether that is making more foliage or preparing to go dormant for the dry season or for winter. As with so many things in gardening, there are pros and cons and we'll leave your choices on deadheading up to you. Bryan and Lauren collect a lot of seed for propagation and sharing. We also deadhead species that have shown tendencies to self-sow too much. In cases of short-lived wildflowers that haven't reseeded as much as we'd like or at all, we often deadhead to lengthen the life of the individual plant, as heavy bloomers and massive seed producers (such as penstemons and columbines) actually exhaust their reserves more quickly if all their flowers are allowed to form seed. Usually leaving one flowering stem to ripen seed is ample, and the rest can be cut off once the flowers finish; the plant's life is often extended a year or two this way.

Native Plants with Notable Winter Interest

Our region has a long winter, often extending into months traditionally considered fall and spring. Planting species that retain their visual appeal and, often along with it, some persistent seed, fruit, or good shelter for wildlife is a win for both creatures and people.

wildflowers

pussytoes *Antennaria* spp.
kinnikinnick *Arctostaphylos uva-ursi*
fringed sage *Artemisia frigida*
creeping grapeholly *Berberis repens*
narrowleaf coneflower *Echinacea angustifolia*
cutleaf daisy *Erigeron compositus*
crispleaf buckwheat *Eriogonum corymbosum*
yellow buckwheat *Eriogonum flavum*
roundleaf buckwheat *Eriogonum ovalifolium*
sulfur flower *Eriogonum umbellatum*
prairie smoke *Geum triflorum*
mat penstemon *Penstemon caespitosus*
silvermat penstemon *Penstemon linarioides*
bladderpod *Physaria* spp.
rock tansy *Sphaeromeria capitata*

grasses

big bluestem *Andropogon gerardii*
ruby muhly *Muhlenbergia reverchonii*
hardy deer muhly *Muhlenbergia rigens*
little bluestem *Schizachyrium scoparium*
golden feather grass *Sorghastrum nutans*
giant sacaton *Sporobolus wrightii*

all cacti and yuccas

shrubs

hardy manzanita *Arctostaphylos ×coloradensis*
silver sagebrush *Artemisia cana*
threadleaf sage *Artemisia filifolia*
big sagebrush *Artemisia tridentata*
Oregon grapeholly *Berberis aquifolium*
desert holly *Berberis fremontii*
littleleaf mountain mahogany *Cercocarpus intricatus*
fernbush *Chamaebatiaria millefolium*
red-twig dogwood *Cornus sericea*
rabbitbrush *Ericameria nauseosa*
common juniper *Juniperus communis*
creeping juniper *Juniperus horizontalis*
winterfat *Krascheninnikovia lanata*
snowberry *Symphoricarpos* spp.

trees

white fir *Abies concolor*
paper birch *Betula papyrifera*
curl-leaf mountain mahogany *Cercocarpus ledifolius*
one-seed juniper *Juniperus monosperma*
Rocky Mountain juniper *Juniperus scopulorum*
Black Hills spruce *Picea glauca* 'Densata'
Colorado spruce *Picea pungens*
bristlecone pine *Pinus aristata*
Taylor's Sunburst lodgepole pine *Pinus contorta* var. *latifolia* 'Taylor's Sunburst'
pinyon pine *Pinus edulis*
limber pine *Pinus flexilis*
ponderosa pine *Pinus ponderosa*
southwestern white pine *Pinus strobiformis*
aspen *Populus tremuloides*
Douglas fir *Pseudotsuga menziesii*
peachleaf willow *Salix amygdaloides*

Another traditional gardening chore is fall cleanup. This probably developed because most regions where gardening has been practiced for a long time are moist, temperate places where there are many trees dropping leaves and needles, and a huge amount of biomass accumulates each year. Leaving all this dead and dying debris around through a wet offseason can promote disease and rotting from dampness and lack of air circulation, and it can allow rodents to take up residence beneath the debris and destroy plant crowns, roots, and tree bark at the bases. Fall cleanup also appeals to long-prevailing tastes for making gardens look controlled and less "chaotic" or "messy." Again, there is no perfectly right or wrong answer to the fall cleanup conundrum. Leaving seedheads up all winter can save many a hungry bird. Insects, reptiles, and amphibians find cover from the elements in plant debris, and many lay their eggs on or in dead-plant material. We recommend leaving much of the dead and dying plant leftovers of the season in the garden over winter for these reasons, so long as leaves don't accumulate more than a few inches deep. If deep or matted, leaves can smother young or sensitive plants and reduce moisture and air exchange at the soil surface. If rodents have taken up fall and winter residence and are destroying the planting, as a colony of voles can do under the snow or beneath the dense duff of a planting in just one winter, then fall cleanup is recommended. If your site is large enough, not too windy, and fire danger isn't high, creating a fall-debris heap or two away from the plantings allows the insects and other creatures some access to the benefits of the dead-plant material—and may eventually turn into some good compost for your vegetables.

Spring cleanup has its own set of options and conundrums. Sometimes there's not enough time once the snow finally melts (and/or it's finally warm enough to work with our hands outdoors) to get everything cut back before plants are already growing through the old, dead duff, which makes it very hard to cut and remove dead duff quickly and well. Then there's the issue that many insects and their broods won't have emerged or hatched yet. Some gardeners, including Bryan, cut the debris and leave it at the base of plants as a mulch—known as "chop-and-drop." This works well in a dense planting exposed to very little wind. Or you can certainly create a spring-debris heap in a separate spot, perhaps enclosed in a compost bin if your site is windy, ensuring that any insect eggs that haven't hatched yet and any overwintering adults that haven't emerged yet have a chance to do so. Some towns have municipal mulching and composting sites where debris can be taken, so at least it gets recycled there and doesn't wind up in the landfill. The best news is that in our dry, harsh climate and our often-lean soils, most plantings don't create the amount of biomass each season that other regions' plantings do. Shrubs and trees are smaller, and many of their leaves and needles tend to blow away. Even our wildflowers tend to be shorter and less leafy than those in moister, more temperate regions. So, we have less seasonal dead-plant debris to come to terms with.

Lauren has worked outdoors physically with plants both professionally and for her own pleasure for more than four decades. Her hands are arthritic, and she doesn't want to spend as much time as in the past on seasonal cleanup in either her professional garden areas or her home garden. She has learned to make use of electric and battery-powered string trimmers and hedge trimmers, but hours of holding even those can wear on an older person's hands, arms, shoulders, and back. She's been moving toward plantings that need less of this seasonal chore, with shorter plants; more groundcovers, succulents, cacti, and fiber plants; and more shrubs. By reducing this labor-intensive cutting back, she saves her energy for other aspects of gardening and lessens the amount of annual biowaste her garden creates.

It's important to know that removing dead biomass during the offseason every year mines the soil of nutrients. Many of such components are replenished if one returns the garden's spent plant material back to its soil. That can be achieved with chop-and-drop, mulching the material with a mower, or composting. It takes additional time to process and put back the clippings, so some people don't. In the past Lauren has composted, and she has tried chop-and-drop with limited success (due to wind and the

Even a casual-looking, naturalistic planting requires tending. Lauren's garden needs less care than most traditional gardens of its size, but what she does is vital to keeping plants thriving, attractive, and in balance with one another.

debris not decomposing quickly enough in her dry plantings). She has hauled off countless truckloads to the municipal mulcher and then added alfalfa pellets to the plantings every few autumns to help replenish the soil. Now with much less cutting back, thanks to different plant choices and planting styles, she's found a good balance that works for her body, lifestyle, and her hopes for her garden.

A final word about managing your plantings: gardening is an ongoing, never-ending process, with cycles and surprises that engage us in the rhythms of regular and seasonal chores and demand we edit, referee, and deal with expected and unexpected growth, death, succession, and change. What our site offers—and what we do with it while we are in a position to steward and tend it—is an ongoing dance between weather, climate, soil, the creatures and plants and their interactions, and our own temperaments, desires, and abilities. Often wonderful, sometimes disappointing, often fun, and sometimes hard, it's an amazing dance so worth dancing.

Reading a Plant Profile

The plants profiled in this book are just a beginning. We've selected a group we are confident will make superb garden and landscape plants when matched to their preferred site and soil conditions. There are so many more natives out there; many of these will make wonderful garden plants too. Our choices reflect wildlife value, availability of plants or seeds, and our extensive experience with them.

◀ Here for a good time rather than a long time, this effusively blooming blazing star is short-lived, putting most of its energy and resources into flowers to produce a single, massive crop of seeds.

Profile category. The plant profiles are grouped into categories that describe the plant's use in the home landscape. Each category has its own section; categories include short-lived wildflowers (which typically live one to five years in the landscape), long-lived wildflowers (which typically live five or more years in the landscape), grasses, cacti and yuccas, shrubs, and trees.

Within each section, every plant profile contains the following data.

Most current scientific name. Older names common at nurseries and in seed catalogs are listed afterward in parentheses. "Spp." abbreviates "multiple species"; "×" indicates a naturally occuring hybrid between species.

Common name(s). Common names are tricky, and many plants have numerous common names. Some who are familiar with these plants may call them by different names or ones that are "officially recognized." The common names we provide are the ones, based on our experience, by which we know them.

Habitat. Includes the USDA hardiness zone rating, based on an average of the annual low for a given location over thirty years (our region falls primarily into zones 3–8); habitats and plant communities where the plant occurs in nature; regional biomes where the plant occurs in habitat; and soil-texture preferences of the plant in cultivation. Use this section to understand the conditions a plant is adapted to and whether your site might be a good fit.

Appearance and uses. Typical dimensions of this plant in cultivation are listed as height × width. Plants significantly taller when in flower have in-bloom height listed after main dimensions in parentheses. Some suggested garden types (meadow plantings) or uses (filler annual) are listed here.

Needs. Any specific light or water needs are called out here. "Sun" indicates six or more hours of direct sunlight; "light shade" indicates four to six hours of direct sunlight, mostly in the morning or dappled sun all day; and "shade" indicates four or fewer hours of direct sunlight. Sites with sun through the heat of the afternoon, even if only four to six hours, should typically be thought of as "sun." Also noted is the type of water regime the plant grows best in—to thrive, not just survive. The range includes the least common type, moist (prefers near-constant soil moisture); moderate (watering approximately weekly rather than within days); low (watering intervals in weeks); and very low (no irrigation needed except in times of unusual drought).

Wildlife icons. These icons indicate categories of insects and other animals for which this plant provides food. Research in this area is ongoing and such interactions vary by time and place. Some interactions have yet to be discovered. These categories include:

bees
birds
butterflies
hummingbirds
moths
other insects

Plants that are larval hosts (provide food) for juvenile insects: caterpillar

Description text. The appearance, character, and cultural preferences of the plant are discussed here, along with any relevant, experience-based information we can share about its care and use in landscapes. Examples of design combinations are provided for each plant to help the reader create gardens as beautiful as they are functional. Some simple ways to propagate each plant—by seed or other relevant methods—is also included in this section, since many native plants are not readily available for sale in all areas, and nursery-grown plants are costly. Seeds are best sown in seedling pots unless noted otherwise; those grown equally well in pots or direct-sown are notated "pot/direct-sow," while those best direct-sown receive only the term "direct-sow." Any necessary seed treatments or other secrets for success are included in parentheses afterward; possibilities include scarification, stratification, light exposure after sowing ("light"), or using only fresh seed. A comprehensive overview of these concepts and techniques is provided in "Growing Native Plants from Seed," beginning on page 38. We've indicated when cuttings are a good option for more experienced growers. When cuttings are specified, set at least one leaf node or more—leaves removed—below the top level of the potting mix. Division is listed for species if it is simple and successful; this remains one of the most homeowner-friendly means of multiplying a healthy plant. After bloom (except in the cases of some grasses—see their section's introduction for guidance), plant crowns can be split in two or more pieces with a sharp shovel and replanted, or dug and teased apart by hand (best when working with brittle roots and bulbs). Suckers—shoots running underground from some shrub species—can be dug and replanted as new plants in a similar manner; they come complete with roots and leaves. Suckers and divisions require extra watering and care after transplant and during establishment, as do seedlings. We hope this additional detailed information on both plant combinations and propagation helps with two of the biggest barriers to those wanting to garden with native plants: how to acquire them when they aren't available to buy, and how to integrate them aesthetically into a planting.

Short-lived Wildflowers

Wildflowers are among the most beloved of our native plants. Smaller in stature than trees and shrubs and also more fleeting, they not only evoke certain wild places but also mark the time of year and sometimes create a once-in-a-lifetime experience, pulling on and holding our heartstrings.

The plants gathered here under the grouping of "short-lived wildflowers" fall into one of three life cycles or scenarios. They can be annual by nature, growing from seed to mature plant that makes more seed and then dies in one growing season. A few are annual by culture, meaning they might be longer-lived than just one growing season in less harsh regions, but in most of our region, it's only once in a blue moon that they possibly overwinter in the warmest parts of our region—or only after an exceptionally mild winter.

The second group of short-lived wildflowers is biennials. These form foliage their first growing season after germinating from seed, and their leaves usually grow in a rosette or circular shape. Then the following growing season—the second year—the plant produces flowers, sets seed, and dies.

The third and last group are short-lived perennials—any plant that lives longer than a biennial but not typically more than five years, whether by its nature, by being difficult to keep happy for long in cultivation, or because it is on the edge of its hardiness in our region and eventually a hard winter takes it down for good.

All these short-lived wildflowers make excellent main players in new and young gardens, growing quickly, blooming at a young age, and often seeding profusely. Some of these plants will continue to thrive and fill in gaps here and there once the long-lived plants in the garden mature. Others don't do well with competition or aren't as at home in the conditions of the particular site, so they diminish and eventually disappear—unless you create a regularly disturbed area for them where you spread their seed, allow them to reseed, don't add more stalwart species, and continually monitor for and pull out unwanted interlopers. Wildflower meadows that don't include perennial grasses are often plantings of this sort.

Most of the wildflowers in this section are profuse seeders. This has its pros and cons. It ensures you have a chance at keeping the species around indefinitely even though its individuals don't live very long. It allows you to share the plants with others. But the seedlings may be overly profuse and aggressive with other plants.

With true short-lived perennials, it's usually wise not to let each plant ripen all the seed it has made, because it allows energy to be diverted back to the parent plant and gives it a chance to live an extra year or more than it would if it ripened every seed. A little ripe seed is usually plenty. So, the common gardening practice of deadheading is important with short-lived perennials to mitigate copious seed ripening and to extend their lives.

As for the annuals and biennials, either leave them standing until the following spring or remove some of the plants that have finished blooming. They won't rebloom, and it's a waste of time to just cut them back when they will die over winter. It's a case-by-case call whether to leave the dead seed stalks up over winter or remove them before they drop all their seed. Many creatures eat seed, and insects often use dead stalks to overwinter or lay eggs in. But on the other hand, if the seedlings typically are too many and hard to remove, it's not worth overwhelming the area and disturbing its balance and diversity. It will save you a lot of time and trouble if you get rid of most of the spent plants and only save a few for ripening some seed.

Abronia fragrans

sand verbena, snowball verbena

zones 4–9 • dry sandy flats, sparse grassland; plains, pinyon-juniper, shrub steppe, foothills • best in sandy or gritty soils

6–18 in. × 18–36 in. • unwatered flower gardens, cactus gardens, chaparral-inspired plantings, seeded wildflower plantings

sun • very low water

One of the most fragrant of our wildflowers; blooms from late spring until the weather cools in earnest in fall. Its gangly, sparse, sprawling habit is much wider than it is tall, but the long season of stunning white three-inch balls of tubular flowers makes up for its lack of form. Flowers open in late afternoon, enticing hawk moths, and carry on through evening and night, closing in the morning except on cloudy days. Sparse foliage with sticky, coarse stems. Typically self-sows a bit, replacing itself in a planting. Prefers a warm or even hot site; give it room to sprawl, bake, and bloom. *Abronia elliptica* (also *A. fragrans* var. *elliptica*) is almost indistinguishable and found wild in the Great Basin rather than on the Great Plains.

Propagation: pot/direct-sow seed (scarify then stratify)
Companion plants: yuccas, chollas, threadleaf sage, purple three-awn

Agastache foeniculum

anise hyssop, blue giant hyssop

zones 3–8 • meadows, forest clearings, watercourse margins; plains, foothills • most soils

4 ft. × 2 ft. • flower gardens, meadow plantings

sun, light shade • moderate to moist

This robust mint relative occurs broadly across the Northern Plains and Black Hills and is native to but uncommon in western Nebraska and the Colorado Front Range. Plants are clumping, not running, and mature quickly to four-foot, swaying specimens topped with spikes of lavender-blue flowers. Provides color and movement all summer, and spent blooms retain their color for some time. Birds are particularly fond of its very small, black seeds and pick them out of the flower spikes as they ripen. Despite this, the plant self-sows in favorable sites; seedlings are easily pulled and tend to not take over. The spearhead-shaped foliage has toothed edges, emerald-green tops, and shimmering, silvery white undersides. All parts of the plant have a licorice (anise) aroma when rubbed or crushed. Other blue-flowering hyssop species, such as nettleleaf giant hyssop (*Agastache urticifolia*), can be found higher in the mountains and on the Western Slope.

Propagation: pot/direct-sow seed (stratify) | **Companion plants:** wildflowers such as swamp milkweed, sneezeweed, meadow blazing star, cutleaf compass plant, partridge pea, and annual coreopsis; grasses like big bluestem, switchgrass, and golden feather grass

Aquilegia chrysantha

golden columbine

zones 4–8 • woodland clearings, canyons; foothills, montane • most well-drained soils

18–36 in. × 15–24 in. • flower gardens, under trees in light shade

sun, light shade • low to moderate water

Grows wild in varied habitats in the southern Rockies and Southwest, making it an exceptionally adaptable garden plant. Lacy, rounded, blue-green leaves form an attractive, ferny clump; in late spring through midsummer, masses of large, starry, bright yellow blossoms arise, brightening shady areas (the plant can also thrive in full sun if given more water). Deadheading finished flower spikes on the front end of the bloom season promotes continued bloom. Leave some spent flowers to seed later in summer if desired; small seedlings transplant readily, and seeds are also easy to grow in pots or flats. *Aquilegia flavescens* (native to the northern parts of the Rocky Mountains) is smaller but similar, with dangling flowers rather than the more out-and-up-facing ones of golden columbine. As is true of columbines in general, golden columbine and its close relatives are poisonous and resistant to animal browsing.

Propagation: seed | **Companion plants:** harebells, Rocky Mountain penstemon, tufted hair grass

Aquilegia coerulea (Aquilegia caerulea)

Rocky Mountain columbine

zones 3–7 • meadows, aspen woods, moist rocky slopes; foothills, montane, subalpine, alpine • most well-drained soils

18–24 in. × 12–18 in. • shady or cool high-elevation flower gardens; under trees that cast light shade

sun, light shade • moderate water

This gorgeous wildflower graces much of the Rocky Mountains' high country in summer and is Colorado's state flower. Lovely, delicate leaves comprise several lobed leaflets that frame the large, two- to three-inch flowers. Blossoms usually have white central petals and blue outer petals (technically sepals) and look like one flower placed on top of another; rarer all-white and all-blue forms can be found. Remove (deadhead) finished flower spikes to prolong flower production. Like most columbines, this plant self-sows and often crosses with other nearby columbine species. Similar in beauty, long bloom time, and wildlife benefits to golden columbine, this plant needs cooler temps and more moisture than golden columbine to thrive, so it's better for gardens at higher elevations and latitudes. It's also poisonous and resistant to browsing by wildlife. Few summer scenes are as refreshingly serene and lovely as a spangle of Rocky Mountain columbine blooming in the dappled shade of an aspen grove.

Propagation: seed | **Companion plants:** shade trees such as aspen, alder, or birch; mountain phlox

Aquilegia desertorum

desert columbine

zones 3–7 • dry meadows, woodland clearings, rocky slopes; shrub steppe, pinyon-juniper, montane • most well-drained soils

15–24 in. × 12–18 in. • flower gardens, meadow plantings, under trees that cast light shade

sun, light shade • low water

One of the finest plants for hummingbirds, this isn't a true desert plant but needs very little water to thrive compared to most columbine species. Deceptively delicate-looking, it makes a superb garden plant, adapting to a wide range of moisture and light levels. Dainty gray-blue leaves give rise to bicolored soft red and pale yellow flowers starting in late spring and on through much of summer. The blossoms are wider, more open, and have more yellow in them than the downward-facing bells of similar western red columbine (*Aquilegia elegantula*). Most important, this plant thrives in drier and hotter conditions, coming from the most southwestern parts of the region; it is also poisonous and resistant to rabbit and deer damage.

Propagation: seed | **Companion plants:** smaller bunchgrasses, such as rice grass and pine fescue; sundrops, sulfur flower

Aquilegia elegantula

western red columbine

zones 3–7 • moist woodland, streamsides, ravines; shrub steppe, pinyon-juniper, montane, subalpine • most moist soils

12–18 in. × 10–15 in. • shaded flower gardens under trees that cast light shade

sun, light shade • moderate water

Demure, charming flowers dangle like bells, with backswept red spurs full of nectar for hummingbirds. Yellow-tipped petals help make this plant's flowers more visible in the shady glens it usually inhabits; it's one of our region's best shade-loving natives, of which there are (compared to sun-lovers) few. It blooms in early summer and continues for longer if kept moist. Resembles *Aquilegia formosa* (aka western columbine), which is native farther west, and its more southwesterly cousin *Aquilegia desertorum*, which has bluer leaves, more wide-spreading red and yellow flowers, and prefers a drier habitat.

Propagation: seed | **Companion plants:** common juniper, creeping grapeholly, boulder raspberry, and wood lily

Argemone polyanthemos

prickly poppy, cowboy's fried egg

zones 3–8 • grassland, disturbed pastures, roadsides, mesas; plains, foothills, pinyon-juniper, shrub steppe • sandy or gritty soils

2–4 ft. × 1–3 ft. • unwatered flower gardens, chaparral-inspired gardens, seeded wildflower plantings

sun • very low water

This late-spring and summer bloomer's huge, white, poppy-like flowers beckon from afar. Their round centers, clusters of golden stamens, explain the charming common name *cowboy's fried egg*. Waxy, lobed blue-green leaves with white veins and thorns clasp the bristled flower stems. A large, sparse, gawky plant, it makes up for what it lacks in form with its flowers and unusual foliage color. Prickly oval pods enclose multitudes of round black seeds, making seed collection dicey. All this armature plus a bitter, staining yellow sap keep it safe from browsing, but the flowers attract many pollinators. Prefers little if any competition from other plants; in denser, more clayey soils, plant it on a slope or berm. The closely related, more compact *Argemone hispida* (bristled prickly poppy) has the same large flowers but paler blue foliage (almost silver with no obvious white venation). It is entirely covered in bristles, yet these are easier to handle than those of *A. polyanthemos*. In many ways, it's a better garden plant, but most seed available is of the larger species.

Propagation: direct-sow seed (stratify) | **Companion plants:** yuccas; threadleaf sage, littleleaf mountain mahogany, fernbush, Apache plume, Palmer's penstemon, silvery lupine, and Geyer's larkspur

Artemisia frigida

fringed sage, prairie sagewort

zones 3–8 • meadows, exposed soil, roadsides; most life zones • most well-drained soils

6 in. × 18 in. (12 to 18 in. in bloom) • perennial gardens, meadow plantings, hellstrips, rock gardens, seeded wildflower plantings

full sun • low to moderate water

Skirting roadsides with a haze of frilly, silver foliage and minute, silver-capped yellow flowers, this gorgeous plant frames wild spaces across our region. Particularly striking en masse or sprinkled through a planting, it adds structure and silver punctuation among wildflowers and grasses. Out of bloom, it keeps a low profile of feathered, aromatic foliage just above the soil surface, where it can be easy to miss. An excellent addition to waterwise perennial gardens, where it can be used like a low-growing grass, a subshrub, or as a texture-rich perennial that unites leafy or busy designs; its pale countenance also makes it ideal for evening gardens. Like other native *Artemisia* species, it is an important larval host for insects and provides food and cover for birds and small mammals.

Propagation: pot/direct-sow seed (stratify, light)
Companion plants: a seeded flower meadow of wild blue flax, scarlet gilia, and tansy aster; in contrast to yuccas and buffalo gourd; among asters and glowing grasses such as ruby muhly or little bluestem; in a "night garden" of evening primroses, angel's trumpet, and snow on the mountain

Berlandiera lyrata

chocolate daisy, chocolate flower

zones 4–8 • roadsides, rocky areas, mesas; plains, foothills • most well-drained soils

15–30 in. × 12–18 in. • hellstrips, seeded wildflower plantings, along edges where fragrance can be enjoyed

sun • low water

These cheerful lemon-yellow daisies with greenish centers and reddish brown undersides bloom from spring till frost, but the best thing about this wildflower is that it smells like milk chocolate in the morning. The velvety, pale gray-green foliage makes a nice foil for the bloom. Shape-wise the plant is coarse and floppy, but the long parade of flowers and their unusual fragrance make up for that. Even the seedheads, whose leftover scalloped green bracts have a blossom-like shape, look like green flowers. Self-sows and, because it's taprooted, doesn't transplant well except when very small. Plant this deer-resistant wildflower where you can smell it—by a doorway, in a courtyard, along a path.

Propagation: pot/direct-sow seed | **Companion plants:** fringed sage or a grass such as ruby muhly, pine fescue, or little bluestem

Castilleja integra

orange paintbrush

zones 3–8 • dry grassland, slopes, mesas, rocky or gravelly sites; plains, foothills, shrub steppe, pinyon-juniper, montane • sandy or gravelly soils

6–12 in. × 6–12 in. • low dry meadow plantings, hellstrips, in native shortgrass lawn

sun • low water

From lush meadows high in the mountains to hot, dry roadsides on the plains, come late spring and summer the flame-shaped, plump flower spikes of numerous paintbrush species bloom spectacularly over much of the mountain west. They rise on stiff stems clothed in often-narrow leaves, sometimes in bouquet-like clusters and in every hue but blue and purple. This group of striking wildflowers is notoriously difficult to tame in cultivation, mainly due to their semiparasitic nature: they require a host plant (such as a grass or sagebrush) to thrive. One of the easiest to tame in the garden, this species' individual plants rarely live for more than a few years in cultivation, but with enough hosts around will often self-sow over time. In trials, Lauren has found her now self-seeding population prefers hosts of fringed sage and various buckwheats to the ample grasses nearby. Two more (whose preferred hosts are fortunately available at nurseries) grow at middle and lower altitudes in the region: *C. chromosa* is native farther west and more red than orange; *C. linariifolia* is the largest, a vibrant vermilion, and Wyoming's state flower.

Propagation: direct-sow seed into host (stratify) | **Companion plants:** blue grama, buffalo grass, buckwheats, or fringed sage

Chamaecrista fasciculata

partridge pea

all zones (annual) • grassland, drainages, rocky places; plains • most soils

1–2 ft. × 1–2 ft. • filler annual in flower gardens, meadow plantings, cottage gardens

sun, light shade • moderate water

Few annuals, especially natives with such a broad range of benefits, are as attractive, versatile, and well-behaved as this one. With just a few years of use, it has become one of the most important annuals in Bryan's gardens, filling in disturbed spaces and fleshing out thin bed margins without fuss. The plant germinates easily, though late in spring, from scattered seed and grows quickly to fill garden holes, complementing grasses and coarse perennials alike thanks to delicate-looking ferny foliage that folds up at night. At the bases of this plant's leaves are extra-floral nectaries (glands producing nectar), which attract a range of insect pollinators. Blooms generously from midseason to frost, steadily producing rich gold, quarter-sized blooms that pepper its full and handsome form. Since this species throws its relatively large seeds from its pods as they shatter, it can spread across a site but rarely becomes a nuisance: individuals don't outcompete most longer-lived plants and are easy to pull out from spots where they aren't desired.

Propagation: direct-sow seed | **Companion plants:** linear, upright grasses such as little bluestem or big bluestem; wildflowers including giant blue hyssop, prairie blazing star, swamp milkweed, ironweed, and azure sage

Cirsium canescens

prairie thistle

zones 3–8 • slopes, meadows, forest clearings; plains, foothills, pinyon-juniper, shrub steppe, montane • most well-drained soils; avoid wet clay

6 in. × 1 ft. (2 ft. in bloom) • rock gardens, meadow plantings, hellstrips

sun • low to moderate water

In American gardening circles, the word *thistle* arrives with a load of baggage. Most of us think of the highly aggressive, rhizomatous Canada thistle (*Cirsium arvense*), which is not Canadian at all, but an introduction from Eurasia. Our native thistles are not like this thuggish titan, and some make attractive, well-behaved garden plants. This handsome native thistle grows in wild spaces with some open soil, from the plains to the montane. Forming a striking, armed rosette of filigreed, silver leaves in its first year, it follows with a branched inflorescence of delicately prickly, white- to pink-blushed pompoms. These plants are monocarpic perennials, meaning they spend one or more years as rosettes, bloom only once when conditions are favorable, and then die after producing seed. Makes an unusual addition to dry meadows and rock gardens, especially where its incredible leaf and plant form can make its way through a veil of tawny grasses. Since it's taprooted, site it once; this thistle won't transplant well. Worth considering as garden plants even if their looks don't capture you, our native thistles are exceptionally valuable plants for local insects.

Propagation: seed (stratify, light) | **Companion plants:** midsized bunchgrasses such as blue and sideoats gramas, pine fescue, ruby muhly, and alkali sacaton; fringed sage, annual buckwheat, plains gayfeather, and snow on the mountain

Cleomella serrulata (Cleome serrulata)

Rocky Mountain beeplant

all zones (annual) • roadsides, barren areas, disturbed sites; plains, shrub steppe, pinyon-juniper, foothills • most soils

2–5 ft. × 2–4 ft. • cottage garden, meadow plantings, seeded wildflower plantings, chaparral-inspired plantings

sun • low to moderate water

In the wild, often seen on the roadside from a car window as a flash of magenta spires among a silver sea of sage. Defying drought, it blooms though the heat of summer in our region, often with little rain. Unusual four-petaled flowers with long, protruding stamens give the plant an almost fuzzy look that makes an interesting textural addition in otherwise-chunky plantings, such as with annual sunflower. Its dramatic, strongly branched, and upright form and its easy movement add a dynamic layer to stiffer plant combinations. More manageable if grown dry; if irrigated regularly, it can quickly grow as tall as its caretaker and is then prone to flopping. While adored by bees, the species is sought out by a diversity of insects. Yellow beeplant, *Cleomella lutea*, is particularly drought-adapted, more compact, and has a lovely yellow flower. It blooms earlier and more briefly than this species. Both species are excellent in low-care wildflower plantings where they can grow and seed with abandon.

Propagation: direct-sow seed (stratify) | **Companion plants:** prickly poppy, angel's trumpet, alkali sacaton, and giant sacaton

Coreopsis tinctoria

plains coreopsis, calliopsis

all zones (annual) • disturbed locations; plains, foothills, has naturalized in pinyon-juniper, shrub steppe, montane • most soils

1–3 ft. × 1 ft. • annual filler, meadow plantings, hellstrips, cottage gardens, seeded wildflower plantings

sun • low to moderate water

This cheery, easy-to-grow wildflower is a versatile addition to meadow and perennial gardens as an excellent filler before longer-lived species have reached full size. Produces more flower than leaves, with masses of half-dollar-sized, golden yellow blossoms that have rusty, red-brown centers. Occasionally, all-red or all-yellow forms can be found. Attractive even before bloom thanks to finely cut, bright green foliage and buds covered with a bronzy metallic sheen, each with a green collar. While typically annual, it can perennialize in the right setting and regardless produces a significant amount of seed; be prepared to deadhead or accept that these plants may spread by self-sowing (especially on bare dirt, with thin perennial cover, or in gravel mulch). Can be established in most gardens simply by throwing seed out, ideally before a winter snow, but in early spring as well. Rake the seed in lightly to reduce losses to birds if sowing in spring, but remember the seeds do need light for optimal germination.

Propagation: direct-sow seed (light) | **Companion plants:** wild blue flax, western yarrow, partridge pea, Rocky Mountain beeplant, snow on the mountain, and black-eyed Susan

Datura wrightii (*Datura inoxia*)

angel's trumpet, thorn apple, sacred datura

zones 5–9 • hot disturbed areas, roadsides, arroyos; plains, pinyon-juniper • most well-drained soils

2–3 ft. × 3–5 ft. • chaparral-inspired plantings, flower gardens, accents near patios or entryways, in courtyards

sun • very low water

A standout for its sheer size and bold texture. A mound of large, velvety, gray-green foliage makes the perfect backdrop for its huge, funnel-shaped white blossoms. These unfurl from elegantly folded, umbrella-like buds in evening, wafting a sweet fragrance, and close the next morning. Late-foraging bees often impatiently chew holes in the still-closed tubes; they return in the early morning, rolling around inside the open flowers, seemingly intoxicated. Blooms throughout summer and fall until cool evenings stop the production of new buds, frost withers the plant, and it dies down to a fleshy taproot. It survives as a long-lived, self-sowing perennial in our region's mildest parts, but in most areas performs as an annual or short-lived perennial. The entire plant is poisonous and potentially deadly. Indigenous peoples brew the roots to induce visions for ceremonies, but this is *not* something to try at home. The seedpods—the thorn apples—are large, round, and covered in bristles. Give this plant loads of heat: by patios, against walls or rocks, along pathways—anywhere you spend time in the evening and can enjoy its beauty and scent.

Propagation: pot/direct-sow seed (scarify) | **Companion plants:** yuccas, chollas, and silver sages; rabbitbrush, winterfat, mountain mahogany, and Apache plume

Dieteria bigelovii (*Machaeranthera bigelovii*)

Bigelow's tansyaster

zones 3–8 • disturbed areas, roadsides; most life zones • sandy or gritty soils

1–4 ft. × 2–4 ft. • seeded wildflower gardens, unwatered flower gardens, meadow plantings

sun • very low water

For many weeks in late summer and fall, this cheerful wildflower festoons roadsides in purple waves and billows. Height varies, depending on rainfall and verge mowing. Flowers grow profusely in great branched mounds, daisylike and a good inch across each with bright yellow centers. A biennial, it takes one year to develop a small foliage rosette and the following year to bloom, after which it sets loads of fluffy seed and then dies. Deer- and rabbit-resistant; grows easily from seed sown directly on-site in fall or spring. Two close relatives deserve mention: summer-flowering, much smaller Tahoka daisy (*Machaeranthera tanacetifolia*) is a true annual, coming up from seed, flowering, ripening seed, and then dying in one growing season. It mingles beautifully with smaller bunchgrasses such as blue grama and has pretty, ferny, gray-green leaves. Hoary tansyaster (*Dieteria canescens*) is larger, has gray, hairy foliage, and blooms later. Any young seedlings that have self-sown into unwanted places can simply be moved to other spots in spring when they are small.

Propagation: pot/direct-sow seed (stratify, light) | **Companion plants:** grasses; shrubby broomweed and rabbitbrush

Erigeron divergens

spreading daisy, cloud daisy

zones 3–8 • grassland, mesas, slopes; plains, foothills • most well-drained soils

4–12 in. × 10–18 in. • chaparral-inspired plantings, hellstrips, low meadow plantings

sun • low water

This wildflower's dainty looks belie its tough and pushy nature. It seeds like mad in many different soils when given bare spots and sun. Introduce it to areas where its progeny won't outcompete less-fertile or smaller species, and you'll be rewarded with charming, long-blooming bouquets of daisies. Typically white, the flowers can be pink or pale lavender, the latter especially as weather cools in fall. All have yellow centers and close on cloudy days and at night. Plants begin their lives as small, neat, flat rosettes of foliage before blooming the following year. Slender, branched stems open a months-long succession of flowers, pausing during the hottest, driest parts of summer if left unwatered.

Unlike similar-looking, longer-lived trailing daisy (*Erigeron flagellaris*), spreading daisy fortunately spreads only by seed, not by runners—but it's nearly impossible to keep spent flowers from forming and releasing copious airborne seed without sacrificing a whole new batch of bloom. Rosettes are thankfully easy to remove where not wanted. Keep this cutie out of more intricate and small-scale plantings such as rock gardens and flower borders, where it will overwhelm other plants.

Propagation: pot/direct-sow seed (light) | **Companion plants:** shrubs, fiber plants, and large, bulky grasses; strong, fast-growing wildflowers such as Maximilian sunflower, horsemint, prairie coneflower, western yarrow, and desert four o'clock

Eriogonum annuum

annual buckwheat

all zones (annual) • sandy prairies, roadsides, areas with sparse or short vegetation; plains, foothills • sandy or gritty soils

2–4 ft. × 1–2 ft. • cottage gardens, meadow plantings, seeded wildflower plantings

sun, light shade • low water

Punctuates sand prairies as a vertical accent, tall and elegant with a silver cast and large, white, many-branched flower cluster held several feet above the ground. Viewed up close, the flower stems and seedheads often feature an understated pink blush that complements the wildflower's statuesque form and reserved coloring. Easy to grow, provided it is seeded on a coarse-textured soil, not clay, and makes a great accent for otherwise-dull spots from late July through September. Native from southern New Mexico to central Montana, it is diverse; local forms may feature colors, size, or other variations not seen in commercial seed. Transplants quite poorly, but germinates and grows with ease if direct-sown early enough—Bryan and Lauren often do so in late winter/early spring on top of existing or before new snow. Viability can be low, so be prepared to throw a good amount of the seed around. Hits its stride as many of our regional garden staples are looking tired, and so can make a reliable and carefree accent to carry plantings through the latter half of summer.

Propagation: direct-sow seed (stratify) | **Companion plants:** stands of warm-season grasses such as little bluestem, deer muhly, and alkali sacaton; plains blazing star

Erysimum asperum

western wallflower

zones 4–8 • dry grassland, sandy prairie, roadsides; plains, foothills, pinyon-juniper, montane • most well-drained soils

6–24 in. × 4–8 in. • meadow plantings, hellstrips, seeded wildflower plantings

sun • low water

One of our earlier and longer-blooming wildflowers, opens in spring and carries on well into early summer. Can be single-stemmed or branched, with rounded clusters of cheerful yellow to orange flowers from a rosette of narrow foliage. Blossoms have a faint, sweetly spicy fragrance.

Erysimum capitatum (prairie rocket) is very similar but is larger, prefers moister conditions, tolerates more shade, and thrives at high elevations. Its subalpine and alpine forms are yellow, lavender, or maroon; lower forms are typically orange or yellow. Both species often rebloom throughout summer when there's adequate moisture. *Erysimum capitatum* var. *capitatum* (sanddune wallflower) is the largest, with bright orange flowers. These western wallflowers self-sow and are easy to grow.

Propagation: seed | **Companion plants:** fringed sage; small bunchgrass such as purple three-awn or rice grass; wild blue flax, narrowleaf penstemon, and prairie verbena

Euphorbia marginata

snow on the mountain

all zones (annual) • grassland, overgrazed pastures, roadsides; plains • most well-drained soils

1–4 ft. × 1–3 ft. • unwatered flower gardens, meadow plantings, cottage gardens

sun • low water

This summer- and fall-blooming annual plains wildflower grows from a single, stout stem that branches near the top, making a domed bouquet of what seem to be white flowers. But it's the whorled bracts and leaves *around* the barely noticeable flowers that have pure white margins, giving the effect of shimmering white flowers. (This same thing is true with its more southerly Mexican cousin, poinsettia, with bract colors of red, pink, orange, or ivory.) The actual flowers, though tiny, attract pollinators. It's important to note that a variegated form of goutweed, or bishop's weed (*Aegopodium podagraria*), is sometimes called "snow on the mountain"; not to be confused with this annual wildflower, it is an aggressively spreading exotic groundcover used commonly in watered shady plantings.

Amid the tawny grasses of late summer and autumn, this plant fairly glows. Large round seeds explode from its capsules. Sticky, poisonous white sap keeps this plant safe from browsing and can irritate skin. Doesn't transplant well, and insists on full sun and a warm spot—the warmer the better.

Propagation: direct-sow seed (scarify or stratify)
Companion plants: midsized grasses; purple prairie clover, butterfly weed, Indian blanket, asters, gayfeather, and goldenrod

Eustoma exaltatum ssp. *russellianum* (*Eustoma grandiflorum*)

prairie gentian

zones 4–9 • pond margins, wetland edges; plains • moist clay soils

1–2 ft. × 1–2 ft. • well-watered border edges, specimen plant

sun, light shade • moderate water to moist

As unmistakable as it is elusive on the High Plains and along the margins of the Rockies. Despite its broad presence across a massive range from central Texas to central New Mexico and north to the Wyoming and South Dakota borders, it occurs rarely, popping up here and there as its relatively infrequent habitat requirements permit. Often, plants appear for a brief time on clay-heavy pond margins after a disturbance and then disappear, not to be seen for years.

This plant's large, satin-sheened, tulip-shaped royal purple flowers stand out in their harsh environment. Centers have boldly contrasting yellow eyes; handsome blue-green leaves are arranged in pairs, and the flower petals twist into elegant, tapered buds before opening. Plants in our region are recognized as subspecies *russeliana*, but *Eustoma exaltatum* occurs across most of southern North America and well into Central America.

Lisianthus, a more garden-adapted relative, was developed by the horticulture industry from this plant and offers an alternative if you can't find prarie gentian seed. Both make superb long-lasting cut flowers, with prairie gentian being one of our finest native flowers for bouquets.

Propagation: seed (stratify) | **Companion plants:** moisture-loving beauties such as wild hollyhock, swamp milkweed, and checkerbloom

Gaillardia pulchella

firewheel

all zones (annual) • roadsides, grasslands; plains • most well-drained soils

10–24 in. × 6–18 in. • cottage gardens, meadow plantings, hellstrips, seeded wildflower plantings

sun • low water

The bright red, yellow, and orange banded daisies of this wildflower bloom from spring to midsummer and in cooler areas until frost. They may be entirely red or yellow but most commonly are orange-red with yellow tips, giving the bright and unusual bicolored effect the wildflower is known for. The felted gray-green foliage is unremarkable, but the flowers make up for it. A true annual, this plant goes to seed and dies after bloom; it also self-sows on-site and is deer- and rabbit-resistant. Unlike most drought-loving wildflowers, makes a good cut flower.

Avoid planting the fluffy and pompom selections common in nurseries: through hybridization, they have sacrificed most of their stamens and pollen for more showy "petals," or ray parts, and therefore have little (if any) food left for pollinators.

Propagation: pot/direct-sow seed (light) | **Companion plants:** small bunchgrasses; Rocky Mountain or smooth penstemons, yellow sundrops, and wild blue flax

Glandularia bipinnatifida var. *bipinnatifida* (*Verbena bipinnatifida*)

prairie verbena, Dakota mock vervain

zones 3–9 • disturbed sparse sites, dry grassland, rocky slopes; plains, pinyon-juniper, shrub steppe, foothills • sandy or gritty soils

6 in. × 1–2 ft. • rock gardens, hellstrips, edges, low dry meadow plantings

sun • low to moderate water

This plant has been subjected to an identity crisis by the botany and horticulture communities; it is sold under several scientific and common names, including (oddly enough) both "Dakota vervain" and "Dakota mock vervain." Know this: a handsome, if slightly wild-looking, low-growing, native verbena in a pot at a nursery is probably a good bet for your garden. Grows vigorously once in the ground, producing low, spreading stems with deeply twice-cut (bipinnate) foliage during the early season. Numerous clusters of magenta to lilac-purple flowers follow in early summer; the plant continues producing them for several months. Stops blooming in response to dry soil yet will continue to flower lightly through summer with modest irrigation. Particularly attractive as a path-edger, near rocks, or as a front-of-bed filler in young gardens. Rose vervain (*Glandularia canadensis*) and Davis Mountains mock vervain (*G. bipinnatifida* var. *ciliata*) are related plants from the margins of our region with similar habit, but rose vervain is less drought-tolerant and Davis Mountains mock vervain is less cold-hardy.

Propagation: cuttings; seed (stratify) | **Companion plants:** low-growing species such as sulfur flower, evening primrose, and purple three-awn; blue grama and fringed sage

Helianthus annuus

annual sunflower

all zones (annual) • roadsides, disturbed areas, overgrazed grassland; plains, foothills, shrub steppe, montane • most well-drained soils

3–10 ft. × 2–4 ft. • filler in neglected bare spots, fencerows

sun • moderate water

This widespread and beloved wildflower's large, chocolate-eyed, golden daisies brighten fields and bring cheer to long drives through the Great Plains from midsummer into fall. Kansas's state flower, its blossoms are typically three to four (and up to six!) inches across. The roughly hairy plant borders on ungainly, with coarse foliage on woody, almost sapling-width, widely branched stems; makes a good cut flower. Avoid pollen-free selections (developed for the cut-flower trade because pollen stains tablecloths), as these have little to no food for pollinators.

This is a true annual, and it self-sows abundantly. The seed is allelopathic, meaning it releases chemicals into soil that inhibit and stunt the growth of other plants nearby. For that reason, and also because they're so large, plant sunflowers away from anything but the toughest shrubs. Prairie sunflower (*Helianthus petiolaris*) is much smaller with narrower foliage; it prefers sandy soils and does better in drier conditions than annual sunflower, but rivals it as a mecca for pollinators and birds. Keep sunflower seedheads and stems up until mid- to late spring: seeds help nourish birds in winter (stiff-branched plant skeletons make great feeding stations), and the semi-hollow, pithy stems serve as important overwintering sites for insects.

Propagation: seed | **Companion plants:** tough shrubs such as leadplant or sumac; giant sacaton grass

Hymenoxys hoopesii (*Helenium hoopesii, Dugaldia hoopesii*)

owl's-claws, orange sneezeweed

zones 3–8 • mountain meadows, slopes, streamsides; montane, shrub steppe, subalpine • medium to moist, well-drained soils

2–3 ft. × 1–2 ft. • perennial gardens, wildflower gardens

full sun, light shade • moderate water to moist

Late-season hikers in our region occasionally come across meadows swimming in seas of brassy gold flowers with long, slender, drooping petals borne on stiff stems. If the meadow is seasonally moist, there's a good chance these are *Hymenoxys hoopesii*. A victim of repeated botanical reclassification complicating the names it may be sold under, it remains one of our most distinctive and dramatic wildflowers and a great garden plant for the mountains and foothills. Leaves are atypically glossy and lush for a wildflower of this region.

Pollinators adore the pollen-rich flowers, which appear late season in the mountains but can be seen as early as May at lower elevations. On lower, warmer sites, plants perform best with regular irrigation. Some forms (like those in the trade from high elevations in Arizona) are reputed to be better for gardens in warmer parts of our region, such as the Front Range, than those collected farther north in the Rockies. Regular deadheading extends the bloom season.

Propagation: seed (light) | **Companion plants:** blue and purple penstemon species, like dusky penstemon

Hymenoxys richardsonii

Colorado rubberweed

zones 3–8 • rocky slopes, dry sparse grassland; plains, foothills, shrub steppe, pinyon-juniper, montane • most well-drained soils

6–15 in. × 8–15 in. • rock gardens, low dry meadow plantings, hellstrips, seeded wildflower plantings, unwatered flower gardens

sun • very low water

In summer in the harshest of places, it's surprising and delightful to see this plant's small yet bushy bouquets of many lemon-yellow daisies blooming when everything else has either finished or is waiting for late-season rains. The jaunty daisies cover the top of the plant and are about an inch across with fringed edges. Narrow, almost needle-like green foliage cloaks the stiffly upright semiwoody stems, making small shrubby forms similar to broomweed and dwarf rabbitbrush but with much earlier, paler yellow flowers. Their yellow has a glowing, cool moonlight quality with an entirely different effect than the warm, rich, strong yellows more common for our region's wildflowers.

Deer- and rabbit-resistant and readily self-sows. Like broomweed, its reputation as a sign of overgrazed pastures has kept it from receiving positive attention as an excellent plant for tough sites, high-summer color, and nectar and pollen.

Propagation: seed (light) | **Companion plants:** tough, low, and bushy wildflowers such as blackfoot daisy and plains skullcap; in a prairie-style planting with purple three-awn, buffalo grass, and blue grama

Ipomopsis aggregata (Gilia aggregata)

scarlet gilia

zones 3–8 • rocky soils, roadsides, meadows, forest clearings; plains, foothills, shrub steppe, pinyon-juniper, montane • sandy or gritty soils

4 in. × 4 in. (up to 2 ft. tall and wide in bloom) • meadow plantings, cottage gardens, seeded wildflower plantings

sun • low to moderate water

Frequently long-lived in nature, this plant's small, feathered, gray-green rosette sits in repose (for one to many years) until it finds its Goldilocks conditions. Once the mix of precipitation, sun, and other variables combine to be "just right," the plant shoots up tall spikes of flashy, tubular red, orange, peach, or creamy yellow flowers. In gardens, where conditions are often more favorable, the plant can flower much sooner, even after just one full season. It is monocarpic, dying shortly after setting seed. In bloom, it is a beacon to hummingbirds, who find food by sight and appreciate this equivalent of a brightly colored restaurant sign.

Bryan, gardening in clay soil, substitutes *Ipomopsis rubra* (standing cypress) for this plant. Native to the Southern Plains, it resembles a taller, denser version of scarlet gilia that is unperturbed by fine-textured soils. On coarser soils, slendertube skyrocket (*Ipomopsis aggregata* var. *tenuituba*), a high-elevation close cousin sporting softer hues of peach, salmon, pink, and white, thrives. Native gilias hybridize, so intermediates crop up in both gardens and the wild.

Propagation: pot/direct-sow seed (stratify) | **Companion plants:** shrubby silver sages and blue desert holly; fringed sage, evening primrose, rice grass, sideoats grama, and pine fescue

Leptosiphon nuttallii ssp. *nuttallii* (*Linanthus nuttallii* ssp. *nuttallii*)

mountain phlox, white stars

zones 4–8 • hillsides, woodland clearings; foothills, montane, subalpine • most well-drained soils

6–12 in. × 12–18 in. • rock gardens, lightly shaded gardens, slope plantings, edges, front of planting

sun to light shade • low to moderate water

This delicate-looking workhorse of a wildflower blooms all summer if not growing in too hot a site. In areas with hot summers, dappled or afternoon shade allows mountain phlox to thrive and produce ongoing flowers. The common names describe the plant well, as it resembles cushion phlox both in leaf and flower shape and is spangled with small clusters of white tubular flowers that look like stars.

The plant forms a casual twiggy mound of rich green, with small, glossy, needlelike foliage in whorls along slender stems. It's sweetly fragrant when bruised or crushed.

Seed is hard to collect, as it ripens flower by tiny flower over a long period of time. Taking early tip cuttings before bloom can be a more reliable source for plants.

Propagation: seed (stratify), tip cuttings | **Companion plants:** silvery lupine, golden columbine, harebells; cool-loving grasses such as tufted hair grass and pine fescue

Liatris ligulistylis

Rocky Mountain liatris, meadow gayfeather, meadow blazing star

zones 3–8 • moist grassland, wet meadows; plains, foothills, rarely shrub steppe and montane • most soils

8 in. × 6 in. (2–5 ft. tall in bloom) • flower gardens, meadow plantings, cottage gardens

sun • moderate water

Of the handful of *Liatris* species native to our region, none is more spectacular in bloom than this one. Typically a single fuzzy, magenta spike, like a feather boa swaying on a stalk. The monarch favorite, its bloom coincides with their migration through our region. In nature, this liatris occurs infrequently but in large numbers in seasonally moist meadows and seeps. Tolerates occasional drought well.

Easily achieves eye-level bloom in a rich or moist soil, but reduces height to adapt to harsher conditions. Produces glossy, narrow, rich green foliage and roots in its first year; blooms heavily in the second. This dramatic accent plant can be short-lived on rich soils or a reliable long-term player on lean soils. It self-sows enthusiastically, but its bulb-like corms can easily be pulled where not desired. Tall and skinny, it makes an excellent cut flower indoors. Outdoors, it weaves among other plants without disrupting them and makes a strong vertical accent late in the growing season. It also delights in fall, sporting vivid orange and red late-season color.

Propagation: seed (stratify, light) | **Companion plants:** big or little bluestem, switchgrass, or golden feather grass; azure sage, ironweed, and sneezeweed

Linum lewisii

wild blue flax, prairie flax

zones 3–8 • dry meadows, roadcuts; most life zones • most well-drained soils

12–24 in. × 8–24 in. • meadow plantings, hellstrips, seeded wildflower plantings

sun • low water

This long-blooming wildflower's wispy demeanor gives little hint of its tough constitution. From late spring well into summer, myriad one-inch, rounded, sky-blue blossoms open every morning, then drop their petals once it gets sunny and hot. On cooler, cloudier days they stay open longer. Occasionally plants have pure white flowers. Scanty needlelike, gray-green foliage and airy slender stems make narrow bouquets topped with clouds of the charming five-petaled flowers.

Can be a pest, as the round seed capsules drop loads of viable seed and seedlings are very hard to pull due to their deep taproots. Cut all but a few plants back by half after bloom to prevent overwhelming seeding where not desired. This also lengthens the plants' lifespan, promoting new foliage and stem growth from the base for next year's display. Deer- and rabbit-resistant.

Visually similar European blue flax, *Linum perenne*, has been planted for reclamation and in gardens here and has become confused with this species in many locations.

Propagation: pot/direct-sow seed | **Companion plants:** blue grama; prickly poppy, blanketflower, larger penstemons, and wallflower; yuccas

Melampodium leucanthum

blackfoot daisy, rock daisy

zones 4 or 5–8 • roadsides, gravelly or sandy badlands, slopes, mesas; plains • sandy or gritty soils

4–12 in. × 12–18 in. • cactus gardens, rock gardens, unwatered flower gardens, hellstrips, along paths

sun • very low water

Native to southern Great Plains and the Southwest. Bushy mounds of dark green, almost-black linear foliage perfectly set off the pure white, papery daisies with yellow centers. Bloom begins as soon as it warms up dependably in spring and continues until frost.

In cooler locations, plant this where it can get some reflected heat from paving, walls, or rocks. It's winter-hardy in zone 4 if given good drainage and a hot location to grow during summer, but it struggles in heavy soil and won't survive winter wet.

Named for its small, dark, foot-shaped seed husks, this plant is rabbit-resistant and self-sows where it's happy. Grow it from fresh seed (in warm conditions and covered well) or from softwood cuttings. Small seedlings transplant easily; mature plants don't due to sparse, deep taproots rather than a fibrous root system.

Propagation: seed; cuttings | **Companion plants:** in a plains-inspired tableau with rice grass, Santa Fe phlox, plains verbena, desert four o'clock, and fringed sage; in a night garden with evening primrose or buckwheat; with cacti and yuccas

Mentzelia nuda

bractless blazing star, stickleaf mentzelia

zones 4–9 • sandy soils, disturbed sites, right-of-ways, rocky places; plains, foothills • sandy or gritty soils

2–4 ft. × 1–2 ft. • rock gardens, dry meadows, seeded wildflower plantings

sun • very low water

Even plant enthusiasts walk right past this plant during the day, when it appears as a stemmy thing about three feet tall with sparse, toothed leaves. Then, like magic in the late afternoon, it becomes impossible to miss as it opens three-inch-wide, cream-colored blooms bursting with fuzzy clusters of stamens at their centers. Still rare in cultivation, it makes a lovely garden addition when placed to highlight the glowing flowers during the evening hours while obscuring its gangly daytime form. Though adapted to grow on coarse, open soils in nature, adapts just fine to heavier soils if grown on a well-drained, dry berm.

Bractless blazing star's columnar (or vase) shape is easily complemented by low, mounding plants or smaller grasses. Lifespan of the plant varies; some live years while others behave as biennials or short-lived perennials. A lean site and well-drained soil extend the lifespans of those with potential to perennialize.

Near relative tenpetal blazing star (*Mentzelia decapetala*) can be used similarly in garden settings; be aware that it has a more triangular form, bigger leaves, and larger flowers spread more evenly across the plant, and it is generally shorter-lived. Both bloom in their second year.

Propagation: pot/direct-sow seed (stratify) | **Companion plants:** threadleaf sage, fringed sage; bushy buckwheat, bush morning-glory, desert four o'clock, and rice grass

Monarda pectinata

plains beebalm, pony beebalm

all zones (annual) • grassland, pine parkland, roadsides; plains, intermountain parks, foothills, pinyon-juniper • most well-drained soils

1–3 ft. × 1–2 ft. • rock gardens, dry meadows, hellstrips, filler annual for new gardens, seeded wildflower plantings

sun • low to moderate water

Most gardeners and hikers in the Rockies are familiar with our native beebalm *Monarda fistulosa*, or horsemint, a showy pink perennial discussed on page 146. Fewer people know about the several lovely annual beebalms, or that one, *Monarda pectinata*, is decidedly native to our region. It appears across the High Plains, throughout the Colorado Plateau, and along the edges of the Rockies, where it makes a lovely, low-growing addition to roadsides and grassy places. Plants flower in late spring (early for annuals) and continue into summer, producing an abundance of white flowers blushing with smoky purple. They protrude in whorls from purple-green papery clusters on their pleasantly mint-scented stems. These handsome plants are low-fuss, long-blooming, and make great filler in vases and gardens alike.

Two near relatives are present at the edges of our region, and both make equally good fillers of roughly similar size and stature: lemon beebalm (*Monarda citriodora*), a lemon-scented annual featuring larger whorls of intense magenta flowers, and the more understated spotted beebalm (*Monarda punctata*), with long-lasting whorls of pink-white bracts and dusty yellow flowers.

Propagation: pot/direct-sow seed | **Companion plants:** purple three-awn grass, evening primroses of all kinds, and wild blue flax

Oenothera rhombipetala

four-point evening primrose

zones 4–8 • sandy disturbed areas, open grassland; plains • most well-drained soils

6 in. × 1 ft. (up to 4 ft. × 3 ft. in bloom) • accent, meadow plantings, mass planting, filler in young gardens

sun • moderate water

Named for its four-pointed diamond-shaped petals, this vigorous biennial rapidly colonizes disturbed sites in the eastern stretches of our region, such as the Sand Hills of Nebraska. Producing a rosette of tapered leaves and a taproot in its first year, the plant erupts skyward in its second, creating a candelabra of glowing, three-inch, lemon-yellow flowers on stems up to four feet high. Blooms begin in mid- to late summer, continue for weeks, and produce enormous amounts of seeds that are popular with songbirds.

Self-sows in gardens, depending on how disturbed the garden soil and plantings are, as more bare dirt and a newer garden encourage more seedlings. Rarely do they compete enough to be an issue.

Like many other plants in this genus, feeds both the larval and adult stages of several hawk moth species and is easy to grow, thriving in a wide range of garden sites provided it receives full sun. Easily grown from seed if surface-sown, and young seedlings transplant well.

Propagation: pot/direct-sow seed | **Companion plants:** silverberry and silver buffaloberry shrubs; snow on the mountain and angel's trumpet; prairie sage

Penstemon angustifolius

narrowleaf penstemon

zones 3–7 • grassland, mesas, slopes; plains, foothills, shrub steppe • most well-drained soils

4–15 in. × 6–10 in. • cactus gardens, unwatered flower gardens

sun • very low water

This spring bloomer's spikes of tubular flowers beckon in patchy grassland, a short but bright sky-blue bouquet of several stems. Pink- and white-flowered forms can sometimes be found. Slender, evergreen, waxy blue-green leaves form a basal rosette and clasp the stiffly upright flower stems.

Removing finished flower spikes to all but one spike prolongs the plant's life; it reserves more energy for renewing basal foliage the next year. One spent spike usually carries numerous seed capsules, so self-sowing is assured in hospitable conditions. Prefers little if any competition from other plants. Small seedlings transplant easily; mature plants don't, as they have only a few large, easily damaged taproots.

Waxleaf penstemon (*Penstemon nitidus*) and sand penstemon (*P. arenicola*) are very similar short, early species, the former with a more northerly native range. Waxleaf penstemon blooms earliest, one of the first wildflowers to open in spring. Both are short but have brighter robin's-egg-blue flowers and slightly wider, more succulent leaves. They prefer highly disturbed, barren areas to grassland and make excellent companion plants in cactus gardens.

Propagation: seed (stratify) | **Companion plants:** spring bloomers such as purple loco, tufted evening primrose, bladderpod, cutleaf daisy, and phloxes

Penstemon barbatus

scarlet bugler

zones 4–8 • dry grassland, rocky hillsides, disturbed areas; foothills, pinyon-juniper, montane, subalpine • most well-drained soils

12–48 in. × 8–24 in. • unwatered flower gardens, seeded wildflower gardens, chaparral-inspired plantings

sun, light shade • low water

Blooms from early summer well into late July and August. Everything about this graceful plant is slender: tall flower stems; sparse, narrow green foliage; and tubular, bright red flowers. It has evolved to attract and allow hummingbirds to feed without much competition. Hawk moths, with their long tongues, also visit, as do tiny bee species that fit into the narrow flowers, but the latter risk being fed to hummingbirds' young. The green foliage forms an evergreen mat that takes on nice plum hues in winter. It tolerates light shade and still blooms well, unusual for a penstemon. Right after bloom, remove all but one stalk down to where the flowers end and there are only leaves.

Compact hybrids of this plant with other species offer coral, pink, white, and even purple flowers. Often these are less hardy; 'Elfin Pink' and 'Coral Baby' are two vigorous, dependable exceptions.

Longer-lived Bridge's penstemon (*Penstemon rostriflorus*) has very similar flowers but a more compact, shrubby habit. It blooms late in summer and into fall, great for late-season color and to extend the hummingbird buffet until migration time.

Propagation: pot/direct-sow seed (stratify) | **Companion plants:** yuccas, silver sages, rice grass, and blanketflower

Penstemon eatonii

firecracker penstemon

zones 4–8 • rocky places, slopes, disturbed areas; foothills, shrub steppe, pinyon-juniper, montane • most well-drained soils

12–30 in. × 8–24 in. • unwatered flower gardens, seed wildflower plantings, hellstrips

sun, light shade • low water

Like its lookalike the scarlet bugler, preferentially attracts hummingbirds to its flashy, tubular, bright red flowers. This wildflower blooms earlier than the bugler—from spring into early summer, with just a little overlap—so by planting both, you can ensure ample hummingbird food from spring through midsummer. In areas with longer, warmer falls, and autumnal rains, it often reblooms.

Coarser, leafier, and less likely to list and flop than its cousin; unlike most penstemons, it tolerates some shade and often grows under high-branched pines in the wild. Both species are inherently hardy, making them superb garden plants even in colder, higher, or more northerly areas.

Deadhead all but one stalk after bloom, preferably the stem holding the least seed capsules. This keeps the plant vigorous and lengthens its life while still allowing it to self-sow. 'Richfield Strain' is an exceptionally heavy-blooming, vigorous selection of firecracker penstemon from Idaho.

Propagation: pot/direct-sow seed (stratify) | **Companion plants:** desert columbine, wild blue flax, fringed sage, and plains skullcap; smaller bunchgrasses such as blue grama, pine fescue, rice grass, and ruby muhly

Penstemon glaber

smooth penstemon, saw-sepal penstemon

zones 3–7 • rocky hillsides, banks, bluffs, roadcuts, dry grassland; plains, foothills, montane • most well-drained soils

8–24 in. × 4–18 in. • unwatered flower gardens, dry meadow plantings, seeded wildflower plantings, hellstrips

sun • low water

Blooms in summer with flowers of an unforgettable clear, vivid blue. Mature plant puts out a handful of thick stems above narrow, evergreen, thick-textured, bright green leaves. The open-mouthed, tubular flowers take up much of the top third to half of the stems. As with most non-shrubby species of the penstemon clan, gives most of its energy to flowers.

Thoughtful deadheading allows the plant to put subsequent energy stores into making new foliage and spend less on ripening seed, resulting in a stronger, leafier, more vigorous plant. Letting the plant ripen a bit of seed (on a single stalk) helps it harden off as it sends seasonal feedback signals to the rest of the plant. A similar but slightly smaller plant with wider, gray foliage is thickleaf penstemon (*Penstemon pachyphyllus*). It is native to the more western and southern parts of the region and has proven to be an adaptable garden plant with perhaps even greater tolerance for very hot and dry conditions.

Propagation: seed (stratify) | **Companion plants:** evening primrose, sulfur flower, blackfoot daisy, and blanketflower

Penstemon grandiflorus

big beardtongue, prairie snapdragon

zones 3–7 • dry meadows, sandy prairie; plains, foothills • sandy or gritty soils

1–3 ft. × 8–30 in. • unwatered flower gardens, hellstrips, dry meadow plantings, seeded wildflower plantings

sun • low water

Blooms in late spring and early summer for only a couple of weeks, but this flowering event is among the showiest of any in our region. Two-inch, broadly tubular blossoms (shaped somewhat like foxgloves or snapdragons) open along thick, stately stems paired with clasping, round, waxy gray leaves reminiscent of florist's eucalyptus. Flower colors vary from lavender (most common) to pale pink, pure white, and deep rose (rare).

Shorter-lived than most penstemons, with a lifespan of typically only two to three years. Prompt deadheading after bloom may prolong its life a year or two. Crosses with other penstemons have occurred in gardens, especially with the more southern red species *Penstemon murrayanus*, which give the resulting hybrids richer flower colors. 'Prairie Jewel' and 'War Axe' are seed strains with a mix of these brighter and deeper rose-, magenta-, and purple-flowered individuals along with the usual lavender, white, and pink.

Propagation: pot/direct-sow seed (stratify) | **Companion plants:** tufted evening primrose, fringed sage, Jones' bluestar, plains verbena, wild blue flax, and small bunchgrasses such as Junegrass and purple three-awn

Penstemon palmeri

Palmer's penstemon

zones 4–8 • arroyos, roadsides, rocky hillsides, disturbed sites; plains, foothills, pinyon-juniper, shrub steppe, montane • sandy or gritty soils

2–3 ft. × 8–24 in. (5 ft. tall in bloom) • unwatered flower gardens, chaparral-inspired plantings

sun • very low water

This is the largest of the hardy penstemons and a sight to behold. In late spring and early summer, each plant sends up several tall stems with big, plump, foxglove-like pale pink flowers along one side of the stems. The flowers smell sweet, another rarity in the large penstemon genus. The plant itself is somewhat shrubby, with beautiful blue-green, waxy oval foliage with toothed margins. The combination of blue foliage, pale pink flowers, and its elegantly tall and slender form give it an ethereal quality despite its commanding size.

Only lives five or six years in most garden conditions. When grown very lean and without much competition from neighboring plants, and with timely annual deadheading before it begins to ripen all its seed, the plant can live a decade.

Propagation: seed (stratify) | **Companion plants:** large yuccas, Apache plume, fernbush, threadleaf sage, and the stately grassy mounds of giant sacaton

Phemeranthus calycinus (Talinum calycinum)

fameflower, flameflower

zones 5–9 • rock outcroppings, rocky soils, buttes and bluffs; plains • sandy or gritty soils

3 in. × 6 in. (8 in. in bloom) • rock gardens, crevice gardens, hellstrips, cactus gardens

sun • very low water

With a daintiness that belies its tough nature, this demure-looking wildflower can be found sporadically in dry areas and on thin soils of the Central and Southern Great Plains. It prefers thin soils because it remains small and doesn't compete well with ground-shading, fast-growing perennials and grasses. So, sticking to thin and lean soils that exclude big, vigorous players is best.

Slow to break dormancy in spring, but dazzles all summer with its glowing magenta, five-petaled flowers bobbing on threadlike stems. Performing best with summer heat, the plant should be sited in a warm microclimate with excellent drainage if grown in cooler parts of our region. The jewel-toned, translucent flowers open only on sunny days. The plant also offers a clean look when out of bloom thanks to low-profile, bright green tufts of succulent foliage.

Self-seeds moderately in gravel mulch, often flowering in its first year. The plant seems to melt in cold temperatures, yet typically returns from the root in spring, along with a flurry of self-seeded offspring nearby. These transplant incredibly easily, so there's always more than enough to spread around and share.

Propagation: seed | **Companion plants:** as a filler among yuccas and chunky, bright-flowering cacti

Physaria spp.

bladderpod, twinpod

zones 3–7 • rocky slopes, open areas; most life zones • sandy or gravelly soils

2–4 in. × 6–8 in. • rock gardens, crevice gardens, cactus gardens

sun • very low water

These sweet little wildflowers are one of the first to open blossoms in early spring. The fragrant, four-petaled, small bright yellow flowers serve as a bee beacon on sunny days as the growing season begins. The flower stems often lie on the ground in a circle around the foliage; at times they are held more erect until they finish and ripen into pretty, greenish, inflated papery seedpods—which loll about for a good month before drying and releasing their seed. Lovely, evergreen silver rosettes of spoon-shaped leaves look like large metallic flowers pasted onto the ground.

Numerous species of bladderpods are native to our region. All typically self-sow in well-drained soils, especially gravel mulch. *Physaria didymocarpa* is native farther north in the region than the common *P. floribunda*, and *P. acutifolia* comes from very high elevations so is ideal for cooler, higher-elevation plantings. All want full sun and are small, so plant them where they won't be swamped by larger plants and can be appreciated up close.

Propagation: seed (stratify) | **Companion plants:** small cacti such as green hedgehog, claret cup, and snowball cacti; cutleaf fleabane and dwarf buckwheat species such as *Eriogonum ovalifolium*; sand lily and dwarf *Phlox kelseyi*

Ratibida columnifera

prairie coneflower

zones 4–8 • meadows, roadsides, clearings; plains, foothills • most well-drained soils

18–30 in. × 18–36 in. • meadow plantings, cottage gardens, seeded wildflower plantings, hellstrips

sun • low water

At lower elevations in our region, it's hard to miss this showy yet airy midsummer wildflower. Individually, it forms an upright, gangly bouquet of daisies; looks best either in mass plantings or threaded through grasses. Tough, dependable, and with a bloom duration of well over a month, it's a workhorse that performs when the weather gets truly hot and dry.

Two distinct races of this plant hybridize when growing near each other: a clear yellow-flowered one and a velvety maroon one. Their hybrids are often bicolored or, more rarely, a lovely amber or copper color. Each daisy's "petals," or ray flowers, hang down from a prominent greenish, thimble-like cone that becomes dark brown as the flower matures, making for an unusual, jaunty daisy look. Flowers have a warm honey fragrance. Slim stems and deeply cut, narrow gray-green foliage lend the plant a spry, casual feel. Self-sows dependably.

Propagation: direct-sow seed (light) | **Companion plants:** with fringed sage, little bluestem, ruby muhly, and blue grama in meadow plantings; with orange butterfly weed, scarlet bugler penstemon, snow on the mountain, and prickly poppy for summer floral panache

Rudbeckia hirta var. *pulcherrima*

black-eyed Susan

zones 3–8 • meadows, roadsides, disturbed areas; plains, foothills, shrub steppe, montane • most soils

10–20 in. × 8–15 in. • flower gardens, cottage gardens, cutting gardens

sun, light shade • moderate water

Blooms from summer into fall for a good two to three months, with large daisy flowers two and three inches across. The brownish, button-like center of the flower contrasts delightfully with the golden orange petals (technically ray flowers). Mid-green stems and leaves are hairy and coarse-textured.

This plant is native over much of the midwestern and eastern parts of North America, including in the Rockies. Seed selections exist in the trade with rusty red or brown floral markings, green centers, or double rows of petals; double petals often make the plant less useful to wildlife, as it can diminish the production of pollen and seed.

Once established, self-sows dependably if given supplemental water and some bare earth without competition from other plants. It's one of the best Rocky Mountain natives for cutting; since it requires a bit more water than most of our natives to thrive, let it share space with vegetables or other cut flowers that need regular irrigation.

Propagation: pot/direct-sow seed (light) | **Companion plants:** adaptable prairie denizens such as purple prairie clover, Rocky Mountain gayfeather, snow on the mountain, butterfly milkweed, and pearly everlasting

Scutellaria resinosa (Scutellaria wrightii)

plains skullcap, sticky skullcap

zones 4–9 • rocky soils, roadsides, areas with sparse vegetation; plains • most well-drained soils

8–12 in. × 1 ft. • rock gardens, meadow plantings, path and patio edges, as a filler, hellstrips, seeded wildflower plantings

sun, light shade • low to moderate water

Deserves greater recognition in our region for its adaptability and lasting beauty in the landscape. It hails from the Central and Southern Great Plains, occuring rarely in the High Plains and adjacent regions but in large numbers where it does. Perhaps it's scarce there because, despite having good vigor, it remains quite small and is easily overgrown by larger perennials and grasses.

Its compact, bushy form makes it a fantastic filler and bed edger, where plains skullcap can seed around to its satisfaction without overtaking the planting. It's also a winner between hardscape, be it paving, rocks, or boulders. The clean, rounded leaves and shapely architecture of these plants soften hard edges and fill in bare spots, producing small but profuse, blue-purple, snapdragon-shaped blooms much of summer. When flowering subsides, cut plants back—or, increase irrigation for a few weeks and they'll resume their floral show.

Propagation: pot/direct-sow seed; cuttings | **Companion plants:** little bluestem or firecracker penstemon; silverleaf evening primrose, blackfoot daisy

Senecio spartioides

broom ragwort

zones 4–9 • disturbed areas, rocky slopes, roadsides, arroyos, sandy flats; plains, foothills, shrub steppe, pinyon-juniper, montane • sandy or gritty soils

3 ft. × 3 ft. • dry meadow plantings, chaparral-inspired plantings, unwatered flower gardens, seeded wildflower plantings

sun • very low water

Numerous cheerful *Senecio* species, also known as ragworts and groundsels, are native to our region. You can find their bright yellow daisy clusters from above treeline down to the plains and from bogs to desert flats. This is among the largest, prettiest, and latest to flower. Its size and bloom time make it special for a myriad of insect pollinators as well as people, offering a visual and actual feast during those last weeks before everything shuts down for winter.

Grows from a deep taproot, branching at the base to form a round, billowing, see-through mound of threadlike stems and leaves. These are a fresh, light green, an unusual and pleasant hue in a dryland planting. One-inch lemon-yellow daisies with similarly thin, threadlike "petals" (ray flowers) open in fall for well over a month.

The plant likes heat during the growing season. Cut back in spring to encourage strong, dense branching; often reseeds a bit in the garden. A very similar but silver-leaved species from yet more southern and southwestern areas is *Senecio flaccidus*. All these groundsels are poisonous to livestock.

Propagation: seed (light) | **Companion plants:** late-flowering lavender tansyasters; bold yuccas and large cacti; many shrubs, hardy deer muhly

Stanleya pinnata

prince's plume

zones 4–8 • dry hillsides, mesas, rocky places; plains, foothills, shrub steppe, pinyon-juniper, montane • sandy or gritty soils

3–6 ft. × 2–3 ft. • unwatered flower gardens, chaparral-inspired plantings, hillside plantings

sun • very low to low water

In late spring and early summer in the most barren and parched wild places, suddenly a great floral drama unfolds as tall stems open spidery yellow flowers in upright foxtail-like spikes, like fluffy candles. Stamens protrude from the four-petaled blossoms, giving the flower stalks their characteristically fuzzy, feathery outline. Flowers ripen to slender, long seedpods on the bottom of the spike while others continue to open, the mix of seedpods and flowers enhancing the feathery appearance. The waxy, toothed foliage, gray-green and also feathery-looking, is concentrated on the lower half of the plant.

Longer-lived in shaly, rocky soils, particularly those with extra selenium, though will grow in most. Dislikes competition; give it space and place it like you would a shrub. It loves sun and heat. Transplant seedlings when small.

Biennial desert plant white prince's plume (*Stanleya albescens*) is much smaller, shorter-lived, and native to very hot parts of the region. The flowers are a creamy white, in some ways even more striking than its larger yellow cousin's because they shimmer and glow, especially at dusk.

Propagation: seed (stratify) | **Companion plants:** Palmer's penstemon, silvery lupine, silver sages, desert mahonia, alkali sacaton, chollas, yuccas, and manzanita

Verbesina encelioides

cowpen daisy, golden crownbeard

all zones (annual) • disturbed sites, overgrazed pastures and fields; plains, foothills, pinyon-juniper, shrub steppe • most well-drained soils

1–4 ft. × 1–3 ft. • seeded wildflower plantings, cottage gardens, fencelines, otherwise forgotten disturbed spots

sun • low water

This annual wildflower ranks with sunflower as a large, coarse, easy wildflower to grow every year for its long display of cheerful daisies and important pollinator benefits. The triangular, felted foliage appears light gray-green due to the short hairs covering it. Leaf edges are toothed, giving the plant a bit more finesse than sunflowers. Yellow one-inch daisies radiate on short stems along the top of plant from midsummer until frost. Native to lower elevations and latitudes, it likes its fair share of heat.

Cowpen daisy gets its name from a propensity for overgrazed, disturbed sites. The whole plant smells quite pungent if rubbed or crushed and is deer- and rabbit-resistant.

Grow this tough, easy-blooming plant in same sorts of places you would consider planting sunflowers—unloved areas where you want something easy, bulky, flashy, dependable, and useful to creatures.

Propagation: direct-sow seed (light) | **Companion plants:** switchgrass, giant sacaton grass, beeplant, snow on the mountain, annual buckwheat, and angel's trumpet

Long-lived Wildflowers

The wildflowers in this section are perhaps the most prized group for a planting. Our region is strikingly diverse in wildflowers in general, and the long-lived ones are easier to design with due to their dependability. All plants included here have the potential to live longer than five years, in most cases many more, with a few species having lifespans greater than the typical human being's.

However, sometimes the plants die sooner. This is part of gardening. In the case of wildflowers, it can be even more of a game of Russian roulette: much less is known about their needs and performance under varied conditions because so few of them have been in cultivation for very long. The best we can do is observe what sorts of conditions they prefer in the wild, which is why we give a lot of information on the native haunts of the plants profiled.

Some people enjoy creating microclimates to suit plants that wouldn't normally like their site. Others prefer to find plants that want conditions that match their site. Most people probably choose to do a bit of both. But even the best-laid plans don't guarantee a happy plant. And sometimes a typically persnickety species may decide to grow and reproduce like mad on your particular spot, like paintbrush does for a few very lucky gardeners.

For people who enjoy magic and surprises, this is all fine. For others who prefer to have some sense of control over the outcome, and those who really suffer when a plant dies, you are the reason we have included propagation information throughout the plant profiles and in "Growing Native Plants from Seed" on page 38. Not only are many of our region's native plants not readily available to purchase, but we need to experiment with them more than with plants that have been grown all over the country for decades and from which we know what to expect. So having the knowledge of how to produce more plants is not only fun, it opens up loads of new plant possibilities while saving money to boot. Just as important, it's empowering having this safety net against too much disappointment. No one likes to see a plant die or feel like they killed it. When you have many baby plants in the wings it's not such a big deal. Plants come and go, sometimes because of what we did or didn't do and sometimes in spite of it. We learn from this. The best gardeners, and pretty much the best people at anything, have failed many, many times. You will also have successes. Grow more of the plants that do well for you. And try lots of new ones. You'll get to enjoy some of the treasures of our region right outside your door and support the web of life at the same time.

Achillea millefolium (*Achillea lanulosa*)

western yarrow

zones 3–8 • meadows, roadsides, disturbed rocky or gravelly areas; all life zones • most well-drained soils

5–15 in. × 12–18 in. or more • dry meadows, hellstrips, seeded wildflower plantings, between shrubs in chaparral plantings

sun • low to moderate water

This widespread wildflower grows native over a large swath of the western United States. In late spring and summer, sometimes into fall, flat-topped clusters of white flowers rise on stiff stems. The finely cut, ferny gray-green foliage is handsome and aromatic. Sends out creeping runners from its crowns and can spread indefinitely in areas with good soil and ample moisture.

Unlike many of our wildflowers, this makes a good cut flower and also dries well. It self-sows a bit; deadhead after bloom. Plants can be mown when planted in a meadow or lawn.

Nonnative European yarrow is taller with greener foliage and less xeric. It spreads with abandon in rich, moist areas. It blooms in white as well as yellow, rust, pink, and red and has escaped into the wild over many parts of North America thanks to being a popular but invasive garden plant.

Propagation: seed (light); division | **Companion plants:** silver sage, horsemint, blanketflower, prairie coneflower, stiff goldenrod, and pearly everlasting; blue grama, alkali sacaton; buffalo grass lawn

Allium cernuum

nodding onion

zones 3–8 • grassy slopes, streamsides, woodland clearings; most life zones • most moist soils

10–18 in. × 8–18 in. • meadow plantings, hellstrips, accent plant, seeded wildflower planting

sun, light shade • moderate water

Native in many parts of North America; probably the most widespread species of native onion on the continent. In summer, nodding buds open clusters of bell-shaped pink, rose, purple, or (rarely) white flowers. The long, flat, linear green foliage has a grassy yet lush texture, filling in around the upright flower stems to make a clean bouquet. All parts of this plant smell mildly of onions when bruised, broken, or crushed and are edible, though deer show little interest in browsing the plant.

In our region, it typically prefers moister areas, but when growing in more moisture-retentive clays it can be quite xeric. Unlike many of our wildflowers, nodding onion makes a good cut flower. It self-sows quite a bit, especially in moister soils.

Propagation: seed (stratify); division | **Companion plants:** tufted hair grass, yarrow, horsemint, and purple prairie clover; dusky penstemon and columbines

Amsonia jonesii

desert bluestar

zones 4–8 • dry slopes, rocky places, grassland; plains, pinyon-juniper, shrub steppe • most well-drained soils

12–18 in. × 12–18 in. • dry meadows, accent plant, hellstrips

sun • low water

Sends up a bouquet of unbranched stems from its almost-woody crown early in the season. In spring, blooms with smoky, dark gray-blue buds that unfurl to tubular stars of a shimmering pale blue. White-flowered forms show up occasionally. Narrow, pale green foliage grows in whorls around the stems, giving the plant a more profuse, robust, and leafy texture than most dryland wildflowers. Leaves turn a warm yellow before falling.

This unique-looking wildflower is slow-growing, getting denser with stems each year and taking about three to five years to reach its prime. It doesn't grow more stems after the initial flush of growth each year, so be careful not to damage stems; they won't be replaced until the next spring. It resents being disturbed or moved and takes a while to grow into the garden star it is, so choose its placement with care.

In thin or coarse soils, typically prefers a bit of extra moisture, but in more moisture-retentive clays it can be quite xeric. Unattractive to deer and rabbits.

Propagation: seed (soak in tepid water until seed sinks)
Companion plants: rice grass; fringed sage, Scott's clematis, native phloxes, locoweed, tufted evening primrose, and cutleaf fleabane

Anaphalis margaritacea

pearly everlasting

zones 2–8 • dry grassland, rocky hillsides, disturbed areas; most life zones • most well-drained soils

10–24 in. × 10–30 in. • meadow plantings, accent plant

sun • low to moderate water

This showy wildflower blooms summer into fall with white, papery flower clusters. The papery parts remain attractive on the plant long after the flowers have finished and dried—well past hard frost—until winter weather bends or breaks the stems. As you might expect from this unusual characteristic, the flowers cut and dry well. Its velvety stems and linear leaves are felted with tiny white hairs, giving the plant a uniquely soft, pale look that blends well with many other plants.

Can spread quickly from root runners in rich, moist soil. In most conditions, is slow to increase and not aggressive. Deer show little interest in it.

Propagation: divisions or seed (stratify, light) | **Companion plants:** summer- and autumn-blooming wildflowers such as horsemint, gayfeather, asters, azure sage, ironweed, and goldenrod; little bluestem and ruby muhly grass; sumac and golden currant

Antennaria spp.

pussytoes

zones 3–8 • thin grassland, rocky hillsides, woodland clearings; most life zones • most well-drained soils

1–2 in. × 10–30 in. and wider over time, (4-6 in. when flowering) • between paving stones, groundcover between shrubs, rock gardens, hellstrips

sun, light shade • low to moderate water

These adorable wildflowers bloom in late spring and early summer with rounded, ivory (or more rarely, pink) flower clusters that resemble kittens' paws and ultimately form fluffy seedheads. These plants' gray evergreen leaves, their greatest asset, grow in rosettes that spread into flat silvery mats over time. Pussytoes thrive in sun or in light, dry shade.

A versatile and delightful groundcover, pussytoes blend well with almost anything. Can serve as a lawn if foot traffic is light or make a fine-textured carpet among companion plants in dappled shade.

'McClintock' is an extra-silver, dwarf form of *Antennaria parvifolia* with tiny, congested, almost-white foliage rosettes, perfect for rock gardens and between paving stones. The plant has a ragged look after bloom, so spent flower stems are best removed. Two of the best species native to the Rockies are: aromatic pussytoes (*Antennaria aromatica*), from the northern parts of the region (small, cute, silvery, likes things dry and rocky, smells of lemons), and rosy pussytoes (*Antennaria rosea*, also charming and petite but with dependably rosy flowers), which prefers a cool, moist spot at lower elevations and latitudes.

Propagation: division; cuttings | **Companion plants:** pine fescue and common juniper; olive-green manzanitas and blue grama

Arctostaphylos uva-ursi

kinnikinnick, bearberry

zones 3–6 • open conifer forests, rock outcrops, slopes; foothills, pinyon-juniper, montane • sandy or gritty soils

3–12 in. × 3–6 ft. • groundcover under trees, with larger shrubs and small conifers, hillside plantings, rock gardens

light shade, shade • moderate water

This low, evergreen shrub is native to such far-flung places as the dunes of Cape Cod, the Colorado high country, and the Austrian Alps. Technically a shrub, it acts more like a groundcover, rarely growing more than six inches tall yet spreading lustily by rooting along its horizontal branches, forming large, dense mats over time. Early in spring, white or pale pink urn-shaped flowers open, then ripen rounded fruit that turns a cheerful bright red and feeds wildlife. The small, rounded, leathery dark green foliage is tidy and often turns rusty red or maroon in winter. Foliage can burn when exposed to extremely cold, dry conditions and strong wind; can also suffer sunburn. A bit of shade protects it and encourages faster, more lush growth than full sun, so plant with a northern or eastern exposure where possible.

Plant early or late; very sensitive to root rot if watered for establishment during the heat of summer. Well-drained soil is a must. Deer love to browse the new growth; protect with netting or wire until mature and well-established.

Propagation: divide self-rooted stems | **Companion plants:** under trees; with silver pussytoes and common juniper

Artemisia ludoviciana

prairie sage, white sagebrush

zones 3–8 • grassland, disturbed areas, roadsides; plains, foothills, montane, subalpine • most well-drained soils

1–3 ft. × unlimited spread • prairie matrix with grasses, around shrubs in a chaparral-inspired planting

sun • low water

One of the most striking foliage plants native to this region and beyond; stems and leaves are felted with pure white hairs, giving the plant a uniquely bright, almost-white appearance that jumps out of a landscape. Narrow foliage and slender stems; flowers in loose spikes are small and barely noticeable. This plant is very aggressive, spreading quickly by root runners. In very dry conditions it is slower to increase. Has a pungent medicinal aroma when bruised, cut, or crushed as well as when wet; people either love or hate it. 'Valerie Finnis' has wider, foliage.

Because of its fast-spreading nature, there are only a few successful ways to grow this plant if you want to maintain any plant diversity. Allow prairie sage to thread through tough, stalwart grasses or mingle with and run around shrubs. Its silver foliage contrasts beautifully with the greens and blues of evergreens or with trees' fall-foliage fireworks. Only a few wildflowers can stand up to this beautiful bully.

Propagation: division; cuttings; seed (stratify, light)
Companion plants: grasses like blue grama, little bluestem, or alkali sacaton; pines and junipers; sumac, Gambel oak, black chokecherry, and American plum; Maximilian sunflower, horsemint, and golden banner

Asclepias incarnata

swamp milkweed, rose milkweed

zones 3–7 • fens, wetland edges, wet prairies and meadows, ditch and stream margins; plains, foothills • most moist soils

3 ft. × 2 ft. • perennial gardens, meadow plantings, moist sites

full sun, light shade • moderate water to moist

Milkweeds are the quintessential butterfly host plant. They, along with the monarch butterfly, introduced many of us to the "host plant" concept. Like showy milkweed (*Asclepias speciosa*), swamp milkweed makes a good host plant for monarchs. Crucially for the gardener, it does this without the inconvenient running tendencies of showy milkweed. Instead, it produces a single crown of deep, fleshy roots, from which its shoots appear in very late spring or early summer. These substantial roots make the species far better at adapting to soils of average moisture than the common name implies.

The biggest challenge in growing this plant is its small, windborne seeds, which seem to delight in casting themselves near and far before taking root. Most individuals produce a dusty pink bloom (*incarnata* means "flesh-like"), but the cultivar 'Ice Ballet' produces a pure white flower. It's likely you will have to grow 'Ice Ballet' from seed if it is to your taste, as plants are not easily available in nurseries.

Propagation: seed (stratify) | **Companion plants:** cutleaf compass plant, sneezeweed, meadow blazing star; golden feather grass and switchgrass; in front of elderberry shrubs

Asclepias tuberosa ssp. *interior*

butterfly milkweed, orange milkweed

zones 3–9 • sandy grasslands, roadsides, railways; plains, pinyon-juniper • most well-drained soils

1–2 ft. × 12–18 in. • meadow plantings, hellstrips, seeded wildflower plantings, perennial gardens

sun • low to moderate water

This spectacular wildflower grows native over a large swath of the eastern United States and into this region. In summer its flat-topped clusters of orange flowers—more rarely yellow or almost-red—open for many weeks, stopping hiker and driver alike with their profusion and glowing color. These also attract insect and even hummingbird visitors, making for a lively, much-frequented hub.

The coarsely narrow, bright olive-green foliage has a lush texture, filling the upright stems to make a bushy bouquet. Come fall, large seedpods split to reveal and release chocolate-brown seeds with silken parachute-like tops that help them disperse on the slightest breeze. The autumnal foliage becomes a nice yellow color and seedpods sometimes turn burgundy.

Butterflyweed needs heat to flourish, so at higher, cooler elevations give it the sunniest, warmest spot available. This subspecies is better adapted to clay soils, while the straight species needs sandy or gritty soils. Deer show little interest in browsing the plant. Unlike many of our wildflowers, makes a good cut flower. It self-sows a bit, especially in loose, gravelly soils.

Propagation: seed (stratify) | **Companion plants:** yarrow, blanketflower, horsemint; leadplant

Berberis repens (Mahonia repens)

creeping grapeholly, creeping barberry

zones 3–8 • rocky hillsides, ledges, forest clearings; foothills, montane • sandy or gritty soils

6–24 in. × unlimited spread over time • chaparral-inspired plantings, casual groundcover with shrubs, slope planting

sun to light shade • low to moderate water

This charming evergreen groundcover has woody stems, technically making it a shrub, but due to its running growth habit and short stature we've placed it here. Spreads by underground roots, with short stems bearing leathery, oval, blue-green leaflets with spiny edges. New foliage is a fresh mint-green or sometimes a soft peach, mutes to a blue-gray with ruddy tints, becomes bright red in fall, and finally sports a handsome deep maroon/purple color in winter.

Clusters of sweetly fragrant, small flowers like miniature daffodils open in spring; their soft butter-yellow contrasts beautifully with the more somber foliage. Flowers ripen to clusters of small, dark blue berries (the "grapes" of the common name), which often have a waxy coating that lightens their hue.

Winter foliage may burn in sunny and windy locations; it recovers easily the following growing season but won't provide winter appeal in the meantime. In areas without reliable snow cover, give it some shade to protect the foliage in the offseason. Grows slowly and is deer-resistant, although deer do relish the berries.

Propagation: cuttings; seed (stratify); divisions | **Companion plants:** pussytoes, mountain and creeping junipers, golden and wax currants, boulder raspberry, snowberry, and dwarf forms of Colorado spruce

Callirhoe involucrata

winecup, purple poppy mallow

zones 4–8 • dry prairies, rocky places; plains • most well-drained soils

6 in.–2 ft. × 3–4 ft. wide • groundcover, filler, hellstrips, meadow plantings, chaparral-inspired plantings

sun • low to moderate water

Of the handful of *Callirhoe* species that grow in the United States, only two have real presences in this region: *Callirhoe alcaeoides*, an attractive, rare resident in Colorado sporting palmate leaves and white, cup-shaped flowers; and this plant, somewhat less refined but far more adaptable, with a range as large as the rest of its genus combined. Found from the Gulf Coast northwest to Wyoming grasslands, it adorns harsh, grassy sites with its deeply lobed leaves and long display of chalice-like, purple-red blooms. Rarely, soft pink and white forms appear in wild populations. The delicate, cupped petals of this species glow when backlit above their mats of green leaves, so consider siting plants where they will receive light in the morning or evening.

Drought-resistant thanks to a large taproot, winecup resents root disturbance, so site with long-term plans in mind—preferably not next to a path or walkway, as the spreading stems are easily damaged by foot traffic. This easy-blooming plant makes for a quick, lightly self-seeding groundcover, useful for filling bare spaces in existing or new plantings with its low, wide-growing stems.

Propagation: seed (scarify then stratify) | **Companion plants:** yucca or cutleaf compass plant; fine-textured grasses such as ruby muhly, blue grama, or prairie dropseed; leadplant

Campanula rotundifolia

roundleaf harebell, bluebell

zones 2–7 • slopes, meadows, streambanks, woodland clearings; all life zones • most well-drained soils

6–12 in. × 6–15 in. • rock gardens, crevice gardens, slope plantings, shaded areas

sun, light shade • moderate water

"Bluebells of Scotland" is another common name for this pretty wildflower, alluding to its wide natural distribution across the cooler and higher parts of the northern hemisphere. Some individuals make small, well-behaved plants while others spread underground and form loose colonies quite quickly, especially if the site is moist.

This dainty-looking but tough little plant blooms all summer. Lavender-blue (or, more rarely, white) bells dangle above slim stems and basal rosettes of small round or heart-shaped green foliage. The more visible, linear leaves along the stems give the plant in bloom a soft, grassy look. Bluebells thrive in cooler temperatures, needing some extra moisture in sunny spots but growing well in quite dry soil in light shade. The plant often self-sows. For plantings not in the higher elevations and latitudes, plant on a north-facing slope or under deciduous trees that create dappled shade.

Propagation: seed (stratify, light); division | **Companion plants:** tufted hair grass, Idaho fescue; fine-textured, white-flowered mountain phlox and columbines; shade trees such as aspen, birch, or alder

Clematis columbiana

rock clematis

zones 4–8 • moist slopes, ravines, cool rocky areas, open woods; foothills, montane • most well-drained soils

4–10 in. × 18–60 in. • accent, hillsides, rock gardens

sun to light shade • moderate water

Named after its affinity for rocky sites, this wildflower creates a lovely effect with its graceful deciduous foliage and stunning flowers flowing among boulders. Grows more like a well-behaved, rambling groundcover than a typical bunching wildflower or the popular vining clematis. Its stems lie on the ground, draping themselves around and over nearby objects.

In spring, show-stopping large blue, pink, or (rarely) white flowers open above leafy, prostrate stems. These can hang down like bells or face upward; either way, there is no mistaking this plant. The lush, bright green three-parted foliage warrants some extra water in drier, hotter, lower-elevation sites. The plant likes the cool root run of a lightly shaded spot or eastern or northern exposure; rocks and rock mulches provide similar root-cooling and moisture-conserving benefits.

Spreads very slowly both under- and aboveground but is not aggressive. Sometimes it takes two long cold periods or two winters to germinate. In the garden, choose a cool spot (ideally on a rocky slope) to show it off best. Close cousin *Clematis columbiana* var. *tenuiloba* comes from higher elevations into the subalpine zone and stays smaller, with a more compact, less sprawling habit.

Propagation: seed (stratify) | **Companion plants:** white, lavender, or pink cutleaf daisies

Clematis hirsutissima

sugarbowls, hairy clematis, leather flower

zones 4–8 • grassland, dry slopes; shrub steppe, foothills, montane, pinyon-juniper • most well-drained soils

10–18 in. × 12–18 in. • low meadow plantings, accent, rock gardens

sun • low to moderate water

Bumblebees forage before most other pollinators, well protected from cold by their hairy pelts and large enough not to be buffeted by spring winds. They savor the blossoms of equally early sugarbowls, which are shaped perfectly to house and feed a large bee and ensure pollination. The big bee must first slip through the narrower "mouth" of the flower to get to the pollen and nectar—this squeeze and effort ensures that the plump furry insect gets covered in pollen.

Similarly hairy against the elements, this cherished wildflower sends forth a bouquet-like bunch of fuzzy stems with finely cut, gray-green foliage that looks like felted wires. These are topped with large, thick, indigo flower bells that also sport a thin layer of felt, giving them a sugar-dusted look. The seedheads are as distinctive and showy as the flowers—silken, wild-haired troll's heads that become fluffier when dry and ready to be dispersed by the wind.

Sometimes needs two winters' worth of cold-moist stratification, making our native clematis species scarce and costly commercially (they take twice as long to produce). However, they're among the longest-lived wildflowers, growing bushier and making more flowers each year.

Propagation: seed (stratify) | **Companion plants:** pussytoes, cutleaf daisy

Clematis ligusticifolia

western white clematis, virgin's bower

zones 3–8 • woods, shrubland, drainages, along watercourses; plains, foothills, shrub steppe, montane • most soils

5–20+ ft. × 5–15 ft. • screening vine for fence, large trellis climber

sun, light shade • moderate water to moist

This vigorous, adaptable vine can be spotted from the High Plains all the way to the Pacific Ocean. In our region, typically a leafy, stemmy vine scrambling up and over large shrubs or up into trees with relatively open canopies. There, it produces an effusive, late-season bloom of fragrant small white flowers with fuzzy stamens. Flowering in such masses that the foliage of the plant is frequently obscured, the blossoms make the vine unmistakable through mid- to late summer. Shortly afterward, a second show develops: fuzzy seeds ripen and cling to the plant for weeks and glow in direct morning or evening light. One of few plants featured in this book that is "dioecious," meaning plants are either male or female; only female plants will produce the attractive seeds. Though the seed is sensitive to drying out when sprouting, this species adapts to a variety of moisture regimes when established and tolerates both full sun and light shade. Plants in richer, deeper soils and that receive more irrigation grow larger and scramble farther. Makes an easygoing cover or screen for large, uninteresting hardscape or infrastructure features, like chain-link fence.

Propagation: cuttings; seed (stratify) | **Companion plants:** American plum

Clematis scottii (*Clematis hirsutissima* var. *scottii*)

Scott's clematis

zones 4–8 • grassland, slopes; plains, foothills, montane • most well-drained soils

10–18 in. × 15–20 in. • accent, rock garden

sun • low to moderate water

Very similar to its kissing cousin sugarbowls but blooms a bit later and for a markedly longer period, up to two months in spring and early summer, making it an even showier garden plant. Unlike sugarbowls' upright bushy bouquet, it grows sprawling stems that continue to elongate, producing new flower stalks as they go. These flowers also have less of the pale, felted outer coating, or "sugar," of sugarbowls' blossoms, and they are more pure blue rather than purple-blue. Scott's clematis has urn-shaped blooms, not fluted bells, and the plant is also less narrow and not nearly as hairy, with small, blue-green oval leaflets. As for similarities, seedheads of this plant are also adorable silky "troll's heads," and the lovely flowers are especially enticing to bumblebees.

As with all our native clematis, needs at least a winter's worth of cold-moist stratification, sometimes two. Seedlings are slow-growing but the plant is exceptionally long-lived. For this reason, our native clematis species are harder to find in the trade and often more expensive, because the crop takes twice as long to produce as many other wildflowers.

Propagation: seed (stratify) | **Companion plants:** white mountain phlox, four-nerve daisy

Cucurbita foetidissima

buffalo gourd, coyote gourd

zones 4–9 • roadsides, ditches, edges of drainages and arroyos, disturbed fields; plains • most soils

1–2 ft. × 10+ ft. • bold accent in meadow planting, slopes, hellstrips, chaparral-inspired plantings

sun • low to moderate water

Like a stegosaurus back rising from a bed of grasses, the large, upright, blue-green leaves of this vine are impossible to misidentify. The out-of-place appearance of these massive, sprawling plants makes more sense when one considers that until a few thousand years ago, the four-inch, stinky fruits of this species were distributed by woolly mammoths and giant ground sloths to yield the plant's present-day range.

Today, it appears at and below 5500 feet as far north as the Nebraska Panhandle, with a range that wraps around the Southern Plains into the Four Corners and south to Mexico. Amazingly drought-tolerant thanks to a giant, club-like taproot, requires little input once established. Precedes its unusual fruits with elegant and attractive (though short-lived), soft yellow, squash-blossom-like flowers. Generally not palatable to people, various parts of the plant are enjoyed by animals, and they have a history of use by Indigenous peoples.

Cleaning seeds from the foul-scented fruits can be a chore. To minimize this, Bryan has simply crushed an old fruit into his home meadow; there, the coarse, geometric leaves make a striking design accent.

Propagation: seed | **Companion plants:** fine-textured grasses, standing cypress, and aromatic aster; fine-textured shrubs such as leadplant, threadleaf sage, rabbitbrush, and Apache plume

Dalea purpurea (Petalostemon purpureus)

purple prairie clover

zones 3–8 • dry grassland, hillsides, roadsides; plains, foothills • most well-drained soils

12–24 in. × 18–30 in. • meadow plantings, flower gardens, seeded wildflower plantings, hellstrips

sun • low water

Makes a fine-textured, upright bouquet in the landscape and is pretty even out of bloom: wiry, slender stems arise from an almost-woody crown, cloaked in threadlike cleft foliage that's a fresh-green. Come summer, tiny rose-purple flowers open, forming plump, knobby, columnar clusters with prominent orange stamens that attract myriad pollinators. Like many prairie wildflowers, is deer-resistant.

This tough yet graceful wildflower ripens copious, viable seed and self-sows quite a bit. It can be difficult to get good seed germination in pots, and the floppy, skinny little seedlings are slow to mature (which may be why the plant is rare in the nursery trade). To encourage generous numbers in a planting, either direct-sow in fall with no pretreatment or scarify seed to direct-sow in spring. Small seedlings can easily be moved early in the season; mature plants resent being moved and have deep taproots, so select placement with extra care. This member of the pea family has roots that fix nitrogen, allowing plants to thrive in and enrich the poorest of soils.

Propagation: seed (scarify); cuttings | **Companion plants:** butterfly milkweed, black Sampson, fringed sage, western spiderwort, Indian blanket, and prairie winecup; ruby muhly and prairie dropseed

Delphinium geyeri

Geyer's larkspur

zones 4–8 • slopes, mesas, hillsides; plains, foothills, pinyon-juniper, shrub steppe, montane • most well-drained soils

2–3 ft. × 12–18 in. • accent, seeded wildflower plantings

sun • low to moderate water

Our region's answer to the short-lived, floppy, demanding (but ever-popular) nonnative hybrid delphiniums. This plant will return for many years with nothing more than good drainage, sun, and minimal competition from grasses. The stunning, rich blue flowers rise on loose spikes in late spring and into early summer. Foliage is fine-textured, gray-green, and mostly at the base. Doesn't compete well in a meadow or prairie-style planting.

Like most of its other larkspur relatives in the genus, this plant is toxic to cattle and other pasture feeders and so has been eradicated on a lot of native ranchland. Our native deer and rabbits avoid it, as will cattle, sheep, goats, and horses if they have plenty of other food—but if you want to enjoy it without worrying about harming livestock, plant it out of their access.

Can be hard to find commercially, probably because it resents transplanting and growing in a pot. Plants ripen copious amounts of large, easy-to-collect, fertile black seed. A plant typically takes three years to bloom from seed.

Propagation: direct-sow seed (stratify) | **Companion plants:** silvery shrubs; prickly poppy

Dryas hookeriana (*Dryas octopetala* ssp. *hookeriana*)

Rocky Mountain avens

zones 2–7 • rocky slopes; alpine • sandy or gritty soils

2–6 in. × 12–20 in. or wider • rock gardens, crevice gardens, slope plantings

sun • low to moderate water

Beautiful large, creamy white flowers with showy yellow centers rise in summer on bare stems above the foliage mat, reminiscent of anemone or single rose blossoms. Flowers rotate to follow the sun, probably to help keep pollen and nectar warmer and easier to collect for pollinators at the very high elevations and exposed places the plant inhabits. Seedheads are as appealing as the flowers—showy, pale, and fluffy, lovely when backlit and similar to those of Apache plume, sugarbowls, and pasqueflower.

Technically a shrub, but its small stature and where it fits best into plantings make it logical to classify it with wildflowers. Grows almost flat to the ground, rooting along its branches and eventually forming large mats. Its leathery leaves are evergreen, narrowly oval, and have scalloped margins and white undersides. This wildflower thrives at cooler temperatures, needing some extra moisture in sunny spots at lower elevations. In warmer regions, plant it on a north- or east-facing slope, or against a large boulder using those same aspects.

Propagation: seed (stratify); cuttings | **Companion plants:** roundleaf harebell

Echinacea angustifolia

narrowleaf coneflower, black Samson

zones 3–8 • dry grassland, rocky meadows and hillsides; plains, foothills • most well-drained soils

10–20 in. × 12–20 in. • meadow plantings, flower gardens, hell-strips, seeded wildflower plantings

sun • low water

Produces a coarse, hairy, upright bouquet of large, pink daisies in early summer. With prominent bristly, rusty maroon centers on stiff stems, these make good cut flowers and continue blooming for well over a month in the heat of summer. The pink "petals" (ray florets) can be droopy or held straight out—flower size and form vary widely. Long, narrow leaves are also roughly hairy, like sandpaper.

Unlike purple coneflower and its many hybrids that thrive in moist loam and clay, needs much less water and prefers poorer, even rocky or gravelly soil. Plants self-sow a bit; seedlings can be moved with ease but mature plants less readily. The dark seedheads turn almost black as they dry and still look great in the dormant season poking through snow. They also serve as stiff, strong bird-feeding stations in late fall through winter.

If you want to propagate a particularly good form, take cuttings of the dark, deep (up to ten feet!), and sparsely branched root during the first half of the growing season.

Propagation: pot/direct-sow seed (stratify, light)
Companion plants: butterfly weed, fringed sage, western spiderwort, prairie winecup, purple prairie clover; smaller bunchgrasses, such as ruby muhly and Junegrass

Epilobium canum ssp. *garrettii* (*Zauschneria garrettii*)

hummingbird trumpet

zones 4 or 5–9 • slopes, rocky sites, canyons, arroyos/washes; shrub steppe • most well-drained soils

4–18 in. × 15–24 in. • groundcover, rock gardens, edges, front of borders, hellstrips

sun • low to moderate water

All members of the now-defunct genus *Zauschneria*—showy red, orange, or peach trumpet-shaped, hummingbird-frequented wildflowers native to western North America—are presently in another genus, *Epilobium*. Regardless of name issues, this wildflower is a champ: tough, long-blooming, and offering much-needed color and nectar from midsummer until frost. This subspecies extends eastward into Idaho, Utah, and Wyoming and is the hardiest of the group. The pale green, oval leaves are unremarkable, but their low profile allows the flower to shine.

Dies back immediately after the first frost, but comes back dependably (even in some warm zone 4 sites, while most of its cousins need zone 6 to be reliably perennial) over a number of years. Attracts its namesake but is surprisingly repugnant to deer. Popular low-growing selection Orange Carpet®, introduced by the late, great Santa Fe plantsman David Salman, has been a Plant Select mainstay for almost two decades and is easy to find in nurseries. This four-inch-tall pancake of a plant can be a groundcover or cascade down a slope.

Propagation: seed (stratify); cuttings; division | **Companion plants:** small shrubs such as winterfat, threadleaf sage, manzanita, and dwarf rabbitbrush; goldenrods and broomweed; smaller grasses such as ruby muhly, little bluestem, and prairie dropseed

Erigeron compositus

cutleaf daisy

zones 2–7 • dry grassland, gravelly or sandy spots, rocky hillsides; all life zones • sandy or gravelly soils

2–4 in. × 4–12 in. • rock gardens, crevice gardens, hellstrips, edges of flower gardens

sun, light shade • low to moderate water

This cute little daisy is one of the first wildflowers to bloom in spring, with a delightful, generous show of typically white (in cooler, higher areas often lavender or pink) daisies, all with yellow eyes. Grows all over the region and continues to sputter bloom all summer and into fall, especially after rains. The flowers open on leafless, solitary stems above a mat of finely divided leaves that vary in color from rich green to gray-green to almost silver and can be very felted or smooth and almost glossy. The leaves are semi-evergreen and actually rise from a taproot to form a basal rosette that continues to widen to create a mat over time.

Cutleaf daisy prefers some afternoon shade in hotter locations. The daisies close on rainy and very cloudy days, reopening in the sun. Plants self-sow quite a bit, especially in gravel. Seedlings move much better than mature plants.

Propagation: seed (light) | **Companion plants:** pasqueflower, sugarbowls, locoweed, lanceleaf chiming bells, tufted evening primrose, phloxes, and any of the early, shorter blue penstemons

Erigeron speciosus

showy fleabane, aspen fleabane

zones 2–7 • meadows, forest clearings; plains, foothills, montane, subalpine • most moist soils

1–2 ft. × 1 ft. • perennial gardens, meadow plantings

sun, light shade • moderate water

Few plants are so ubiquitous across our region; occurs in a massive spread up and down the Rockies. Also occurs at most elevation ranges in our region, indicating a durable, easygoing nature. Attractive to, and a superb food source for, various fly species and other flying insects. Also attractive to hikers, though not as a snack; its numerous, many-petaled flowers blanket mountain meadows and aspen groves with a lovely lavender haze in midsummer.

Grow this plant in part shade at lower elevations to keep it looking its best longer. Plants bedraggled by especially hot or dry summers can recover if cut back hard and watered deeply a few times. Some degree of cutting back can benefit plants in cooler sites, too, and serves to reduce their vigorous seed set. In higher-elevation areas, plants thrive in full sun and part shade alike. Hybridizes readily with close relative three-nerve fleabane (*Erigeron subtrinervis*), so intermediate forms can be found where the two grow together, wild or cultivated.

Propagation: seed (light), division | **Companion plants:** horsemint, wood lily, columbines, and dusky penstemon; flowering shrubs such as rockspray or mock orange

Eriogonum corymbosum

crispleaf buckwheat

zones 4–8 • dry grassland, mesas, rocky slopes; foothills, pinyon-juniper, shrub steppe, montane • sandy or gritty soils

1–4 ft. × 1–3 ft. • unwatered flower gardens, hellstrips, with shrubs and yuccas in chaparral-inspired garden

sun • very low water

This shrubby buckwheat can make quite a show in late summer and fall in even the driest sites, blooming in great billows, and then after as the tiny flowers remain colorful even as they mature, dry out, and ripen seed. Comes in many colors, from white, pink, and rose to yellow and all shades in between. As the flowers age they often become reddish or peach before ultimately turning a rusty brown. The small, gray-green leaves are semi-evergreen, narrowly oval, and have a dry, crinkled feel, hence the common name.

To keep the plants vigorous and shapely, cut them back by half in spring when removing last year's flower clusters and when you can see there is new growth starting to push. Make sure this plant gets superb drainage, and don't water after establishment except in the driest, hottest spots and/or years. Plants self-sow a bit, especially in gravel. Seedlings move much better than mature plants due to deep taproots. Crispleaf buckwheat does best in warm, sunny locations.

Propagation: seed (stratify) | **Companion plants:** yuccas and pricklypear; sages, fernbush, Apache plume and littleleaf mountain mahogany; pinyon pines and junipers

Eriogonum flavum

yellow buckwheat

zones 3–6 • mesas, rocky slopes, outcrops, ledges; most life zones • most well-drained soils

2–4 in. × 6–12 in., up to 10 in. tall with flowers • rock gardens, crevice gardens, in cactus plantings, hellstrips, edge plant

sun • very low water

Compared to many buckwheats that are much more particular about site and soil, this pretty species is very adaptable, growing in rocky, dry, barren areas at most elevations. Its rounded clusters of luminous, moonlight-yellow flowers are cheerful for several weeks in late spring and early summer and glow at dusk and dawn and on cloudy days.

Yellow buckwheat has a lot going for it despite its demure size, with a tidy habit, evergreen foliage, and flowers that continue to look good after they have gone over and are drying and making seed. The narrowly oval foliage varies from gray-green to silver and is felted. The silver-leaved forms are especially attractive blending with the soft yellow flowers. Basically, this plant looks like a small, gray-leaved version of sulfur flower (*Eriogonum umbellatum*), with shorter, smaller flower clusters and a slightly earlier bloom time.

Propagation: seed (stratify) | **Companion plants:** cacti, blackfoot daisy, cutleaf fleabane, small penstemons, and purple three-awn

Eriogonum ovalifolium

roundleaf buckwheat

zones 3–7 • rocky slopes, ledges; most life zones • sandy or gritty soils

1–3 in. × 6–12 in. • rock gardens, crevice gardens, cactus gardens, between paving stones

sun • very low water

This is one of the cutest members of the large, mainly western North American buckwheat tribe. The small, evergreen, rounded-to-oval foliage is silver (almost-white) and grows in clustered rosettes forming a mound or small patch. Dense round spheres of flowers hover slightly above in late spring and early summer, like little lollipops. Colors range from ivory and yellow to pink, peach, and crimson.

Roundleaf buckwheat requires minimal water. It also grows beautifully in crevice gardens or any dry, sunny planting where it can be seen up close and not smothered by larger, more aggressive plants. An alternative method of propagation is to take rosette cuttings from a mature mound in early spring before budding, or soon after bloom is finished.

Eriogonum bicolor is a similarly small and charming gray-leaved plant with pink to white pompoms. *Eriogonum shockleyi* is another diminutive, silver-leaved roundleaf buckwheat, with an array of flower colors similar to this plant's and even shorter-stemmed rounded flower heads; it's a true gem but very hard to find seed of.

Propagation: seed (stratify), cuttings | **Companion plants:** small cacti

Eriogonum umbellatum

sulfur flower

zones 3–8 • sage meadows, woodland clearings, rocky hillsides; most life zones • most well-drained soils

6–12 in. × 12–20 in., 4–8 in. taller with flowers • rock gardens, unwatered flower gardens, slopes, hellstrips

sun, light shade • very low water

This exceptional plant is truly a four-season wildflower. Bloom begins in early summer with distinctive ball-shaped clusters in an eye-catching moonlit yellow. As they dry and age, they turn rusty orange or sometimes even bright red before dropping seed and disintegrating a couple months later. The foliage makes a handsome, refined mat of rounded-to-oval, evergreen leaves arranged in rosettes. Rich olive-green during the growing season, it turns rust, maroon, or sometimes bright red in fall and winter.

Adapts well to light shade, though fall and winter foliage color is less pronounced in shaded sites. Several selections are available commercially: Plant Select's Kannah Creek® boasts dependably red fall and winter foliage, while it is the flowers of High Country Gardens' 'Poncha Pass Red' that age to a true red. A dwarf higher-elevation form, *Eriogonum umbellatum* var. *porteri*, makes a perfect plant for between paving stones, in rock gardens and crevice gardens, and among small cacti. A similar species for similar applications—matted buckwheat, or *E. caespitosum*—is also tiny with yellow pompoms (almost luminescent on summer evenings) and green foliage.

Propagation: seed (stratify); cuttings | **Companion plants:** penstemons, evening primroses, wild blue flax, silvery lupine, plains verbena, rice grass, cacti, and yuccas

Gaillardia aristata

blanketflower

zones 3–8 • meadows, shrubland, roadsides; plains, foothills, montane • most well-drained soils

1–2 ft. × 10–18 in. • unwatered flower gardens, meadow plantings, hellstrips, seeded wildflower plantings

sun • low water

The amber or clear yellow daisies of this flashy wildflower have contrasting reddish centers, blooming heavily in late spring and summer and then often sputter blooming until frost. At high elevations, this plant is at its best in late summer. Large, solitary flowers sport fringed edges and rise on stiff, hairy stems; they make good cut flowers and range from two to three inches across to as large as four inches. Hairy, coarse, somewhat-ungainly gray-green foliage is best masked by companions. Self-sows mildly and spreads a bit from slightly wandering roots. Deer and rabbits avoid the plant.

'Amber Wheels' is an extra-large-flowered and floriferous selection with a butterscotch color that was selected by plantsman Larry Vickerman.

The common *Gaillardia* selections found in the nursery trade are usually hybrids between the annual and perennial species *G. pulchella* and *G. aristata* and aren't as long-lived as the straight perennial species. Many selections have more "petals" (ray flowers) at the expense of the disk flowers that produce pollen and nectar, so though appealing in their variety, they are often much less valuable to pollinators.

Propagation: seed (light) | **Companion plants:** fringed sage; small grasses such as purple three-awn or blue grama

Gentiana parryi

Parry's gentian

zones 3–8 • forest clearings, meadows, streamsides; montane, subalpine, alpine • most moist soils

6–15 in. × 8–18 in. • rock gardens, lightly shaded gardens, flower gardens

sun, light shade • moderate water to moist

In late summer or early fall (depending on elevation and latitude), this plant's large, upright bell-shaped flowers open, clustered at the tip of unbranched stems, making a lovely, floppy bouquet. This already-striking wildflower is even more special and surprising because it blooms in that rarest of floral colors, deep sapphire blue. The jewel-like blossoms are precious treasures to experience on a late-season mountain hike. Rich green, narrowly oval foliage clasps the stems all the way up to the flowers, with leaves neatly arranged in alternating pairs. Flowers close on cloudy days and in wind, but even then the large, navy-blue tubes are lovely.

Pleated gentian (*Gentiana affinis*) is quite similar and late to bloom but grows in drier sites, needing less moisture to thrive than this plant. All gentians make loads of extremely fine, almost dust-like seed that can take two years to germinate. The seedlings are tiny and slow-growing but tough. Both seedlings and mature plants can be moved easily.

Propagation: seed (stratify) | **Companion plants:** jamesia, pearly everlasting, and compact forms of red stem dogwood

Geum triflorum

prairie smoke, old man's whiskers, purple avens

zones 3–6 • grassland, slopes, streamsides; foothills, shrub steppe, montane, subalpine, alpine • most well-drained soils, can briefly withstand waterlogged soil in spring

6–10 in. × 15–20 in., with flowers 12–15 in. • meadow plantings, accent

sun to light shade • moderate water

One of the earliest of the larger wildflowers, charming prairie smoke blooms in mid-spring. Clusters of nodding flowers rise on abundant wispy stems above the foliage mat, varying in color from washy peach to dusty pink to rich coral rose. These ripen to feathery pinkish seedheads that fade to tan before drying and dispersing in the wind. When backlit, the seedheads shimmer diffusely. In the wild this plant typically grows in patches and colonies where there is spring moisture, and the backlit effect gives the plant its picturesque common names.

Pretty, ferny green foliage makes a slightly hairy mat that is evergreen except in the coldest winters without snow cover, with a bonus of ruddy red fall color. The foliage makes a slowly expanding mat over time. Prairie smoke does best in cooler sites, and deer tend to avoid it. Thick, woody, dark brown rhizomes can be divided in spring or summer to make more plants.

Propagation: division; seed (stratify) | **Companion plants:** pussytoes and pearly everlasting; wild iris and tufted hair grass

Gutierrezia sarothrae

broomweed, matchbrush, snakeweed

zones 3–8 • dry grassland, roadsides, slopes, disturbed sites; plains, foothills, pinyon-juniper, shrub steppe, montane • sandy or gritty soils

8–15 in. × 12–18 in. • dry meadow plantings, seeded wildflower plantings, chaparral-inspired gardens, hellstrips

sun • very low water

This small, fine-textured subshrub's stiff but slender woody stems form a defined, perfectly rounded mound. The threadlike, bright green foliage contrasts with the predominant sage-greens, grays, tans, and silvers typical of dryland flora. Small golden flowers form clusters atop the stems in late summer and fall, creating yellow billows for weeks. Looks a lot like dwarf forms of rabbitbrush but blooms a bit earlier, and its foliage is even finer, stiffer, and a brighter green. Historically used to treat snakebites by Indigenous and Spanish-speaking peoples. Trim a mature plant back by a third to half in spring as growth commences to keep it shapely, sturdy, and less likely to splay.

This plant's curvaceous green domes are wonderful accents among the scruffy, often-amorphous textures and shapes of the dry garden, and it also provides nice winter form and texture. It contrasts beautifully with the starker architectural kings of the dry garden—cacti and yuccas—and is also lovely with similarly fine-textured grasses because of contrasting form and movement (grasses sway and are linear while broomweed is a stalwart twiggy mound).

Propagation: seed (light) | **Companion plants:** cacti and yuccas; fringed sage, plains gayfeather, Tahoka daisy, and blackfoot daisy

Helenium autumnale

common sneezeweed

zones 3–8 • moist meadows, streamsides, arroyos, roadsides, woodland clearings; plains, foothills, pinyon-juniper, shrub steppe, montane • most moist soils

2–4 ft. × 2–3 ft. • meadow plantings, flower gardens, cutting gardens

sun • moderate water

Unlike most Rocky Mountain natives, sneezeweed needs regular moisture and makes a superb subject in low areas, in drainages, by downspouts, or anywhere a rain-garden planting makes sense. This large, showy wildflower blooms in late summer and early fall. And no, this plant doesn't cause sneezing—except when the flowers are dried, ground, and used as medicinal snuff. Fresh-green, narrow foliage clasps lanky stems, topped by a spray of tidy, plump daisies with cleft edges and prominent button-like centers. These are usually a sunny yellow, often with an orange or rusty tint and at times entirely amber or bronze. The tall flowering stems make excellent long-lasting cut flowers. Plants, especially the flowers, are toxic to and generally avoided by livestock as well as deer.

Propagation: seed (light) | **Companion plants:** big bluestem, switchgrass, Indian grass, cutleaf compass flower, Rocky Mountain gayfeather, and pearly everlasting

Helianthus maximiliani

Maximilian sunflower

zones 4–9 • grassland, arroyos, fencerows; plains • most well-drained soils

5–10 ft. × 3–5 ft. • with shrubs, along fences and walls

sun • low to moderate water

Come autumn, these stately golden pillars of daisies are traffic stoppers. Throughout the growing season, narrow, hairy gray-green foliage cloaks the stiff upright stems. Flowers then open on short branches facing outward all along the stems, creating this dramatic vertical display of gold.

Like most sunflower species, this wildflower has wide appeal and is especially valuable to birds and pollinators of all sorts. It self-sows a lot and spreads slowly by short rhizomes. It's on its best behavior in dry, poor soils where it grows less floppy and seeds less aggressively than it does in rich or moist soils.

Lauren made the northern selection 'Dakota Sunshine' for regions in Colorado and northward, because it is a bit shorter and significantly earlier-blooming. (Plants from the more southern part of the range typically don't flower until well into October, which in the north is often too late for much of a floral show before winter.)

Plant in rougher areas with shrubs as part of a hedge or screen, or near driveways or walls.

Propagation: seed (stratify); division; cuttings
Companion plants: giant sacaton, azure sage

Iliamna rivularis

streambank wild hollyhock

zones 3–7 • forest clearings, stream edges; foothills, montane • most soils

2–6 ft. × 1–3 ft. • traditional garden borders and beds, meadow plantings

sun • moderate water to moist

Reminiscent of the common garden hollyhock, a non-native plant, this native analog makes a close substitute, though at a quarter the scale. Plant height varies with age, site, and water availability, but all produce handsome, broad, deeply lobed leaves and large, cupped, soft pink or white flowers. Rarely seen in gardens.

Occurs from the Four Corners region all the way into Canada at moderate elevations; relatively uncommon in the wild. The plants are shade-intolerant despite preferring moist soils, and moist soils foster the growth of trees, so this plant has a problem. The solution is its exceptionally long-lived seeds—possibly viable for more than a hundred years—that sit dormant in the soil, awaiting a disturbance event like a fire or flood to clear the site of trees. Once unshaded, seeds grow quickly and plants bloom profusely to recharge the soil's seed bank.

In the garden, plants grow well and long in full sun with minimal competition; situate them in meadow openings, along drainages and swales, in traditional garden beds, or (as was customary for some settlers) around an outhouse to indicate the building's purpose.

Propagation: seed (scarify then stratify) | **Companion plants:** horsemint, swamp milkweed, and tufted hair grass

Ipomoea leptophylla

bush morning-glory, man-root

zones 4–8 • grassland, roadsides, banks, sandy, silty, gravelly spots; plains • sandy or gritty soils

2–3 ft. × 3–5 ft. • unwatered flower gardens, chaparral-inspired gardens

sun • very low water

This odd-looking but beautiful plant makes a loose, arching mound with narrow, willow-like foliage. Its high-summer parade of large two- to three-inch, funnel-shaped, rose-pink blossoms lasts a couple months. To synchronize with pollinator activity, flowers are open in the morning and then close before the heat of the day sets in.

Bush morning-glory gets its other common name from its root, which is the size of a hefty thigh. This storage organ allows the plant to grow large in droughty climates, soils, and during the hottest time of the year. But it takes time to grow this root—usually at least three years are needed from seed to bloom, and two or three more for the plant to become its resplendent full-grown self. (Only relocate mature plants when they're dormant, and handle the root with great care.)

At first frost, this plant's ultra-sensitive foliage dies down to the ground. It's one of the last wildflowers to emerge in spring, protecting its vulnerable new growth from late-spring frosts common in our region.

Propagation: pot/direct-sow seed (scarify) | **Companion plants:** small shrubs such as winterfat, sages, leadplant and rabbitbrush; prairie winecup, blackfoot daisy, snow on the mountain, and silverleaf evening primrose

Iris missouriensis

wild iris, western blue flag

zones 3–7 • seasonally wet meadows, along watercourses and drainages; most life zones • most soils

18 in. × 2 ft. • perennial gardens, meadow plantings

sun, light shade • moderate water

One of our most beloved mountain wildflowers, instantly recognizable thanks to its large and familiar flowers that appear like cool blue rivers across mountain meadows and silver sagebrush seas in late spring. Synchronized to bloom with available snowmelt, this dramatic display disappears as quickly as it begins. Within just a couple of weeks, plants are entirely green and making seed in preparation to endure the typically dry period before summer monsoon.

Thanks to its seasonally wet-dry meadows of origin, the plant is tolerant of periodic waterlogging but won't bloom well if dry before flowering. After bloom, tolerates brief drought once established but suffers if dry for long in hot environs. Just like its larger relative the bearded iris, this tough plant sprouts from fibrous rhizomes (horizontal, leafless stems at or below ground level that store food and water) and can be divided as its flowering concludes.

Consider using this wildflower as a garden perennial, where its clean, vertical form complements messier or lumpier partners in the front of the border and its soft blue flowers pair beautifully with pale yellow, pink, and white.

Propagation: division; seed (stratify) | **Companion plants:** woolly cinquefoil, shrubby potentilla, prairie smoke, and golden currant

Leucocrinum montanum

sandlily, starlily

zones 3–8 • dry grassland, woodland clearings; plains, foothills, pinyon-juniper, shrub steppe • sandy or gritty soils

3–6 in. × 5–10 in. • rock gardens, crevice gardens, buffalo grass lawns, cactus gardens

sun • very low water

This lovely little wildflower is among the earliest to bloom, offering nectar and pollen before all else. Gray-green, narrow, grassy leaves create a lax mound of foliage that frames the pure white flowers nestled in the center, which shine like stars. Individual plants vary a great deal in flower size and width of the petals; the best can be two inches across. Blossoms are fragrant, especially on cloudy days and in the morning and evening. A mature plant can produce dozens of flowers over several weeks, and the individual flowers are waxy and long-lasting. Foliage dies back to the ground before midsummer.

The seed is very hard to collect, as it forms at the base of the spent flower tube that is often at or even below ground level—the flowers themselves have no stems, they rise above the foliage thanks to their long tubes.

Propagation: seed (stratify) | **Companion plants:** buffalo grass lawns; pasqueflower, sugarbowls, green hedgehog cactus, and snowball cactus

Liatris punctata

plains gayfeather, plains blazing star

zones 3–8 • dry grassland, hillsides, roadsides; plains, foothills, shrub steppe • most well-drained soils

10–18 in. × 15–24 in. • unwatered flower gardens, low meadow plantings, seeded wildflower plantings, hellstrips

sun • low water

Come late summer when much of our native flora is taking a rest, this plant's iconic feathery rose-purple flower spikes appear, along with monarch butterflies that always seem to find them. Blossoms open starting from the top of the stem down, the opposite of how most flower spikes bloom. A mature plant sends up a dozen or more stems from a swollen woody corm, with whorled, dark green, narrow leaves that superficially resemble pine needles, creating handsome, stiff-stemmed, fine-textured, dark green bouquets that make the perfect foil for the flashy flower spikes.

Fluffy, wind-dispersed seeds follow; the shimmering white, seed-laden stalks are almost as lovely as when purple with bloom. Belowground and from the base of its corm, sends down a taproot that can reach depths of up to a hard-to-fathom twelve feet or more into the subsoil, making this wildflower exceptionally rugged and long-lived.

Plants self-sow, especially in loose, gravelly soils. Older plants move best when dormant or just starting growth in spring.

Propagation: seed (stratify, light) | **Companion plants:** small shrubs such as winterfat, fringed sage, dwarf rabbitbrush, and broom snakeweed; blackfoot daisy, snow on the mountain

Lilium philadelphicum

wood lily, prairie lily

zones 3–8 • moist meadows, aspen groves, woodland clearings; foothills, shrub steppe, montane • moist, well-drained soils

15–24 in. × 6–8 in. • cool or shaded flower gardens

sun to light shade • moderate water

This sumptuous wildflower is rare in the wild, and what a treat to run across a patch of them in full bloom. In early summer, four-inch orange-red flowers open with brown freckles toward their centers, looking like wide-open tulips. Leaves are narrow, rich glossy green, and scattered and whorled around the unbranched stems. A plant can have several flowers at the top of a stem, but just one is more common.

Wood lily grows from a small, scaly white bulb. Unlike many of our native plants, it likes humus-rich soil, so treat it like you would a classic English garden perennial such as a peony or delphinium—give it good soil and regular water, and site it where it stays relatively cool in summer. This plant doesn't like to dry out completely, whether it's a tiny seedling or a mature individual.

Propagation: seed (stratify); division of bulb scales
Companion plants: columbines, tufted hair grass, wax currant, and mock orange; in hot-summer areas, under aspen, alder, or birch

Lupinus argenteus

silvery lupine

zones 3–8 • seasonally wet meadows, forest clearings, slopes, roadsides, shrubland; plains, foothills, shrub steppe, montane • most well-drained soils

2 ft. × 2 ft. • flower gardens, meadow plantings, chaparral-inspired plantings, seeded wildflower plantings

sun, light shade • very low water to moist

In Colorado's North Park, running through swaying fields of silvery lupine is an experience etched in Bryan's fond memories of a plant-rich childhood that helped fuel his growing interest in native flora. Ubiquitous throughout the Rocky Mountain region and a bit variable in looks due to hybridization, this plant has it all: handsome, unique foliage; glowing floral displays; drought-tolerance; and longevity. Flowers in a massive flush in early summer, beginning just after our native iris finishes, often growing in the same habitat and with flowers a similar color. Its numerous, shimmering blue flowers create dense spikes around often-reddened stems and rise above their one-of-a-kind, umbrella-like, fuzzy, pale leaves. In large populations, pure white and soft pink forms can be found. After the flowers, bean-like pods form that split upon drying to launch seeds.

Resents transplanting; does best while still small to minimize disturbance of its long, brittle taproot.

Propagation: seed (sow fresh seed; scarify, then sow stored seed) | **Companion plants:** shrubs such as manzanita, threadleaf sage, or Apache plume; yuccas; taller early penstemons such as Rocky mountain penstemon, firecracker penstemon, plains snapdragon, and smooth penstemon; in a night garden with evening primroses, mountain phlox, and sulfur flower

Mertensia lanceolata

lanceleaf chiming bells, narrowleaf bluebells

zones 3–6 • dry grassland, open slopes; most life zones • most well-drained soils

6–15 in. × 6–12 in. • rock gardens, accent plant

sun to light shade • low water

Spring wildflowers are extra beloved, probably because they follow a long, cold season devoid of active growth, offering color and lively change. Finding this plant's first sky-blue, nodding flower clusters on a hike just after snowmelt mud has finally dried is one of spring's finest things.

This pretty little plant is one of the earliest wildflowers to bloom and carries on longer than most other ephemeral spring treasures, typically blooming for well over a month. Not to be confused common-name-wise with mountain harebell or roundleaf harebell (*Campanula rotundifolia*).

Leaves are narrow and gray-green, and a mature plant in a good site forms a small, lax bouquet of flowering stems. The plant can go dormant by midsummer, especially in hotter, drier sites. It often self-sows lightly in loose soils, and small, young plants move well if the entire long taproot is dug. Deer tend to avoid this plant.

There are several other bluebells native to our region; some only thrive in high-elevation areas and/or with ample moisture and cool temperatures. The longest bloomers and most adaptable are this plant and its close cousin *Mertensia oblongifolia* (oblongleaf bluebells).

Propagation: seed (stratify) | **Companion plants:** cutleaf daisy, silver pussytoes

Mirabilis multiflora

desert four o'clock, giant four o'clock

zones 4–8 • sparse grassland, roadsides, gravelly flats; plains, foothills, pinyon-juniper, shrub steppe • most well-drained soils

1–2 ft. × 3–5 ft. • chaparral-inspired plantings, shrub companion, seasonal groundcover, hellstrips

sun • very low water

This dramatic, coarse-textured plant looks like a shrub but dies down to the ground each fall after frost, resprouting again quite late in spring from a starchy, thick taproot. Foliage is oval/triangular and a pretty, soft blue-green. In midsummer, covers itself for the next couple of months with funnel-shaped, one-inch rose-magenta flowers that open in the afternoon (hence the name) and close in the morning. Astonishing growth is produced by mature plants in dry, lean soil, thanks to their huge roots. These take several years to develop, though, before a young plant reaches mature splendor.

Drab off-white-flowered forms occur rarely and are not very showy. However, when present they often hybridize with the common magenta forms and throw some nice, pink-flowered seedlings.

Plants self-sow in gravelly sites. Likes heat, so in cooler areas plant it in your sunniest spot. Deer- and rabbit-resistant yet supports hawk moth caterpillars, which can make a visible dent in the foliage in a few days' time.

Propagation: seed (scarify or stratify) | **Companion plants:** banana yucca, buffalo gourd, angel's trumpet, threadleaf sage, leadplant, giant sacaton, and cholla

Monarda fistulosa var. *menthifolia*

horsemint, wild bergamot, western beebalm

zones 3–8 • meadows, streamsides, draws, woodland clearings; plains, foothills, shrub steppe, montane • most moist soils

15–40 in. × 3–4 ft. • meadow plantings, casual lightly shaded plantings

sun to light shade • moderate water

A floral paradise for myriad pollinators. For many weeks in summer, rose-pink, lavender, or occasionally white tubular flowers open in a tight, rounded cluster. Individual flowers have protruding threadlike stamens and styles that give them an appealing fuzzy look.

Narrowly oval leaves clasp the square stems in pairs, and all parts of the plant are freshly aromatic when crushed, just like culinary mint. Also shares mint's aggressively spreading roots, so most wildflowers can't survive having horsemint as a close neighbor. Foliage can get powdery mildew (which won't harm the plant but makes leaves look shabby and mottled) in late summer if the plant is drought-stressed or sited in spots with poor air circulation.

Combine this beautiful bully, which is exceptionally valuable to wildlife, with larger, stalwart shrubs, similarly aggressive wildflowers, or dense clumping grasses.

Propagation: seed; cuttings; division | **Companion plants:** western yarrow and prairie sage; tufted hair grass, golden feather grass, and big bluestem; mock orange and snowberry

Oenothera cespitosa

tufted evening primrose, gumbo lily

zones 3–8 • rocky soils, roadsides, exposed bedrock; plains, foothills, shrub steppe, pinyon-juniper • most soils

3–12 in. × 6–24 in. • rock gardens, unwatered flower gardens, path and patio edges, hellstrips, cactus gardens

sun • low water

Despite their delicate, crepe-paper-textured petals, all evening primroses are tough; this one inhabits some of the coldest and driest parts of our region. To succeed, it has developed into a variety of forms, from a one-foot-high, woody-stemmed subshrub with hairy leaves to a smooth-leaved, low-growing, running form, to—in extraordinarily harsh locations—just a tuft of leaves arising directly from the soil.

The common name *gumbo lily* was popularized by rancher and plantsman Claude Barr and refers to the plant's ability to grow in the plains' challenging sticky clay soils. Barr, who gardened in the Dakota Badlands, was one of the first to showcase the plant in writing: "these flowers, 2½ to 4 inches wide, open so rapidly in late afternoon that the movement of their unfolding may be watched" (an adaptation to the rapidly changing weather typical of this region).

The four-petaled flowers open in the evening and fade with rising daytime temperatures; the blooms open pearly white and melt to rosy pink, indicating to visiting pollinators which flowers have the freshest pollen and nectar. Flowers remain attractive well into the morning hours and on cloudy days.

Propagation: seed (stratify) | **Companion plants:** blue penstemons; flowering cacti

Oenothera hartwegii (*Calylophus hartwegii*)

Hartweg's sundrops

zones 4 or 5–7 • grassland, rock outcroppings, barren soils; plains • most soils

18 in. × 2 ft. • rock gardens, unwatered flower gardens, hellstrips, low meadow plantings

sun • low to moderate water

One of two plants in this book recently moved from the genus *Calylophus* to *Oenothera*, the other being lavender-leaf sundrops (*Oenothera lavandulifolia*). Both are exceedingly water-thrifty plants that share an intimate relationship with hawk moths, feeding all life stages of the insect in exchange for pollination. Both also captivate passersby for weeks with luminescent, four-petaled flowers that seem to melt in the heat of day, transforming their glowing, crepe-paper-like, lemon-yellow petals to soft, apricot-orange crinkles by afternoon.

To find the best ways of using these similar plants, it helps to know their differences: Hartweg's sundrops is a larger, twiggier plant. It's slightly less cold-hardy, though still hardy to at least -30°F, and is far more tolerant of clay soils than its petite cousin. Its larger habit makes it a better plant for waterwise flower gardens, which also help reduce its spindly legs. Cut back hard after its heavy bloom concludes in early to midsummer to encourage a denser, more attractive form. Often, this tactic results in a light rebloom, too. Self-sows lightly in favorable settings.

Propagation: seed, cuttings | **Companion plants:** taller penstemons; white yarrow, fringed sage, plains verbena, and creeping globemallow; rice grass and yucca

Oenothera lavandulifolia (Calylophus lavandulifolius)

lavender-leaf sundrops

zones 4–7 • rock outcroppings, bare soil, dry grassland and shrubland; plains, pinyon-juniper • sandy or gravelly soils

6 in. × 1 ft. • crevice gardens, rock gardens, paver/flagstone accent, hellstrips, cactus gardens

sun • very low water

The second of two plants in this book that were formerly in the genus *Calylophus* and are now *Oenothera*, it shares the beacon-like yellow bloom of its larger cousin, Hartweg's sundrops, and serves hawk moths equally well. This is the more petite of the pair, a trait that helps it endure the alternately cold/hot, dry/windy tops of limestone buttes and bluffs in the High Plains. Its restrained growth habit also makes it more refined, as it grows slowly into a fine-textured, gray-green tuft over years, forgoing the twiggy stems of its near relative. The plant is an exquisite stress tolerator; it remains handsome through summer, flowering with minimal inputs.

However, conservative growth and exceptional stress-tolerance make it poorly suited to lush garden borders and rich soils; it succumbs to competition from bigger neighbors in the former and rots in the latter. Situated properly, it blankets itself in large (up to two inches across) flowers in early to mid-spring and tapers off as summer heat arrives. With occasional waterings, plants continue to bloom sporadically through most of summer.

Propagation: seed (stratify) | **Companion plants:** claret cup and hedgehog cacti; plains verbena, narrowleaf penstemon, cutleaf daisy, and rock tansy

Oenothera macrocarpa ssp. *fremontii*

narrowleaf evening primrose

zones 4–8 • mesas, rocky slopes, outcrops, ledges; plains, foothills • most well-drained soils

4–8 in. × 12–15 in. • edges, unwatered flower gardens, rock gardens, hellstrips, seeded wildflower plantings

sun • low water

This pretty, low-growing plant opens luminous moonlight-yellow flowers for many weeks from late spring through midsummer. The two- to three-inch-wide blossoms absolutely glow at dusk and dawn and on cloudy days, closing during the hottest, sunniest times of day. Narrow foliage varies from gray-green to silver. This bloom timing synchronizes with the activity of various species of hawk moths found in the lower elevations of the region. Forms that have silver foliage are especially attractive with the soft yellow flowers.

Can become a bit of a pesky self-sower where it's happy, as the seedlings are very hard to dig out due to enormously long taproots that break off easily. The plant likes heat and, when grown at higher elevations, needs a spot with some reflected warmth to thrive.

Lauren and plantsman Scott Ogden selected an especially narrow-leaved, silvery form that Lauren named 'Shimmer'; it was chosen as a Plant Select offering in 2023. One of Lauren's signature design uses of native evening primroses is along paths, where they serve garden visitors on an evening stroll as lantern-like floral wayfinders.

Propagation: seed, cuttings | **Companion plants:** larger cacti, blackfoot daisy, penstemons, and purple three-awn

Oenothera macrocarpa ssp. *incana*

silverleaf evening primrose

zones 4–9 • rocky soils, roadsides, exposed bedrock; plains • most well-drained soils

8 in. × 2 ft. • rock gardens, low meadow plantings, path and patio edges, unwatered flower gardens, hellstrips, seeded wildflower plantings

sun • low to moderate water

Four-inch flowers glow like yellow limelights for a show that begins promptly at dusk. The scene, involving a nectar-rich floral tube, a long proboscis, and the nick of time, is reenacted for months across our region with the repeat appearance of hawk moths at nightfall. Each act ends promptly the next day when flowers succumb to the hot sun.

This easygoing plant makes attractive, loose, low and wide mats with spear-shaped silver leaves and reddened stems. Remarkably adaptable and dependable in the garden, it flowers exuberantly from late spring through summer and does so with extra vigor given a bit of supplemental water. If left to produce seed, the plant flowers in a heavy first flush and then lightly afterward, self-sowing on soils with good moisture or finer, claylike textures. The seeds are large and flat, borne in showy four-winged seedpods. Lauren uses this plant liberally along paths as a signature in her designs; it serves as floral landscape lighting.

Propagation: seed; cuttings | **Companion plants:** angel's trumpet and fringed sage; hummingbird trumpet, plains skullcap, blue penstemons, rice grass, and blue grama

Oxytropis lambertii

purple locoweed

zones 3–7 • roadsides, dry hillsides, sandy or gravelly sites; most life zones • sandy or gritty soils

4–12 in. × 8–12 in. • unwatered flower gardens, dry meadow plantings, hellstrips, rock gardens, crevice gardens

sun • low water

In late spring and early summer, this beautiful wildflower spangles large areas in varied latitudes and altitudes with its glowing, ruby-magenta flower spikes. Silvery green, fine-textured leaves form mats of rosettes and make the perfect foil for the bouquet-like show of bright blossoms. The flowers are highly popular with diverse pollinators, attracting them with rich color and a light honey fragrance.

Purple locoweed absorbs selenium from soils and concentrates the element in its tissues, making itself toxic to grazing livestock. Unlike many other poisonous plants that taste or smell bad, this plant appeals to many domestic grazing species' palates, especially horses; they can become addicted and die from it. (The common name refers to the bizarre behavior that stricken animals exhibit.) Be sure not to plant it where livestock have access.

The hairy, silvery foliage rots easily when watered overhead, so conventional nursery culture has not been successful with this plant despite its beauty and widespread presence in the wild. There, it often crosses with white locoweed, resulting in hybrids with pretty, soft pink flowers that are usually larger and in denser spikes than their darker parent.

Propagation: pot/direct-sow seed (scarify) | **Companion plants:** tufted evening primrose, early-summer-blooming blue penstemons

Oxytropis sericea

white locoweed

zones 3–7 • grassland, meadows, slopes, rock outcrops; most life zones • most well-drained soils

10–15 in. × 12–15 in. • low dry meadow plantings, rock gardens, hellstrips

sun • low water

Blooms in spring, a month or so before purple locoweed. Its pea-shaped flowers are larger and its spikes are fatter than its darker-colored, later-blooming relative's. Flowers are usually a pure white but can also be almost yellow or washy lavender. In some populations where hybridization between purple and white locoweed has probably occurred, clear pink and rose variants pop up.

This wildflower has larger, somewhat less silver, and more profuse foliage than purple locoweed and tends to grow in better soil and less-disturbed plant communities where its silky, hairy leaves and stems and white flowers shimmer from a great distance, contrasting with the early fresh-green growth of grasses.

Propagation: pot/direct-sow seed (scarify) | **Companion plants:** narrowleaf penstemon and indigo sugarbowls

Penstemon caespitosus

mat penstemon

zones 3–8 • rocky hillsides, ledges, dry meadows; foothills, shrub steppe, montane • sandy or gritty soils

1–3 in. × many feet in width over time • rock gardens, hillside gardens, groundcover between shrubs or flagstones, hellstrips

sun • low water

Has a very different look than most cold-hardy penstemons native to the Rocky Mountains and Great Plains: instead of making upright spikes of flowers above the foliage, it lays low to the ground; even when in bloom, the flowers appear as if they are lying on top of the leafy mat. This peculiar growth habit lends it to very different uses in plantings than other penstemons.

Blooms in late spring, covering its foliage with a spangle of blue or lavender flowers that sport prominent white throats. Tiny evergreen leaves, rounded to oblong to sometimes almost linear, look much like creeping thyme. The plant spreads by rooting along and layering its creeping stems, creating an ever-widening mat. This little but mighty penstemon makes a great crack-filler between casual, widely spaced stepping stones and a charming year-round groundcover between shrubs.

The Plant Select program now includes a selection called Waggon Wheel®, which has made the plant much more available.

Propagation: cuttings; division | **Companion plants:** manzanita, littleleaf mountain mahogany, golden and wax currants, and Apache plume

Penstemon linarioides ssp. *coloradoensis*

silvermat penstemon, toadflax penstemon

zones 4–8 • dry rocky slopes, woodland clearings; foothills, montane, pinyon-juniper • most well-drained soils

6–12 in. × 8–15 in. • unwatered flower gardens, rock gardens, planting edges, hellstrips

sun • low water

This little shrubby penstemon is a year-round asset to any sunny, dry planting where it won't be overwhelmed by bulkier, more aggressive plants. Pale lavender-blue flowers open in spring and carry on through early summer, in many short, one-sided spikes above narrow, gray leaves. When out of bloom, the plant resembles a tiny rabbitbrush or lavender, and the evergreen leaves cloak the fine-textured shrublet through winter. Less exacting in its site requirements than many of its clan, it only calls for a bit of trimming off its spent flower stalks (like lavender), mainly to keep the shrubby form shapely and show off the silvery leaves. Makes a beautiful edging to plantings.

The late plantsman David Salman introduced a fine selection through High Country Gardens that he named 'Blue Lips', with brighter blue flowers and more contrasting white throats. Plant Select offers a very silver form called Silverton®. Handsome Crandall's penstemon (*Penstemon crandallii*) has similar linear foliage, but green rather than silver, and plants grow more flatly mounded with deeper blue flowers. Notably, unlike this plant, it doesn't tolerate clay.

Propagation: cuttings; seed (stratify) | **Companion plants:** yellow and white evening primroses, cutleaf daisy and sulfur flower, or with pink phloxes and purple locoweed

Penstemon strictus

Rocky Mountain penstemon

zones 3–8 • open grassland, rocky hillsides, disturbed areas; most life zones • most well-drained soils

12–30 in. × 8–30 in. • flower gardens, hellstrips, seeded wildflower plantings

sun, light shade • low water

This popular, robust penstemon blooms early to midsummer with abundant, deep indigo-blue flowers in thick spikes. Elongated emerald-green foliage forms an evergreen mat, providing a handsome presence year-round.

Right after bloom, remove all but one stalk down to where the flowers end and there are only leaves, and preferentially save the stem holding the least seed capsules. This has several benefits: the plant's energy stores go into making new foliage rather than ripening seed, resulting in a stronger, leafier plant. Allowing the plant to ripen some seed helps signal it to harden off. Lastly, the few seed capsules left offer the chance of seedlings but not at the expense of the parent.

Seed germinates better after being stored dry for a year or two. Exceptionally tolerant of most soil types, including heavy clay, and a wide range of moisture regimes (but still must have good drainage, especially in winter). A rare white form found in northern New Mexico by plantsman Kenny Sanchez, Blanca Peak®, is part of the Plant Select program.

Propagation: seed (stratify) | **Companion plants:** sulfur flower, white and yellow evening primrose species, fringed sage, paintbrush, Indian grass, prickly poppy, and four-nerve daisy

Penstemon virens

blue mist penstemon

zones 3–7 • hillsides, ledges, disturbed rocky areas; most life zones • most well-drained soils

6–15 in. × 12–18 in. • flower gardens, rock gardens, hillside gardens, hellstrips

sun, light shade • low water

Probably the most iconic penstemon of Colorado's Front Range, this carpets steep and rocky spots throughout the foothills and mountains there in late spring and early summer. Its small, profuse, densely clustered flowers are an ethereal soft blue, and the plants' overall fine texture combined with the color gives patches a truly misty look. More rarely, pink or white variants can be found. Fresh-green, narrow leaves cloak the slender stems and make rosettes along the ground. The plants spread by short runners that form new rosettes, making sizeable mats over time.

Similarly fine-textured, compact, and blue, littleflower penstemon (*Penstemon procerus*) is much more widespread in the wild, growing over much of the mountain West on into the Cascades and Sierras. It has also proved to be a very adaptable garden plant, unlike many in the genus, sharing with blue mist penstemon a tolerance for light shade, competition by neighboring plants, and more moisture than most cold-hardy penstemons.

Propagation: seed (stratify); cuttings | **Companion plants:** wild iris, cutleaf daisy, Colorado blue columbine, Junegrass and sulfur flower

Penstemon whippleanus

dusky penstemon, Whipple's penstemon

zones 2–7 • meadows, rocky slopes, mountain forests; foothills, montane, subalpine, pinyon-juniper • most well-drained soils

8–20 in. × 8–18 in. • slightly shaded or cool flower gardens, rock gardens, slopes

sun, light shade • moderate water

This unique-looking high-elevation penstemon blooms in summer. Its exact timing depends on elevation and warmth; it opens later at cooler, higher elevations and latitudes. Unremarkable oblong green foliage rosettes give rise to stems topped with large, dangling flowers clustered in dense mopheads. These blossoms come in hues quite unusual in summertime flowers: mysterious deep purple, rich maroon, or ivory. The entire plant is also covered in small hairs, perhaps as protection from high-elevation winds and strong summertime ultra-violet light.

Dusky penstemon needs more water and cooler temperatures than most of our region's penstemons to thrive. In warmer parts of the region, give it some shade or a northern or eastern exposure.

As with any floriferous species that's easy to deadhead, don't let most of the flowers ripen seed; this preserves the plant's energy for foliage and flower production in subsequent seasons. Right after bloom, remove all but one stalk down to where the flowers end and there are only leaves, and preferentially save the stem holding the least seed capsules.

Propagation: seed (stratify); division | **Companion plants:** golden or blue columbine, white yarrow, and showy fleabane

Phlox kelseyi

marsh phlox

zones 3–8 • meadows, seasonally wet spots; plains, foothills, shrub steppe, pinyon-juniper, montane • most seasonally moist soils

1 in. × 15–20 in. • rock gardens, crevice gardens, between flagstones

sun • moderate water

This petite, mat-forming wildflower covers itself in open-faced lavender, purple, or occasionally white tubular flowers in spring. Several other lovely native mat-forming phloxes grow in our region, but of the tiny ones this species has the widest adaptability to soil types and summer heat, provided it gets some extra moisture. Eventually its mats create a slowly spreading groundcover, but perhaps a better role for it is to star as a specimen plant in intimate garden settings. There, its narrow, short, needlelike foliage and sweet flowers can be appreciated close-up. It's also a manageable plant to grow between paving stones, where, again, it can be enjoyed while on a slow ramble.

Phlox species are notoriously hard to collect seed from because the seed ripen over time, and the plant expels them as soon as they ripen. Dogged collectors resort to putting paper bags over plants for days to catch maybe a dozen seeds.

This little gem of a phlox looks great between rocks, whether they be pavers, rock-garden boulders, or closely sandwiched crevice-garden stones.

Propagation: seed (stratify); cuttings | **Companion plants:** sugarbowls, prairie smoke, and wild iris

Phlox multiflora

Rocky Mountain phlox

zones 3–8 • grassy slopes, sagebrush meadows, woodland clearings; foothills, shrub steppe, montane • most well-drained soils

1 in. × 12–18 in. • rock gardens, unwatered flower gardens, path edges, hillside plantings, hellstrips

sun • low water

This spring-blooming wildflower is one of the showiest of our region's phloxes, making sizeable low mats completely covered in large, rounded, flat-faced, five-petaled pale pink, lavender, or white blossoms. It's the largest flowered native phlox in our region. As with all phloxes, the flowers offer nectar protected inside the narrow tube behind the showy flower face to accommodate long-tongued insects of many species. Rocky Mountain phlox has a rich, sweet fragrance to entice pollinators from afar and in lower-light conditions at dusk. Narrow, needlelike foliage is much less prickly and stiff than that of marsh phlox, and this plant is larger and more adapted to dry soils. Marsh phlox is altogether a more diminutive plant with richer flower colors.

As is true for most phlox species, Rocky Mountain phlox roots easily and quickly from softwood cuttings.

Propagation: cuttings; seed (stratify) | **Companion plants:** fringed sage, blue and pastel penstemons, Scott's clematis, locoweed, silvery lupine, plains verbena, and desert bluestar

Phlox nana

Santa Fe phlox

zones 4–8 • mesas, rocky slopes, outcrops, ledges, roadsides; plains, foothills • most well-drained soils

4–8 in. × unlimited spread • chaparral-inspired plantings, low dry meadow plantings, hellstrips

sun • very low water

Of the many phlox species native to our region, none have this one's prolonged bloom. Maddeningly hard to find because propagation has been so difficult and the plant rarely roots from cuttings. The late Santa Fe plantsman David Salman cracked the code when he found a local selection that roots easily; he named it 'Perfect Pink'.

Spreads underground, forming open patches over time. Has a floppy, sparse habit with scruffy narrow foliage that gets tattered and brown by midseason—but the warm pink flowers just keep coming. Probably the longest-blooming perennial wildflower of our region, alongside silverleaf primrose. To make more of the plant, dig up and transplant pieces that have some roots on them once the phlox has fully established on your site.

Santa Fe phlox likes heat during the growing season. At high elevations and latitudes, it should be given some reflected heat off rocks, walls, and/or pathways. Its relative *Phlox longifolia* is very similar in appearance but less of a runner and blooms for a much shorter period in late spring and early summer. Both are somewhat rabbit-resistant.

Propagation: division | **Companion plants:** silverleaf evening primrose; shrubs, chollas, large pricklypears and yuccas

Potentilla hippiana

woolly cinquefoil

zones 3–8 • grassland, meadows, shrubland, forest clearings, roadsides; plains, foothills, shrub steppe, montane, subalpine • most soils

6 in. × 1 ft. (1 ft. in bloom) • meadow plantings, rock gardens, along path and paver edges, hellstrips, seeded wildflower plantings

sun • low to moderate water

An adaptable, easygoing, and variable plant present throughout most of our region. In early spring it starts to form handsome mats of texture-rich, woolly silver leaves with toothed edges. By late spring or early summer, small, simple yellow flowers, sometimes in large numbers, open well above the foliage. This wildflower hybridizes with other native cinquefoil species, making it quite variable, with some forms much more visually striking than others. *P. hippiana* var. *effusa* is among the showiest, with intensely silver foliage and a cloud of small, five-petaled yellow flowers above silvery, wirelike stems; Bryan has found it a breeze to grow from seed he collects on his family's ranch.

The best forms of this plant shimmer as low-floating, silver-yellow clouds of flowers on roadsides in late spring into early summer. As is often the case, seeing the plant in the wild sparks ideas on how to use it in the garden. Plants self-seed moderately in suitable conditions (without overpowering their neighbors), making them great additions in grassy plantings.

Propagation: pot/direct-sow seed (stratify) | **Companion plants:** buffalo grass, bunchgrasses; wild blue flax, wild iris

Pulsatilla nuttalliana (Pulsatilla patens, Anemone patens)

American pasqueflower, prairie crocus

zones 3–7 • rocky slopes, dry grassland; plains, foothills, montane, subalpine • sandy or gritty soils

4–12 in. × 6–12 in. • rock gardens, unwatered flower gardens, edges, hellstrips

sun • low water

Our native pasqueflower, South Dakota's state flower, is a favorite wildling for its large flowers and super-early spring appearance, often with snow still on the ground. Adorably furry all over as if dressed for the weather. Showy pale blue, icy lavender, or (rarely) pink flowers up to three inches across appear before the foliage emerges, their bells opening upward. Centers are bushy crowns of golden stamens bees love; the fluffy seedheads (similar to those of sugarbowls and prairie smoke) shimmer in the bright, silvery seasonal light. Narrow cut foliage pushes up as the plant ripens seed. The entire plant is even more magical with backlighting; consider this when siting it.

Like most plants from higher elevations and latitudes, likes cooler temperatures and benefits from some afternoon shade in summer. Planting between deciduous shrubs or under a deciduous tree is ideal in warmer areas, offering shade after the plant has bloomed and leafed out. Regardless, usually goes dormant later in summer, even in cool climates.

Trim the fluffy plumes off the seed before sowing; grows slowly, sending up several flower stems each year, and becomes a veritable bouquet after five or more years in the ground.

Propagation: seed (stratify) | **Companion plants:** deciduous shrubs or trees

Salvia azurea

azure sage

zones 4–9 • roadsides, grassland, swales, ditch banks, seasonally moist soils; plains • most well-drained soils

3–5 ft. × 2–3 ft. • meadow plantings, back-of-border perennial

sun • low water to moist

This is a "stop the car!" plant. No wildflower in our region displays such intensely blue flowers at such height and girth. Come August, sky-blue flower spikes open near eye level, swaying along roadsides above green and gold grasses. Occurs in a broad swath from Texas to the Colorado border and north into the Nebraska Panhandle, a true zone-4 plant. Thrives on heat and doesn't risk late snow or frost, so is very late to emerge in spring.

Lays low early in the season, making humble clusters of green shoots with clean but somewhat-tousled foliage before hitting its stride later. Cutting the plant back by half in early to midsummer reduces its ultimate height and floppiness and helps it develop a fuller form. Culling the many seedlings of this vigorous self-sower is difficult due to their deep, wiry roots. Resist temptation to deadhead, though: songbirds love the seeds.

The blues of azure sage vary by population, from sky blue to deep cobalt. 'NeKan', named for its origin on the Nebraska-Kansas state line, is a vigorous selection with light blue flowers.

Propagation: seed; cuttings | **Companion plants:** large grasses such as golden feather grass, switchgrass, or giant sacaton; Maximilian sunflower

Sidalcea neomexicana

New Mexico checkermallow

zones 4–9 • wet meadows, seeps, fens, forest clearings; plains, foothills, shrub steppe, montane, subalpine • most moist soils

3 ft. × 2 ft. • border perennial, meadow plantings, cottage gardens

sun, light shade • moderate water to moist

Found in nature from plains to subalpine, though always with seasonally wet feet; keeps a low profile in such settings, hiding in the foliage of the grassy meadows it prefers. Only once these plants bloom do they become easy to spot, adorning grassy places en masse with soft pink, cupped flowers on lean stems. Can make a splendid perennial for wet and moist gardens, where its cheery blooms adorn meadow gardens and cottage garden borders alike in midsummer.

Plants cultivate with ease, though they resent transplanting due to brittle taproots and require soils that remain moist through heat. Up close in the garden, their unique and handsome foliage is worthy of appreciation, too. Plants produce two different leaf shapes: a rounded, scallop-edged leaf that arises from plant crowns, and a delicate, deeply cut leaf produced by the flowering stems.

Like a number of our native mallow family members, checkermallow is an excellent insect host plant. It can be challenging to find in nurseries.

Propagation: seed (scarify then stratify) | **Companion plants:** finely textured grasses such as tufted hair grass and prairie dropseed

Silphium laciniatum

cutleaf compass plant

zones 3–9 • wet meadows, seeps, draws, ditches; plains, foothills • most moist soils

4 ft. × 4 ft. (up to 8 ft. tall in bloom) • border perennial, meadow plantings, cottage gardens, accent plant

sun • low water to moist

Instantly recognizable, cutleaf compass plant makes quite the garden conversation piece. It is simply huge, with richly green, deeply lobed leaves that can reach over three feet long. These spectacular, jungle-evoking leaves explain its common name: once mature, they align themselves so that their blades face east-west and their sides point north-south, probably to reduce water loss from their large surface area under the hot prairie sun. Its leaves are most dramatic when viewed from east or west.

A fantastic bed anchor, accent, and statement plant in informal plantings, its size and coarseness can make it tough to shoehorn into smaller or more formal plantings. Adapts to drought by developing massive, plunging taproots, and so is best allowed to develop slowly and with deep, occasional waterings. Though worth growing for the foliage alone, it also produces a floral display in midsummer: four-inch, yellow daisylike flowers on lanky stems. Like sunflowers, this plant provides both table and meal for songbirds with its exceptionally tall, stout stems.

Can be challenging to find for sale in our region. Be patient with seedlings, which develop extensive root systems for several years before flowering.

Propagation: seed (stratify) | **Companion plants:** big bluestem and golden feather grass; anise hyssop, horsemint, and meadow blazing star

Solidago rigida (Oligoneuron rigidum)

stiff goldenrod

zones 3–9 • grasslands, roadsides, gravelly sandy or rocky spots; plains, foothills, montane • most well-drained soils, tolerates periodically wet soils

15–36 in. × 15–36 in. • flower gardens, meadow plantings, seeded wildflower plantings

sun • low water

This widespread, very successful group of native North American wildflowers is also one of the most important late-season food sources for pollinators and birds. Their iconic, showy yellow flower heads in high summer and fall and their often-aggressive growth habit earned them undeserved blame for pollen allergies. The real culprit is ragweed, *Ambrosia artemisiifolia*, whose green flowers are barely noticeable and bloom around the same time.

Grows throughout the midwestern prairies, but on the Great Plains and in the Rockies there is a shorter, tougher variant, ssp. *humilis*, with the same bold, gray-green, sandpapery basal foliage and large, flat-topped golden flower heads on a more compact plant. Unlike most of its cousins, stiff goldenrod doesn't spread underground. In late summer it sends up flowers on sturdy upright stems (hence the name *rigida*), attracting insect pollinators. As the seeds set, big white fluffy seedheads feed many species of birds, especially songbirds. These showy white feeding stations contrast beautifully with the fall foliage in orange or rusty hues.

Often reseeds and can be problematically weedy (and look floppy) in rich, moist soils, so best to plant in drier, poor soil.

Propagation: seed (stratify, light); division | **Companion plants:** bunchgrasses, ironweed, azure sage, and liatris

Sphaeralcea coccinea

creeping globemallow, cowboy's delight

zones 4–8 • grassland, dry hillsides, roadsides, disturbed areas; plains, foothills, pinyon-juniper, shrub steppe, montane • sandy or gravelly soils

4–10 in. × unlimited spread • low meadow plantings, chaparral-inspired plantings, hellstrips

sun • very low water

This charming wildflower carpets many parts of this region with striking orange blooms in early summer, making sizable patches from fast-spreading underground roots. It's our slightly less dramatic version of the West Coast and Southwest deserts' orange and gold poppies, yet more dependably blooming, even in drought years. Resembles a tiny orange hollyhock, to which it is related. Short spikes of small, open-faced ruffled flowers rise on stems with pretty, deeply cleft, scalloped foliage that varies from gray-green to silver.

Grow it dry and limit overhead watering, as the foliage is subject to fungal attack if grown in too humid, damp, or shaded conditions. Sunny, windy, dry, and harsh is perfect. Many taller, orange-flowered cousins are native farther south and west. Most don't have its cold hardiness but are similarly tough, rambunctious, and beautiful. Germination can be spotty, especially with older seed. Expect it to be staggered over a period of several weeks. Spreads aggressively; best to combine it with small shrubs rather than other wildflowers.

Propagation: seed (scarify then stratify); division | **Companion plants:** threadleaf and fringed sages, dwarf rabbitbrush, and leadplant; rice grass, buffalo grass, blue grama, and wild blue flax

Sphaeromeria capitata (Artemisia capitata)

rock tansy

zones 3–7 • dry slopes, rock outcrops; shrub steppe, foothills, montane • most well-drained soils

1–3 in. × 12–18 in. • rock gardens, sloped plantings, cactus gardens

sun • very low water

Cute as a button, this tiny sagebrush relative's evergreen, cleft gray foliage grows in small rosettes that form dense, flat mats. When wet or rubbed, the leaves smell a lot like their iconic larger cousins. Yellow pompom-like flowers bloom in late spring, held stiffly a few inches above the mat of foliage. This plant is technically a minute, spreading subshrub, or in gardener language, a woody groundcover.

Rock tansy is bone-hardy but resents overhead watering during hot weather and can easily rot with such treatment. During very dry periods in summer when some extra hand-watering may be helpful or even necessary, be sure to water early in the first part of the day so the plant's foliage can dry off quickly in the sun before it gets too hot out.

Propagation: seed (stratify, light); cuttings | **Companion plants:** smaller-statured dryland plants such as lavender-leaf sundrop, small buckwheats, phloxes, short penstemons, pasqueflower, four-nerve daisy; paintbrush species; smaller hardy cacti such as snowball cactus, claret cup, hedgehogs, and pincushions

Symphyotrichum ericoides (Aster ericoides)

white heath aster

zones 3–8 • fields, ditch banks, roadsides, floodplains, shrubland; plains, foothills, montane • most soils

1–3 ft. × 3 ft. • hellstrips, meadow plantings

sun • low to moderate water

The scientific name of this plant references visual similarity to the genus *Erica*, or heath/heather—small, needle-leaved, evergreen plants from moist places in northern Europe. In culture, heath and heath aster couldn't be more different; rather than a bog, heath aster excels in dry, hot spaces with little help, provided the plant's roots find deep water or receive occasional irrigation. This fine-textured, unfussy perennial is common in weedy fields, along roadsides, and in grassland, where it sits as an overlooked green whisk until erupting with clouds of minute, daisylike flowers in late summer and early fall.

Somewhat challengingly keen to proliferate, doing so by both wind-distributed seeds and runners. Rarely do plants become so dense as to outcompete good-sized native flora that prefer similar growing conditions, even in a garden, but can be a nuisance. As with most native asters, though, it is exceptionally valuable to wildlife.

The cultivar 'Snow Flurry' makes a fantastic prostrate groundcover, rarely exceeding four inches tall; *Symphyotrichum falcatum* (white prairie aster) is similar but with larger leaves and fewer, larger flowers.

Propagation: division; seed (light) | **Companion plants:** autumnal grasses such as blue grama, little bluestem, and ruby muhly

Symphyotrichum laeve (*Aster laevis*)

smooth blue aster

zones 3–8 • meadows, seasonally wet drainages, watercourse edges; plains, foothills, montane • moist loam or clay

2–4 ft. × 1–2 ft. • meadow plantings, flower gardens, cottage gardens

sun, light shade • moderate water to moist

One of the earliest-blooming asters in our region, with some forms flowering one or even two months before most other native asters. Attractive, tapered, notably smooth leaves line upright, sometimes-purple stems that can grow to almost four feet in regularly watered gardens. Shapely and easygoing, it hails from as far south as Mexico and as far north as Canada.

Most commonly takes a column or vase-shaped form, topped in late summer and early fall with rounded sprays of dozens of one-inch, smoky blue to purple daisies with yellow-orange eyes. Strong yet supple stems give stands of this plant an impressive amount of interest through movement, with flowers swaying fluidly across the landscape. Attractive, bronzy bracts beneath the fuzz-laden seeds of smooth aster complement late-season grasses beautifully in understated, texture-rich plantings. Despite appearing in seasonally wet places in nature, it tolerates periodic drought without fuss in garden settings. Growing it in moderately dry conditions is an excellent tactic for throttling back its sometimes overly enthusiastic self-seeding tendencies. Has exceptional wildlife value, including for small mammals.

Propagation: seed (light) | **Companion plants:** pearly everlasting; midsized grasses such as tufted hair grass or ruby muhly

Symphyotrichum oblongifolium (*Aster oblongifolius*)

aromatic aster

zones 3–9 • roadsides, meadows, drainages; plains, foothills, montane • most soils

1–3 ft. × 2–3 ft. • hellstrips, flower gardens, seeded wildflower plantings, meadow plantings

sun • low water to moist

A versatile and attractive native aster with exceptional presence in the garden. Plants are robust and full, creating sizeable, rounded mounds several feet high and across of handsome, fine-textured foliage that has a distinctive, spicy smell when crushed. This species blooms in mid-fall when most garden displays are long gone, their fresh-green, round forms smothered in hundreds of starry, amethyst (or, more rarely, pink) flowers.

Speaking broadly, two different forms of this plant exist in our region, with a form from the central prairies (most common in the horticulture trade) achieving the large, round shape, and a second form from wild spaces in the Southern Rockies and adjacent prairies as well as the Black Hills and South Dakota Badlands areas. This latter form remains shorter. All forms of this plant spread by both seed and runner, sometimes aggressively, though to varying degrees. Deer and rabbits tend to avoid the plants.

Propagation: seed (stratify, light); division; cuttings | **Companion plants:** golden feather grass, little and big bluestems; sumacs; ruby muhly

Tetraneuris scaposa (Hymenoxys scaposa)

four-nerve daisy, plains yellow daisy

zones 4–9 • roadsides, disturbed areas, rocky slopes; plains, pinyon-juniper • most well-drained soils

4–8 in. × 10–15 in., 8–15 in. tall in bloom • rock gardens, unwatered flower gardens, cactus gardens, hellstrips

sun • very low water

This tough little plant blooms heavily in spring and early summer and then sputter blooms into fall, especially if there are late-season rains. Its green, grassy foliage makes semi-evergreen tussocks, above which a multitude of warm yellow daisies hover on many slender naked stems, lending a very fine texture to the entire plant. The flowers, with fringed edges, seem like they're floating and are about an inch across—quite large for the plant's size.

Four-nerve daisy self-sows a bit, and small seedlings can be transplanted with care. Older plants don't move or divide well at all.

This wildflower is similar to Colorado rubberweed (*Hymenoxys richardsonii*) but is less shrubby, longer-lived, and the flowers are typically a warmer, less lemony yellow. Paler yellow and almost-white forms of four-nerve daisy exist. Its small size and neat habit throughout the year make for a nice edging plant, and it also looks great in unwatered rock gardens.

Propagation: cuttings; seed (light) | **Companion plants:** plains skullcap, blackfoot daisy, purple three-awn, tufted evening primrose, cacti, and yuccas

Thermopsis montana (*Thermopsis divaricarpa*)

mountain goldenbanner

zones 3–7 • seasonally moist meadows, aspen and ponderosa woods; foothills, montane • well-drained soils

1–3 ft. × 2 ft. • hellstrips, shrub and tree groves, meadow plantings

sun, light shade • moderate water

One of the most common and well-known early-season yellow flowers of our foothills and mountains; makes a vigorous and easy-to-grow garden plant. Plants produce attractive, richly green leaves in threes and top their many stems with glowing spikes of yellow pea flowers in late spring and early summer.

We have observed that many butterfly and moth species make use of some of our region's most rapidly growing and spreading native plants to lay their eggs. Vigorous plants such as this, which can sustain rapacious caterpillar feeding while still producing lots of healthy leaves to meet their own needs, make dependable hosts. In the garden, this wildflower's shoots come up in a diaspora from the mother patch, so it's best situated with neighbors that put up a fight or out in the back forty where its running habit can be a benefit for covering bare soil.

Transplants respectably from a pot but less so if divided. If dividing, do so in early spring and keep large pieces of root and running stem attached.

Propagation: seed (scarify) | **Companion plants:** trees and shrubs such as aspens, bigtooth maple, alders, rockspray, and boulder raspberry

Thermopsis rhombifolia ssp. *rhombifolia*

prairie goldenbanner

zones 3–7 • grassland, shrubland, dry places; plains, pinyon-juniper, shrub steppe • most well-drained soils

6–12 in. × 1 ft. • hellstrips, meadow plantings, chaparral-inspired gardens, cottage gardens

sun • low to moderate water

Few are familiar with this plant despite its taller cousin, mountain golden banner, being a beloved high-country wildflower. More tolerant of heat and limited precipitation, this remains half the height of its relative—or smaller, if conditions dictate. It flowers earlier, typically in mid-spring. These yellow pea-shaped flowers are so bright and large, they act like a beacon to early foraging bees and winter-weary people to come close, in the way that traditional spring harbingers such as crocus do.

Like its relative, this cheery, large-flowered, and vigorous plant runs, though it forms somewhat-looser, more open colonies. This difference, combined with the reduced stature of prairie goldenbanner, make it somewhat more suitable for combining into plantings, though it can still become a nuisance in more manicured plantings or those with delicate residents. An excellent meadow plant, where it fills in gaps and competes with weeds while putting on an all-out spring bloom display that can compete with any European-style daffodil meadow. Afterward, it keeps a low profile with attractive, three-part leaves and a low form.

Propagation: seed (scarify) | **Companion plants:** buffalo and blue grama grass; shrubs

Tradescantia occidentalis

western spiderwort

zones 4–8 • dry sandy meadows, rocky slopes; plains, foothills, shrub steppe, montane • most well-drained soils

12–20 in. × 15–20 in. • meadow plantings

sun to light shade • low water

This unusual-looking wildflower bears sizeable, three-petaled, soft blue flowers in loose clusters that open in the morning, then close and finish later in the day. More blossoms open each day, starting in early summer and continuing for many weeks. There are a number of North American native spiderworts; this species needs less moisture than most and also doesn't spread underground by rhizomes like some others do. The distinctive gray-green narrow foliage looks almost grassy from a distance but is folded down the middle and droops and bends in many directions.

Western spiderwort self-sows; seedlings form long taproots quite quickly, making them hard to dig out in a planting where they're not wanted. For this reason this plant is best in a naturalistic, casual composition with other tough plants that can stand their ground.

Propagation: seed (stratify) | **Companion plants:** midsized grasses such as little bluestem, hardy deer muhly, and alkali sacaton; western yarrow, black Sampson, butterfly weed, and horsemint

Vernonia fasciculata

prairie ironweed

zones 4–9 • river valleys, wet meadows, grassland; plains • most soils

4–6 ft. × 2–3 ft. • meadow plantings, cottage gardens

sun • moderate water to moist

The origin of this plant group's common name is a mystery; theories range from rusty stem and seedhead colors to "tough as iron" stems that stand up through winter snows to deep, tenacious roots that defied the plow.

Notable among regional natives for its refined beauty, this ironweed is slow to wake in spring but decisive once it does. Produces tall, narrow shoots with attractive, toothed leaves encircling purpled stems. Flattened clusters of fuzzy, royal-purple, button-like flowers open late in the season. Rusty-hued fuzzy seedheads follow; the plant self-sows.

When this plant's unique, vase-shaped, vertical form sways in grassy plantings or perennial borders, the effect is as interesting as its brief bloom. Hosts several insects, including the American painted lady butterfly. While the Southeast and Midwest offer numerous native ironweeds, only a few are present and landscape-worthy in our region. *Vernonia marginata* (southeast corner of our region) presents a more petite alternative; *Vernonia baldwinii* (Colorado Front Range and Central Plains) is similar to but leafier than prairie ironweed.

Propagation: seed (stratify, light); divison | **Companion plants:** azure sage and sunflowers; taller grasses such as big bluestem, switchgrass, and golden feather grass

Xanthisma spinulosum (Haplopappus spinulosus, Machaeranthera pinnatifida)

cutleaf goldenaster

zones 4–8 • sandy plains, rocky outcrops; plains, foothills, shrub steppe, pinyon-juniper, montane • sandy or gritty soils

3–6 in. × 8–15 in. • unwatered flower gardens, cactus gardens, rock gardens, low meadow plantings, hellstrips

sun • very low water

This highly variable species is common across a wide swath of the Great Plains and intermountain west. The shorter, denser high-plains form is definitely garden-worthy and more appealing than the rangier, less finely textured forms of the species or the more common hairy false goldenaster, *Heterotheca villosa*, to which it otherwise bears many similarities. Finely cleft, almost fringed gray-green foliage makes a low, spreading mound throughout the growing season and, in late summer, sends up loads of bright yellow daisies for several weeks.

Cutleaf goldenaster likes to bake and prefers dry soils that heat up in summer. It reseeds mildly.

This plant's compact form, fine-textured foliage, and unusual water thriftiness make it an excellent companion for cacti.

Propagation: seed (stratify, light) | **Companion plants:** small bunchgrasses such as blue grama and purple three-awn; yuccas and cacti

Zinnia grandiflora

Rocky Mountain zinnia, prairie zinnia

zones 5–8 • mesas, rocky places, roadsides; plains • most well-drained soils

4–8 in. × 10–15 in., larger over time • unwatered flower gardens, rock gardens, crevice gardens, hillsides, hellstrips

sun • very low water

This pretty little workhorse of a wildflower blooms midsummer into fall. Golden, rounded to almost square flowers, typically with orange or red centers, literally cover the entire plant. The papery flowers persist and remain attractive long after they have finished producing nectar or pollen, finally turning tan late in the season. Narrow, sparse, gray-green needlelike leaves line the slender, floppy stems.

Prefers dry, heavy clay—relishes it. Self-seeds and runs underground very slowly from a deep, woody taproot, eventually forming mats and colonies. Doesn't like life in a pot and doesn't move well, so should be transplanted from pots into the ground when small.

Because this wildflower prefers warmth, it's an especially good candidate for planting with rocks for reflected heat and also to show off its small, cascading form. Deer- and rabbit-resistant.

Plantsman David Salman's selection 'Gold on Blue', a Plant Select winner, has gold rather than reddish centers and extra-large flowers, plus the foliage sports a distinctly blue tint. It's a larger and more vigorous plant than the typical forms seen in the wild.

Propagation: cuttings; seed (light) | **Companion plants:** rice grass, purple three-awn, blackfoot daisy, pussytoes, fringed sage, plains gayfeather, hummingbird trumpet, cacti, and yuccas

Grasses

It's been a long time coming, but North Americans have finally embraced grasses as not only the dominant players that they are in many of the world's wild ecosystems and our food production, but now for landscapes and gardens as well. As we question our historic default to planting lawns everywhere, we've started to replace traditionally thirsty, hungry, and maintenance-dependent turf grasses with other grass species. But we've also taken aesthetic and ecological cues from the vast grasslands of our continent and are creating prairie and steppe plantings, bioswales, and orchestrated borders filled with wonderfully diverse and resilient bunchgrasses, including loads of native grass species.

The Rocky Mountain region as defined in this book includes plant communities where grasses are ubiquitous, whether among shrubs in steppe zones; between and beneath tree groupings in savannas and open woods; as main components of plains, prairie and alpine meadows; or as intermittent players in desert and high-alpine environments. Their tenacity and adaptability; ease of care; importance as food, shelter, and habitat for many birds, larval insects, and mammals; seasonal personalities; textural beauty; and lovely response to wind and light all make them an absolute must for inclusion in our planting plans, whether as accents, lawn alternatives, or main players in design matrices. We've selected primarily bunching grasses rather than those that run because—with the exception of alternative turf applications—bunching grasses are usually better garden denizens than runners.

The basics for understanding and succeeding with the grasses we profile in the following pages are simple. First, grasses have a predilection for growing in either cool or warm conditions. What months of the growing season are cooler or warmer vary in our region depending on elevation and latitude, and these grass distinctions also don't necessarily mean a so-called warm-season grass won't grow at higher elevation, or a cool-season grass will sulk in the more southerly and lower parts of the region. That is true for some species and not for others. It is more important to know these predilections to understand when a plant is actively growing and looking its best and is most responsive and successful when faced with being planted, divided, or moved. An actively growing grass can handle these stresses better, but on the other hand will be less able to handle lack of water or sunlight or temperature extremes while in this state of active growth. So, it's good to know whether a grass is a warm-season or a cool-season grower.

The other thing to know is that grasses are by their nature resilient and require little care, but in the absence of natural grazing or fire, they need to be cut back during or at the end of their dormant period to allow new growth to expand unimpeded. And dry grasses are very flammable. In areas where wildfire is an issue—which is the case in much of our region at some time of the year—it makes sense to cut back grasses close to structures or at the bases of other flammable plants as soon as the grasses dry out. It's sad to have to remove dried textures, forms, and colors that could add a lot of interest as well as wildlife habitat, but the trade-off—fire safety—makes the decision a no-brainer.

That said, our choices of grasses and options on how to use them to enhance our spaces are expanding exponentially. It's one of the most exciting recent developments in North American horticulture. Outdoor spaces, whether municipal, corporate, public, or private, are transforming thanks to these wonderful plants.

Andropogon gerardii

big bluestem, turkeyfoot

zones 3–8 • remnant prairie, revegetated sites, deep rock crevices, seasonally moist meadows, watercourse edges; plains, foothills • most soils

2–4 ft. × 2–3 ft. (4–8 ft. in bloom) • meadow plantings, beds and borders, screening grass

sun • low to moderate water

An iconic and essential species of the tallgrass prairie, where it provides food and shelter for numerous other organisms in the ecosystem. Long-lived, it gains steam gradually, showing little foliar growth its first couple years, instead focusing on developing a deep, drought-resistant root system. As it matures, achieves impressive size, vigor, and stress-tolerance and begins to bloom more heavily with silvery, three-pronged flowers that resemble a turkey's foot.

Makes an attractive, richly green or grey-blue tuft of medium-textured, flowing leaves. Some forms, especially in drought or heat, feature striking purple streaking or patching, and all have fiery fall color that rivals even the best of autumn's tree displays. A more muted ruddy coloration persists through winter. Quite tolerant of dry conditions, but looks and performs best with occasional deep watering. Requires summer temperatures that regularly reach or exceed the lower 80s for robust growth, so not suited to high-mountain communities.

Typically grows as a bunchgrass in the West, only occasionally producing short runners on some sites.

Propagation: divisions; seed (stratify) | **Companion plants:** anise hyssop, sneezeweed, smooth blue aster, cutleaf compass plant, ironweed, or azure sage

Aristida purpurea

purple three-awn

zones 4–8 • dry grassland, rocky or sandy plains, slopes, roadsides, disturbed areas; plains, foothills • sandy and gritty soils

6–15 in. × 8–15 in. • accent in unwatered plantings, dry meadow plantings, hellstrips

sun • very low water

When seen in the wild, the wispy, shimmering, rosy-tinted hummocks of purple three-awn waving easily in the slightest breeze may make you want to fill your property with them. This lovely small, fine-textured bunchgrass deserves planting for its good looks, low-water use, creature benefits, and tolerance for poor soil. However, this attractive native is universally disliked by ranchers and livestock owners because, soon after its late-spring bloom, the flowers ripen to tan seed with sharp ends that easily embed in clothes and animal fur and can poke curious animals' eyes and noses. Avoid planting purple three-awn in areas where people and animals walk through or graze frequently.

This graceful, petite grass is short-lived and usually self-sows. It is a warm-season grower and one of the better grasses for a low-growing dryland meadow matrix, as it blends beautifully with short wildflowers. Also makes a wonderful textural accent in a cactus planting or dry rock garden to play off their coarser, more static forms and textures, and adds motion and stunning backlighting effects.

Propagation: seed; division | **Companion plants:** blackfoot daisy, sand verbena, sundrops, evening primrose, gaillardia, Santa Fe phlox, globemallow, and plains verbena; cacti

Bouteloua curtipendula

sideoats grama

zones 3–9 • roadsides, dry grassland, washes, draws, rocky places; plains, foothills, pinyon-juniper, shrub steppe • most soils

1–2 ft. × 1–2 ft. (3 ft. in bloom) • hellstrips, meadow plantings, cottage gardens

sun • low to moderate water

A lovely, midsized to small grass that is unfussy and vigorous yet well-behaved, not seeding excessively nor spreading aggressively by runners. While the leaves of this plant are coarser than most other small grasses in the Rockies, this species forms a serene, mounded shape that mellows busy plantings and provides good visual filler between large or messier-looking neighbors. Mid- to late summer brings an understated and reliable spray of tapered, pendulous flowers held in rows along arching stems that inspired the common name. Often, flowers bear minute but striking orange anthers that extend from the florets and appear before the flowers of larger warm-season grasses.

This excellent wildlife plant serves as a host for insects and a grain source for both birds and mammals. It is adapted broadly to the continent and exhibits diversity in form across its range; Southwestern forms are generally more clumping, while forms from farther east produce more runners.

Grows quickly, transplants well, and is one of our easiest-to-grow native grasses, adapting well to nursery pot culture, and a variety of landscape settings.

Propagation: seed; division | **Companion plants:** late-blooming daisies such as blanketflower, spreading fleabane, and chocolate flower; fringed sage and prairie thistle

Bouteloua dactyloides (*Buchloe dactyloides*)

buffalo grass

zones 3–10 • widely distributed on clay and limestone-based soils; plains, foothills • most soils

6 in. × unlimited spread • lawn replacement, filler layer in meadow gardens, hellstrip turf replacement

sun • low to moderate water

Historically one of the two dominant grasses of the High Plains shortgrass prairie, alongside blue grama. Unlike that more upright, clump-forming grass, buffalo grass keeps a low profile, spreading quickly by runners along the soil surface in summer. Use of this grass as a native lawn has recently surged thanks to its excellent drought-tolerance and wildlife value (including for mammals). Bryan finds it makes an excellent understory and filler in meadow plantings featuring larger grasses and wildflowers (those with dense foliage). There, this shade-avoidant grass quickly covers sunny bare patches, reducing weeds and reducing erosion. This works best with range, not sod-type buffalo grass cultivars, and perennials should be established for at least a year before adding buffalo grass.

Individuals of this species compete with one another, so seeded plots are patchier (ideal for understories); plug plantings, being one clone, form denser, more even turf. While not as aggressive as Kentucky bluegrass, it is a competitive spreader with surface runners that can quickly overrun, smother, and shade out young companion plants, especially those with low rosette foliage.

Propagation: division; seed (stratify); plugs | **Companion plants:** shortgrass prairie natives such as fringed sage, broomweed, plains yucca, silvery lupine, and plains blazing star

Bouteloua gracilis

blue grama

zones 3–9 • grasslands, shrublands; prairie, shrub steppe, pinyon-juniper, montane • most well-drained soils

6–12 in. × 12–18 in. (to 30 in.) • lawn replacement, hellstrips, low-water mixed plantings, meadow plantings

sun • low to moderate water

One of the most widespread grasses in American landscapes today. Rose to fame in the 2000s with the introduction of 'Blonde Ambition', a selection made by New Mexico plantsman David Salman that quickly became known for its uniquely blonde-colored flowers held perpendicular to their wiry stalks. Both this cultivar and the straight species have become well-known for their superb adaptability (thriving in most moisture regimes and soil textures), reliable mid- to late-season floral display, and excellent winter interest.

Among our hardiest warm-season grasses ('Blonde Ambition', though, prefers zone 4 and warmer). Makes a top-notch filler, textural accent, wildlife plant, and lawn replacement; shares space better than buffalo grass, which will outcompete many wildflowers with its aboveground running habit. Smaller and faster to mature then many other warm-season grasses, it's among the best for compact garden spaces, water-thrifty gardens, and locations demanding a line-of-sight for traffic, such as hellstrips. Especially handsome if backlit late season when it turns a tawny gold.

Near-cousin *Bouteloua hirsuta* (hairy grama) is similar but smaller. The two have hybridized in the wild, producing additional durable and petite grasses, notably David Salman's introduction 'Zig Zag'.

Propagation: seed; division | **Companion plants:** fringed sage, asters, or evening primroses

Deschampsia cespitosa

tufted hair grass

zones 3–8 • meadows, seeps, fens, ditch banks, watercourse margins; plains, foothills, shrub steppe, montane • most moist soils

1 ft. × 1 ft. (3 ft. in bloom) • mixed-flower gardens, meadow plantings

sun, light shade • moderate water to moist

A major component of moist mountain meadows (and other environments with reliable early-season moisture) across the northern hemisphere. Thanks to its early flush of growth, this grass achieves its zenith by early summer, long before most ornamental grasses. In bloom, tufted hair grass makes a lovely upright, arching specimen, with finely textured, flowing florets like elegant clouds atop shiny, sleek stems and lush emerald-green foliage. This cool-season grass completes bloom by mid- to late summer and retains its spent flowers, presenting the gardener an opportunity to break up plantings with its shimmering, long-lasting golden seedheads.

Intolerant of dry soils when grown in full sun, especially at lower elevations. At cooler, higher elevations and latitudes, can tolerate a drier regime if winter snowpack recharges soil moisture in spring. Vigorous at lower temperatures and adapted to a short growing season, it's one of the best native grasses for mountain areas. Plants transplant easily and divide best during cooler parts of the growing season. Appreciates a soil rich in organic matter, though it tolerates leaner soils with reliable irrigation.

Propagation: seed; division | **Companion plants:** midsea-son bloomers coneflower, cutleaf compass plant, or bee-balm; columbines

Eriocoma hymenoides (Achnatherum hymenoides, Oryzopsis hymenoides)

rice grass

zones 3–8 • dry grassland, desert, rocky slopes; plains, foothills, shrub steppe, pinyon-juniper • sandy or gritty soils

15–24 in. × 12–18 in. • accent, unwatered meadow plantings, cactus gardens, hellstrips

sun • very low water

Among the region's most water-thrifty, showy native grasses, this lovely plant expands clouds of tiny flowers in airy panicles in late spring and early summer, going from pale green to straw as they ripen seed. Seedheads persist to create a lovely effect for months into winter. Leaves are sparse, narrow, long, and wiry.

A cool-season grower yet prefers warm soil and sites. Short-lived in gardens, it reseeds mildly, especially in gravel and sandy soil; the selections 'Nezpar' and 'Paloma' are longer-lived. Cut it back in late winter or early spring to about four inches to encourage new growth and remove last year's tawny dried remains.

As with many grasses, this plant is quite deer-resistant but with rabbits not so much. Collecting seed is tricky as it is hard to tell when it's too early or too late; be extra observant and consistently check.

Propagation: division; seed (stratify) | **Companion plants:** yuccas and cacti; penstemons, silvery lupine, chocolate flower, plains verbena, and wild blue flax

Festuca arizonica

Arizona fescue, pinegrass

zones 4–8 • grasslands, ponderosa pine forest, mountain meadows; foothills, montane • most well-drained soils

10–18 in. × 12–18 in., flowers another 1–2 ft. higher • meadow plantings, groundcover, accent, hellstrips, under trees

sun to light shade • low water

A great alternative to the popular, beautiful but weedy and short-lived Mexican feather grass (*Nassella tenuissima*), with a similarly appealing wispy look. This species is longer-lived, more cold-hardy, and doesn't produce massive numbers of unwanted seedlings.

A fine-textured grass, it adapts to most soils and to varying light and moisture conditions; it's one of very few grasses that does well in light, dry shade. It grows actively during the cooler parts of the growing season, and it's best to sow seed in the early spring while it's still cool.

The hair-like, olive to gray-green foliage makes lax, arching mounds, and in early summer, small flower panicles open on tall, slender, upright stems. These panicles then dry and persist into winter. Foliage is beautiful in the dormant season, eventually fading to blonde in most parts of our region. Cut back as low as possible in late winter to allow the new growth to push up unimpeded.

Propagation: seed; division | **Companion plants:** under trees and between shrubs with pussytoes; columbines, wild blue flax, asters, yarrow, hummingbird trumpet, and silvery lupine

Koeleria macrantha (Koeleria cristata)

Junegrass

zones 3–7 • dry grassland, woodland clearings, rocky slopes; plains, foothills , shrub steppe • sandy or gritty soils

6–12 in. × 6–12 in. (24 in. in bloom) • rock gardens, low-prairie plantings, naturalistic gardens

sun, light shade • moderate water

In late spring or early summer before the weather heats up, the pale green, sometimes purple-tinged flower clusters of this widespread North American grass open to silver spikes that glisten and sparkle when backlit. By midsummer these ripen to long, thin, tan pipe-cleaner-like cylinders holding the seeds. When not in bloom, its narrow silhouette of blue-green leaves in small, upright clumps is visually quiet and unassuming.

Stays attractive for longer in cooler climates; in hot sites the foliage becomes ratty and semi-dormant by midsummer. Be sure to cut it back low to the crown in early spring before the new growth emerges for best vigor and presentation.

Junegrass makes one of the best-behaved grassy companions for more delicate wildflowers, as it's not competitive with either seeding, overall size, or root system. It plays nicely with the likes of other springtime lovelies and can take a bit of dappled summer shade, especially in hot climates. Ideally, plant it in a location where some backlighting can awaken the shimmer of the flowers in bloom. The grass also makes an airy addition to early bouquets.

Propagation: seed (light) | **Companion plants:** pasqueflower, sugarbowls, and prairie smoke

Muhlenbergia reverchonii

ruby muhly

zones 5–9 • grassland, shallow-soiled hardpan with seasonal moisture; plains • most well-drained soils

15–18 in. × 18–24 in., flowers rise 12 in. above foliage • accent, meadow planting, mass planting, hellstrips

sun • low to moderate water

In autumn, clouds of airy, rosy flowers hover in great masses above the foliage of this long-lived southern Great Plains native, then ripen seed and dry to ruddy tan and persist all winter. This warm-season grower makes fine-textured, arching mounds of gray-green foliage and doesn't die out in the center with age.

The robust, handsome, and hardy Plant Select form in the trade, known as Undaunted® ruby muhly, was introduced by Lauren and Texas plantsman Scott Ogden. Hardier and more xeric than its better-known pink, coarser, more upright relative Gulf muhly, it's also more attractive, hardier, and more robust than the Texas hill country seed strains of *Muhlenbergia reverchonii* available. Ruby muhly likes it hot, so place it near reflected heat from pavement, rocks, or walls. Performs best at lower elevations and/or lower latitudes; is one of the most clay-tolerant native grasses. Cut ruby muhly back to the crown in spring to allow new growth to emerge unimpeded. Divide in early summer. Ideally, plant ruby muhly where it will receive either morning or evening backlighting; its flowers glow spectacularly.

Propagation: division; seed (light) | **Companion plants:** manzanita, silver sage, pearly everlasting, asters, datura, and snow on the mountain

Muhlenbergia rigens

hardy deer muhly, deer grass

zones 4–8 • grasslands, rocky arroyos and streambeds, open forests; plains, foothills • most well-drained soils

2–3 ft. × 3 ft., flowers 1–2 ft. above foliage • accent plant in low-water planting, meadow planting, chaparral

sun • low to moderate water

This stately southwestern bunchgrass has a bold texture and upright, arching form. Long, narrow, silvery flowering spikes rise above the leaves in an open spray like fireworks from late summer through fall. They sway in any breeze. Linear seedheads turn tawny and remain attractive through winter. Long-lived and remains mostly evergreen in mild winters and protected sites. In colder areas, foliage turns golden in fall; its blonde hue persists through winter.

Native range in the region is only in northern New Mexico and the Four Corners area, and most of the plants sold in the Southwest and Texas aren't hardy in zones 4 or 5. In 2012, Lauren brought a wild-plant division from that area to her Fort Collins garden. It thrived and proved hardy for more than a decade, through −30°F, and is now a Plant Select introduction named Sure Thing™.

Unless it is evergreen, cut the foliage mound to the ground in spring each year. Divide in spring or early summer. Its year-round texture and form provide excellent wildlife cover, habitat, and food and make a handsome contrast to shrubs or as lively repeated linearity in a modern-style planting.

Propagation: division; seed | **Companion plants:** buffalo gourd, broomweed, asters, sages, broom ragwort, rabbitbrush, winterfat

Panicum virgatum

switchgrass

zones 3–10 • roadsides, draws, drainages, watercourse margins, ponderosa parkland; plains, foothills • most soils

2–4 ft. × 2–4 ft. (3–8 ft. tall in bloom) • cottage gardens, meadow plantings, foundation plantings, seasonal screening

sun • moderate water to moist

Native to all but three states, switchgrass finds its stronghold in the Great Plains. In late summer, it forms elegant sprays of airy stems and glossy seeds above foliage with an upright, vase-shaped form. Leaves are long, of moderate width, and make a tuft at the plant's base in addition to keeping a presence on the stems. Switchgrass is a relished food source for birds and small mammals and serves as a larval-host plant for skipper butterflies.

Thanks to thick, stiff stalks, foliage holds up well to snows, so plants can be left standing through winter for visual interest and wildlife benefit. Notable for its diversity, with forms ranging from the petite, three-foot-high 'Cheyenne Sky', with red-blushed leaves and fall color to match, to the eight-foot-tall behemoth 'Heavy Metal', featuring massive leaves with a steely blue sheen. This texture-rich species makes a great visual break for big-leaved or busy plantings and presents particularly well behind mounded forms, like those of many native asters.

Propagation: division; seed | **Companion plants:** desert olive, silverberry, leadplant, rabbitbrush, and sumac; Maximilian sunflower, azure sage, sneezeweed, cutleaf compassplant, and ironweed; as a screen with Rocky Mountain beeplant and sunflower

Schizachyrium scoparium

little bluestem

zones 3–10 • grassland, meadows, roadsides, watercourse margins, draws, drainages, pine parkland, mesas, canyons; plains, foothills, pinyon-juniper • most soils

1–2 ft. × 1–2 ft. (2–4 ft. in bloom) • cottage gardens, perennial borders, meadow plantings, foundation plantings, hellstrips

sun • low to moderate water

Little bluestem is an exceptional grass, nearly as versatile in our landscapes as it is ubiquitous across the continent. Like many prairie grasses, this plant starts slow and isn't willing to risk damage by late frost, breaking ground in late spring and growing slowly and steadily into an understated but attractive green or blue-green tuft until summer temperatures arrive. With summer's heat, this warm-season grass gains size and color more quickly, often taking on reddish, metallic, or opalescent hues and a more substantial form as it begins to bloom in late summer. In autumn it finally turns a rich red, fading to russet after hard frost. Unlike many of our native grasses, this bunchgrass remains narrow and upright, with unbranched, linear stems that form a neat column and provide inspiration for the epithet *scoparium*, meaning broom-like.

Little bluestem serves wildlife of all sizes, providing seed for birds and small mammals, tolerating browsing well after establishment, and as a larval host for insects.

Propagation: division; seed | **Companion plants:** pearly everlasting; stiff goldenrod and asters; sumac, Gambel oak, golden currant, and junipers; fringed sage

Sorghastrum nutans

golden feather grass

zones 3–9 • grassland, roadsides, watercourse margins, pine parkland, canyons, rocky soils; plains, foothills, pinyon-juniper • most soils

3 ft. × 2–4 ft. (4–6 ft. in bloom) • cottage gardens, perennial borders, meadow plantings, foundation plantings, accent

sun • low to moderate water

This plant and big bluestem are sometimes confused. Both are large, upright, medium-textured, warm-season grasses from remnant tallgrass prairie—but they have different forms and cultural preferences. Golden feather grass takes on a more assertive presence than big bluestem's gentle, tall, swaying form. It erupts from a central point, producing long, stiff, silver-blue to green leaves with a strongly upright habit. The inflorescences appear above their leaves as glowing, warm-toned feathery tufts that taper at their tops and wiggle in breezes on remarkably stiff stems. This long-lived grass excels in dry, rocky, and moderate soils, filling out quickly to a substantial size and providing reliable fall color. Self-sows on sites it finds particularly suitable.

Cultivars of note include 'Thin Man' from David Salman and 'Indian Steel'; most are selected for a silver-blue leaf and narrow, upright habit.

Makes an excellent garden accent, where its clean foliage and contrasting flowers punctuate plantings and look great in bands and waves. Plant them in a location where their flower heads are backlit by morning or evening light to show them off.

Propagation: division; seed | **Companion plants:** cutleaf compass plant, sneezeweed, and swamp milkweed; sumac, Maximilian sunflower, azure sage, and ironweed

Sporobolus airoides

alkali sacaton

zones 4–9 • roadsides, gravelly or thin-soiled locations, seasonally wet places; plains • most soils

1 ft. × 2 ft. (2 ft. in bloom) • meadow plantings, hellstrips, mass plantings

sun • very low water to moist

The genus *Sporobolus* offers several fine-textured, adaptable grasses to regional gardeners. Of the two smaller offerings, this one is seen more frequently in the wild. Common along roadsides, gravelly places, and in dense, seasonally saturated soils, it's remarkably tolerant of what are usually considered challenging soils, including those with extremely fine textures, high salts, or that stay very wet or very dry.

Plants present as somewhat-scruffy mounds early in the season, with thinner foliage cover than most other grasses. Follows its spring foliage flush with a cloud of very fine flowers, held two to four feet above the ground. Midsummer blooms range widely from blonde to dark brown to pink; in most cases, their color changes rapidly as flowers mature, with any but blonde-tan being fleeting by the time seeds begin to mature. Plants make great bird feeders thanks to prodigious seed production. Clumping rather than running, this grass can make a low-fuss accent, matrix grass, or mass planting, though it can appear less refined than other options. Reseeds in preferred conditions, naturalizing on some sites.

Propagation: seed; division | **Companion plants:** yarrow, fringed sage, or aromatic aster; cowpen daisy, prairie sage, ironweed, or angel's trumpet

Sporobolus heterolepis

prairie dropseed

zones 3–8 • seasonally moist meadows, pine parkland; plains to montane • most soils

2 ft. × 3 ft. (3 ft. tall in bloom) • mixed borders, meadow plantings, accents, hellstrips

sun, light shade • moderate water to moist

Hands-down one of the best grasses available for irrigated plantings in our region. Highly adaptable to a variety of soil types and moistures, performs equally well after establishment in seasonally wet/dry clay as in loamy, rich garden soils, matching or surpassing the adaptability of even the most widespread introduced grasses. With deep, woody roots, it is slow to establish but exceptionally dependable and long-lived, enjoying a lifespan more like a shrub than a grass. Can surpass fifteen years without any hint of dying out in the center of the plant.

Offers aesthetics to match its cultural versatility: plants are fine-textured and symmetrical, developing into shapes like giant Koosh balls. Leaves are delicate, arching, and fresh-green with a sheen; they move beautifully in a breeze. Attractive sprays of diaphanous, tiny golden flowers in late summer are particularly lovely when backlit in the morning or evening. One of very few grasses that are fragrant, it's variously described as smelling like coriander, buttered popcorn, or Juicy Fruit gum. In fall, its color transformation ranges from a pleasant butterscotch-gold to arresting warm ambers and fiery orange-red.

Propagation: seed, division (mid-spring only) | **Companion plants:** butterfly milkweed, purple prairie clover, narrowleaf coneflower, and nodding onion; dwarf sand cherry

Sporobolus wrightii

giant sacaton

zones 4–8 • roadsides, arroyos, disturbed areas; plains • most well-drained soils

4–8 ft. × 3–5 ft. (up to 10 ft. tall in bloom) • accent, chaparral-inspired planting

sun • low water

It's unusual in our harsh climate to find something as large and profuse as this bunchgrass that's not a tree or shrub. Even more unusual is to be able to grow it with so little moisture. Plant this for its imposing good looks, low-water use, important role as cover and food for wildlife, as well as tolerance of poor soil. Gray-green, semi-evergreen leaves form a lax fountain-like foliage clump. One- to two-foot-long tawny plumes rise high, yet loose and graceful, on a spray of tall stems above the foliage in late summer. Flowers, patterned like fish bones or feathers, persist through autumn into winter; they're especially beautiful wearing snowflakes or hoarfrost.

This warm-season grower wants summertime heat—otherwise it isn't fussy. It is deer-resistant and tolerant of salt. Cut the plant back as far as possible in late winter. (Wear gloves, as the sharp foliage edges can cut skin.) Divide it in late spring or early summer.

Late New Mexican plantsman David Salman made 'Windbreaker', an even larger and more robust form, available through High Country Gardens. It makes a great accent or casual hedge.

Propagation: seed, division | **Companion plants:** banana yucca, Maximilian sunflower, Apache plume, leadplant, and rabbitbrush

Cacti and Yuccas

These rank among the most water-thrifty and long-lived of our native plants. The unique looks of cacti evolved to adapt to extreme dryness, strong sunlight, and intense grazing pressure. Stems have become thickened for massive water storage and leaves modified into protective and shading spines. Large, showy flowers in often brilliant hues serve as long-distance beacons where pollinators and plants are few and far between.

Mail-order cactus nurseries offer several of our region's native species. Be wary of any large specimens, as these are often dug from the wild.

Cacti grow easily from seed sown in warm temperatures. It takes a few years for the seedlings to size up for planting and flowering maturity, but unlike softer, faster-growing types of plants, cactus seedlings are quite self-sufficient and without a doubt the cutest. Young seedlings of pricklypears and chollas don't resemble the mature plants—they have more numerous and softer spines and are often elliptical or cigar-shaped.

Don't transplant cactus seedlings into the garden until they are about an inch in size or more. Smaller plants are not only hard to keep track of outside of their pots, they also can rot or dry out more easily, and with their smaller, softer spines they're more readily consumed by hungry and thirsty rabbits. Growing chollas and pricklypears from pad and jointed-stem cuttings works faster than seed if you don't need a large number of new plants. Do this during the warm part of the growing season, and allow the cut ends to dry and callus for a week or two, then stick them in a pot of well-drained potting soil or straight into the ground.

Be sure not to overwater cacti, as they are extremely susceptible to rotting, especially after potting or planting in the garden. Unlike with other plants, it's best to wait a couple weeks to water them in, allowing any small injuries to the roots or plant's body to callus and heal. Potting and planting should occur when the cactus is naturally actively growing, so it gets busy rooting and is less likely to rot once watered. Potted cacti do need more water more regularly than cacti growing in the ground, as the latter rarely need anything beyond what comes from the sky. Potted cacti also appreciate diluted mild fertilizer such as kelp or fish emulsion when they're actively growing. Don't up-pot them until they have almost grown to the rim of the pot; they do best undisturbed in small pots for several years as long as they get a bit of extra water and food.

Most padded pricklypear cacti have more than just spines to protect themselves—clusters of tiny hair-like glochids are often dotted over their surface. These are more irritating than spines because they are barely visible, come off the plant and into your skin or clothes at the slightest touch, and are harder to see to remove.

Barbeque tongs are excellent tools for planting cacti and weeding close to them. Avoid gloves, as glochids and spines embed in them, rendering them useless. Unlike the smaller ball-shaped or columnar cactus species, most padded cacti are fast-growing and increase exponentially—each pad makes more which in turn then make more. All you need is one or a few pads to start. These can root along both their edges and the areas where their spines cluster when actively growing, making sizeable, sprawling clumps in only a few years.

Cacti are considered succulents, but not all succulents are cacti. We profile one succulent, fameflower, ***Phemeranthus calycinus***, in the short-lived wildflowers section, as it fits better there in terms of general garden appearance and role.

Yuccas are also simple to grow from seed. Smaller, younger transplants are not as cold-hardy and are often browsed by various mammals. Mammals are less inclined to browse mature plants, except in severely dry years. So it's a good idea to either purchase larger, older plants or keep younger, smaller ones potted and in a protected place for a few years before planting them into the ground. Grow seedlings in pots until they have at least a dozen leaves, which can take two to three years.

Cylindropuntia imbricata (Opuntia imbricata)

tree cholla

zones 4–9 • dry grassland, overgrazed pastures; plains, pinyon-juniper • most well-drained soils

4–6 ft. × 5–6 ft. • accent for unwatered plantings, chaparral-inspired plantings, foundation plant

sun • very low water

Our largest cold-hardy cactus, long-lived tree cholla looks like nothing else in the wild or planted landscape. Matte gray-green, it reads ashen and shadowy from a distance, forming a large, dense, much-branched succulent shrub, sometimes with a purple cast in winter. Cylindrical stems have ripples of bumps all along them, and the plant defends itself from browsing with barbed spines as well as clusters of tiny, hair-like spines that detach easily on contact and can be very painful without fingernails, tweezers, or sticky tape to remove them pronto.

In early summer, ruffled magenta flowers glow like stained glass when backlit. Squarish green fruits ensue, then turn yellow before drying and persisting through winter.

Give tree cholla a sunny, wind-protected spot against a south or west wall in areas where it's marginally cold-hardy or where summers are cool.

'White Tower' has greenish white flowers. More compact Santa Fe cholla, *Cylindropuntia* ×*viridiflora*, has apricot flowers. Spineless 'Inermis' is only hardy to zone 5. Shorter Anasazi cholla, C. ×*anasaziensis*, has soft pink flowers.

Propagation: cuttings; seed | **Companion plants:** large yuccas, angel's trumpet, sages, Apache plume, crispleaf buckwheat, desert four o'clock

Echinocereus mojavensis (*Echinocereus triglochidiatus, Echinocereus coccineus*)

claret cup, scarlet hedgehog, three-spine hedgehog, kingcup cactus

zones 4–9 • dry sites, especially among rocks, sometimes on cliff faces; foothills, montane, pinyon-juniper, shrub steppe • most well-drained soils

4–12 in. × 1–3 ft. • rock gardens, crevice gardens, accent in unwatered plantings

sun • very low water

For this book's purposes, this flashy group of visually almost-inseparable native cactus species is lumped together. Claret cups are the largest of the hardy non-padded cacti and can make quite a statement. They're also among the least fussy of the non-padded species to grow in garden conditions. Bright green, ribbed, cylindrical stems sport spines up and down their longitudinal ridges. These can be very stout or fine, and range in color from cream to gray to tan, brown, and reddish brown to almost black. Mature plants can have a couple hundred stems, reaching a yard in diameter. Such a glorious plant may be a century old or more.

Clusters of large, bright scarlet to reddish orange flowers with contrasting prominent chartreuse stigmas in their centers bloom in late spring. Individual flowers last for several days, unlike most cactus flowers. Fruits are large and rounded, usually green until dried out but sometimes yellow, pink, or crimson.

A spineless form, *inermis*, grows more compactly with the added attraction of white-furred bumps, known as areoles, where the spines would protrude in the more common forms.

Propagation: seed | **Companion plants:** winterfat, smaller yuccas, smaller penstemons, lavender-leaf sundrops

Echinocereus reichenbachii

lace hedgehog cactus, pink-flowered hedgehog

zones 4–9 • very dry sites, rocky slopes, mesas; plains • sandy or gritty soils

2–8 in. × 8–15 in. • rock gardens, crevice gardens, winter-proof containers and troughs

sun • very low water

A small, intricate cactus; can be solitary or clustering. Stems grow into elongated cylinders with a profusion of very short spines that bend back toward the plant, making it less prickly than most cacti. Tiny spines form starry shapes that follow the ribs, making an attractive striped or spiral pattern. Spines are often so dense that they give a lacy appearance. The spines can be white, tan, brown, black, or even maroon.

In late spring, stunningly large, two- to four-inch pink to magenta flowers top the plants, dwarfing the stems. In the wild, these signal from a distance, drawing pollinating insects to the otherwise-diminutive, easily overlooked plants.

Many subspecies and varieties exist. In the colder range of its tolerance, look for plants grown from seed of hardier forms. Plant in a warm, protected spot near the sunny side of a building with rocks close by and rock mulch, to help insulate it and give it the extra heat it wants year-round. Subspecies *perbellus* has done well in plantings in colder areas. Rabbit- and deer-resistant, probably due to its super-dense spines.

Propagation: seed | **Companion plants:** small, exceptionally water-thrifty plants such as fameflower and all but the largest buckwheats

Echinocereus viridiflorus

green-flowered hedgehog, prairie hedgehog cactus

zones 3–7 • dry grasslands, rocky barrens, mesas; plains, foothills, pinyon-juniper, shrub steppe • sandy or gritty soils

2–6 in. × 3–12 in. • rock gardens, crevice gardens, winter-proof containers and troughs

sun • very low water

Among the first plants to open flowers on the prairie, sending up clusters of greenish yellow to lime-green flowers from the sides and the top of the stem. On cloudy days, the flowers glow and can be seen from quite a distance. If you bother to get down on your knees or stomach to smell them and don't mind competing with the bees, the reward is a sweet, lemony fragrance.

This small cactus has squat, cylindrical stems, often solitary but sometimes may grow in clusters or branches. The short, profuse, but not terribly prickly spines vary from white to yellow to maroon to black, and sometimes segregate into separate color bands, making a striking striped effect.

Looks and feels right at home planted in a rock-garden setting. When planted in winter-hardy pots or troughs, its intricate spines and scented flowers are brought especially close to enjoy. It's so small and blooms so early that it really needs a spot where it won't be overlooked or crowded out by other plants.

Propagation: seed | **Companion plants:** cutleaf daisy

Escobaria missouriensis (Neobesseya missouriensis)

Missouri pincushion cactus, Missouri foxtail cactus, Christmas cactus

zones 3–9 • dry grasslands, mesas; plains, foothills, pinyon-juniper, shrub steppe, montane • most well-drained soils

1–3 in. × 2–12 in. • rock gardens, crevice gardens, winter-proof containers or trough gardens

sun • very low water

In the wild, this little cactus can grow as a solitary stem or in wider clusters of stems. It hides among grasses most of the time, but what a sweet surprise to find! Its round, bright red fruits—which may have reminded European settlers of red holly-berry holiday decorations—give it a common name "Christmas cactus," not to be confused with the popular tropical houseplant.

To protect itself from winter weather, this petite cactus pulls itself down into the ground and shrinks to ground level or below. Come late spring, it reemerges and plumps back up. A ring of starry, often-striped flowers opens, intriguingly colored in shades of straw, greenish yellow, caramel, pink, or peach. Pale, not-very-prickly spines grow from tubercles all over the rounded plant. Round green fruits ripen to showy bright red over a period of a year, becoming quite sweet (to the delight of the birds who eat them).

Give this a special spot without close plant companions. Rock or crevice gardens and winter-proof containers and troughs are ideal. Otherwise, you'll probably miss the sweet display of flowers and maybe even the fruit, though the latter often persist for many months.

Propagation: seed | **Companion plants:** fameflower

Escobaria vivipara (Coryphantha vivipara, Mammillaria vivipara)

pincushion cactus, ball cactus, prairie beehive cactus

zones 3–7 • dry grasslands, rocky knolls, hillsides; plains, foothills, shrub steppe, pinyon-juniper • sandy or gritty soils

1–6 in. × 2–15 in. • rock gardens, small accent plant in unwatered plantings, winter-proof containers and troughs

sun • very low water

This showy small cactus is widely distributed in the wild across the Great Plains, from Canada to Texas. The shape of the plant varies; often grows as a solitary, barrel-shaped stem up to four inches in diameter. Other individuals form clusters by sprouting baby stems, in some cases producing a multitude of tiny spiny balls in dense companionship, forming bumpy "baskets" a foot across.

Each stem is covered with tubercles, prompting another common name: nipple cactus. Spines grow from the tips of these protuberances in varying shades of white, gray, tan, rust, brown, or black, covering the plant to protect it from being eaten and to shade it from the harsh sunlight and intense heat it experiences over much of its range. In late spring, large, pointy-tipped, bright pink flowers open, making a striking floral crown that can easily be seen from a distance. The fruit is green and tasty.

Propagation: seed | **Companion plants:** petite fameflower

Opuntia aurea

golden pricklypear, yellow beavertail cactus

zones 5–8 • mesas, buttes, rocky desert; pinyon-juniper • sandy or gritty soils

1 ft. × 3–5 ft. • accent plant for unwatered plantings, hellstrips

sun • very low water

Handsome and heavy-textured with large, flat, paddle-shaped pads. In early summer, stunning three-inch yellow, apricot, or rose-pink flowers attract myriad pollinators. Pads have a gray-green color, sometimes with purple undertones, but come winter they turn a striking plum-purple. Though almost spineless, pads have clusters of tiny, hair-like glochids dotted over their surface that can be more irritating than spines because, barely visible, they're harder to remove.

Many mammal and bird species eat the plant's pads, fruit, and seeds.

Planting on berms or slopes in moister regions helps the plant avoid rot. One of the hardiest (into zone 4) and most purple-padded selections is 'Coombe's Winter Glow', with bright magenta flowers. Plantsman Kelly Grummons has introduced some gorgeous hybrids of this species that boast good hardiness, more and larger flowers, fewer spines and glochids, and some rebloom after the early-summer flush. Several also have extra-purple-flushed foliage that turns deep, rich hues in winter. These hybrids are called Walk in Beauty™ and are available through mail-order.

Propagation: cuttings; seed | **Companion plants:** water-thrifty yucca, winterfat, and white evening primrose; long-bloomers blackfoot daisy and fameflower

Opuntia fragilis

brittle pricklypear, brittle cactus

zones 3–7 • dry grassland, overgrazed pastures, open ponderosa pine forests; plains, foothills, pinyon-juniper, shrub steppe, montane • sandy or gritty soils

1–3 in. × 12–18 in. • low-growing accent plant for unwatered plantings

sun • very low water

This plant breaks easily into small pieces that attach to unwitting animals, hitching rides over many miles to colonize a huge range mirroring that of bison—from Texas and Arizona to Manitoba and British Columbia.

Smaller and hardier than most pricklypears; the plump, oblong, inch-and-a-half-long joints eventually make patches close to two feet across but only a few inches high. Sparse but large and beautiful yellow flowers open early to midsummer, visited by a host of diverse insects. Many mammals and birds eat the seeds and stems.

Probably the best garden form is the near-spineless, aptly named *Opuntia fragilis* 'Potato', with even more rounded stems that turn quite purple in winter, perhaps in response to sunlight, as they lack the shading spines provide. With its plumper stems and lovely winter color, 'Potato' offers an interesting, unarmed texture; easy care; and longevity for sunny, low-water or no-water plantings.

Hybridizes in nature with other pricklypear species, sometimes retaining the cute qualities of the abundant, fine-textured, smaller stems of this parent while taking on the more profuse flowering and blossom-color variety of the other parent.

Propagation: cuttings; seed | **Companion plants:** small dryland grasses such as rice grass and purple three-awn

Opuntia polyacantha

plains pricklypear

zones 3–7 • dry grassland, overgrazed pastures, buttes and mesas, open ponderosa pine forests; plains, foothills, pinyon-juniper, shrub steppe, montane • sandy or gritty soils

6–12 in. × 15–24 in. • low-growing accent plant for unwatered plantings

sun • very low water

This variable cactus is abundant in our region, with a huge range from Canada down into Texas and Arizona. Pads lay prostrate on the ground (hard to see unless blooming), but in rocky and barren sites, this plant becomes a focal point. Mature plants have many thick, two- to four-inch rounded or oval pale green pads, with mainly white or gray spines on both sides. In some varieties, the spines are so dense they look like white hair.

Large, silky, shimmering flowers are yellow, orange, or rose-pink and bloom in early summer. The stamens in the flower centers actually bend toward touch, helping myriad insect visitors with pollination. (Use your fingertip or a small stick to demonstrate this fun attribute for kids.) Many mammals and bird species eat the seeds and stems; the mature fruit is dry.

Brown-spined pricklypear, *Opuntia phaeacantha*, grows native in a much smaller range here and generally has fewer spines and larger pads. More important, the fruits (aka *tunas*) ripen to a beautiful maroon red and make great jam. Its flowers range from clear lemon-yellow through peach and pink.

Propagation: cuttings; seed | **Companion plants:** small dryland grasses such as rice grass and purple three-awn

Pediocactus simpsonii

snowball cactus, mountain ball cactus

zones 3–6 • high-elevation dry sparse grasslands, on slopes, grassy clearings between pines; foothills, montane, pinyon-juniper, shrub steppe • sandy or gritty soils

2–6 in. × 2–6 in. • rock gardens, crevice gardens, winter-proof containers and troughs

sun to light shade • low water

Who would expect to see a cactus at high elevations, especially one that looks like a softball about to roll down a mountainside? The highest-elevation cactus native to our region, this thrives under deep snow cover in ski country as well as on windswept high plains and mesas.

An adorable little plant with fine but dense spines that vary from brown to pure white (the latter forms are the "snowballs" of the clan). One of the earliest plants to bloom, with little bouquet-like clusters of pink, rose, and (more rarely) white, cream, or pale yellow flowers at the center and top of the ball. Blooms later at higher elevations and latitudes, but always at the beginning of the flowering season.

Doesn't take well to intense sunlight and heat, so prefers some afternoon shade in summer at hotter, lower elevations. Grows as a solitary specimen and never gets sizeable, so needs an intimate space and only diminutive companions. A grouping of three or four has more impact than one, unless framed by rock in the drama of a crevice garden. Often seed successfully in loose soil and gravel mulch, eventually forming a small pack.

Propagation: seed | **Companion plants:** cutleaf daisy

Yucca angustissima

narrowleaf yucca

zones 4–8 • dry grassland, dry shrubland; pinyon-juniper, shrub steppe • most well-drained soils

12–18 in. × 2–4 ft. (2–4 ft. in bloom) • accent for low- and no-water plantings, hellstrips

sun • very low water

With strongly textural foliage, beautiful symmetry, and stunning white flowers, this plant stands out, especially at dawn and dusk. One of the region's smaller yuccas, its leaves are the truest green and the finest-textured; it's an especially good garden plant. As more rosettes sprout from the rootstock, it forms a dense, multi-headed shrub.

In early to midsummer (most years), mature plants send up a thick stalk of large, white bell-shaped flowers high above the foliage. Buds and stalks often have a smoky purple tint. Large, green fruits dry and persist through winter and the next season.

If any prickly, pokey yucca can be "cute," the similar but often smaller and hairier species *Yucca harrimaniae*, dwarf yucca, deserves it. The cutest have leaves only six inches long, edged with loads of curly white fibers. Produces the same gorgeous, white, bell-shaped flowers as its bulkier cousins.

Give these smaller species a special spot up close, where their diminutive but architectural forms can be appreciated best, and also where the fibers' textures can be backlit.

Propagation: seed (stratify) | **Companion plants:** cacti, blackfoot daisy, fringed sage, various buckwheats, and creeping globemallow; evening primrose, plains skullcap, and other very xeric, low-growing plants

Yucca baccata

banana yucca, datil

zones 4–9 • dry grassland, slopes, mesas; plains, foothills, pinyon-juniper • most well-drained soils

2–3 ft. × 3–6 ft. • accent for unwatered plantings

sun • very low water

The boldest of our yuccas, with thick, broad, spine-tipped leaves two to three feet long and edged in white fibers, giving it a softer look. Sword-like leaves, often curved, range from powder-blue to gray to olive-green. The large, sharp, stiff points on their tips don't give, so seasoned gardeners "dehorn" this yucca, cutting off the tips with pruners. Do this every year with new leaves; it's well worth the time to avoid a painful encounter.

Over time, forms a branched shrub because it clusters, sending out offsets that mature into rosettes. Luscious, fat spikes of large, waxy, white bell-shaped flowers open from peachy pink buds in early to midsummer; stalks don't rise much above the foliage. The fleshy, edible fruits look like short, fat, four- to five-inch green bananas. Any uneaten by animals dry and persist through winter.

Give this stately plant room to be seen—and not felt. In a dryland planting, its sculptural form contrasts with scruffier shrubs. Botanical variety *vespertina* has pale blue, extra-straight foliage and a more formal character; it's slightly less cold-hardy than some of the gray and green forms.

Propagation: seed | **Companion plants:** sages, winterfat, sand verbena, penstemons, evening primroses, blackfoot daisy

Yucca glauca

plains yucca, soapweed yucca

zones 3–8 • dry grassland, slopes; plains, foothills, montane • sandy or gritty soil

18–24 in. × 2–4 ft. (to 3 ft. in bloom) • accent for unwatered plantings, hellstrips

sun • very low water

Gray-green to blue-green, this yucca's evergreen-foliage rosettes punctuate the serene grasslands and dry prairies of our region like fireworks. It is the hardiest and most widespread of our native yuccas. For a short period in early summer, with some bloom years more dramatic than others, it sends up spectacular, dense spikes of large, creamy white, sometimes rose or maroon-tinted flowers that shimmer. These ripen to large, woody fruits that hold through winter and often for more than a year.

The stiff leaves are about twelve to eighteen inches long with white margins. Fine, long, hair-like fibers often peel from the edges of the foliage, especially down near the center of the rosette, giving the plant a softer, nest-like look. Like other yucca species, defends itself from browsing by means of a sharp spine on the tip of each leaf. The rosettes cluster over time, making a handsome shrub.

Give plains yucca a backdrop of a sunny wall or rock, or place it silhouetted on top of a slope to showcase its form. Its low-water needs also make it ideal as a foundation plant.

Propagation: seed (stratify) | **Companion plants:** threadleaf sage, rabbitbrush, and Apache plume; cacti and penstemons

Shrubs

In this region of short growing seasons, temperature extremes, scant moisture, and mostly lean soils, the line between trees and shrubs is more blurred than for regions with more gentle climates, generous moisture, and deeper, rich soils where many native trees flourish. To be placed in the following profile section as a shrub, a plant typically grows twigs and leaves to fill in around its main stems from quite near the base on up to the top.

In our region, and anywhere trees don't dominate plant communities, shrubs have an outsized role as major ecosystem players. Besides offering foliage to feed larval insects, flowers for pollinators, and fruit for other wildlife, shrubs create vital places for myriad creatures. They provide shelter and protection from predators and during bad weather and winter, and safe, hidden spots for raising young.

Shrubs have long been garden stepchildren—not as imposing as trees and not as cute and soft as wildflowers. Aesthetically, many houses fit more casually and naturally into the surrounding landscape without the traditional shrubby foundation planting, that ubiquitous "parsley around the turkey," and it's easier to blend outdoor living spaces between such a house and the wider landscape without it. Shrubs get thoughtlessly rammed up against the base of buildings, often under the eaves with little chance to receive any natural rainfall or snow. In fire-prone areas, if they are planted quite close to structures (or underneath needled evergreen trees), they must be cleaned out of extra twigs, dead material, and fallen foliage to limit tinder for safety. It's time we pull most shrubs away from the prison of the foundation and out into the landscape.

Shrubs need little if any regular management and are generally quite long-lived, so for folks who don't like to garden much, or have less time or strength to do so, they are a wonderful low-input alternative to grasses and wildflowers that typically need more ongoing care and periodic replacement. Pruning shrubs just for pruning's sake makes less sense in demanding climates like ours because a plant must work harder to grow at all and has a shorter time each year to do so. With the natural beauty of our region luckily still close at hand, naturalistic unpruned-plant shapes give a sense of place. That's not to say a person can't prune a shrub that takes well to it if their heart is set on that. But for the most part, pruning only tired, misshapen, and dead wood is what's necessary to keep a shrub attractive, vigorous, and less of a fire hazard. Time most pruning during the first half of the season when the plant is actively growing, when you can see what parts of the shrub aren't performing well anymore. If the shrub produces flowers or fruit with good wildlife benefits that don't form until midsummer or later, then it's a good idea to save more of the pruning for during the dormant season. Less-than-ideal late-summer and fall pruning promotes new growth at a time when the plant should be slowing down and sending its resources back into the existing wood and roots, rather than into soft new shoots and leaves that will be more vulnerable to soon-to-be cold temperatures and snow and ice breakage.

Amelanchier alnifolia

western serviceberry, Saskatoon serviceberry

zones 2–6 • slopes, canyons, woodland clearings, streamsides; most life zones • most well-drained soils

8–10 ft. × 8–15 ft. and wider over time • wildlife shelterbelt, casual hedge or screen

sun, light shade • low to moderate water

This large, suckering, deciduous shrub is a hub for and valuable to many forms of wildlife. Narrow-petaled, fragrant white flowers bloom in spring after foliage emerges, followed by shiny, rounded, dark blue (almost-black) fruit clusters in summer. Fruits are favored by people as well, with a delicious flavor like blueberries and almonds. Oval, blue-green leaves often have paler undersides and turn yellow and amber, sometimes red, in fall.

Selections include 'Obelisk' for a narrow, columnar form and 'Regent' for a wider, shorter form with larger, more profuse fruit. Utah serviceberry (*Amelanchier utahensis*) is generally more xeric and finer-textured than western serviceberry, and the two species intergrade in the wild where their ranges overlap.

This shrub is slow-growing both in a pot and in the ground. Deer relish browsing this plant, so protect it with a cage or fencing until it is sizeable.

Ideally grown in groups and let loose to sucker and form dense, good-sized colonies for wildlife food, cover, and to ensure there's enough fruit to go around that maybe you can eat some yourself.

Propagation: seed (stratify) | **Companion plants:** Rocky Mountain juniper and mountain rockspray

Amorpha canescens

leadplant

zones 4–7 • roadsides, woodland clearings, grassland; plains, foothills • most well-drained soils

3–4 ft. × 3–5 ft. • accent, companion shrub in meadow planting, chaparral-inspired planting

sun • low to moderate water

This airy-textured, deciduous shrub's tiny gray leaflets set off a crown of indigo flower spikes with contrasting, bright orange stamens in summer. As the flowers form seed, they retain a plummy color that remains attractive for several weeks.

Dies back a bit every winter, so needs spring pruning. Can be treated almost like a semiwoody perennial: cut it back by a third, half, or to the ground after an exceptionally hard winter. New growth sprouts very late in spring; wait until globular silver buds appear so you'll know where to cut. Blooms on old and new wood (unlike its smaller cousin dwarf indigobush, which blooms only on old wood), so usually still blooms after intensive pruning.

Sometimes spreads by rhizomes and forms colonies over time—slowly; colonies take decades or more to form in the wild. Often self-sows (though not as much as dwarf indigobush), but seedlings have long taproots even when small, making them hard to remove. If seeding becomes problematic, remove the spent flowers before seed ripens.

Propagation: seed (scarify then stratify) | **Companion plants:** rabbitbrush, Apache plume, and fringed sage; bluestem, ruby muhly, and alkali sacaton; winecup, evening primroses, butterfly weed, and blanketflower

Amorpha nana

dwarf leadplant, dwarf false indigo

zones 3–7 • grassland; plains • most well-drained soils

1–3 ft. × 1–3 ft. • small accent, companion shrub in meadow planting, hillside planting

sun • low to moderate water

This compact little shrub has neatly arranged, tiny green leaflets slightly larger than its silvery cousin leadplant's, but the overall plant is about half the height. The flowers are a bit more purple than indigo but similarly attractive—dense, upright spikes with showy golden stamens. Spent flowers and seedheads also remain attractive, but self-seeding can become an issue. If it does, cut off the spent flower spikes before they ripen seed.

Unlike leadplant, dwarf false indigo has very little winter dieback, even after brutal winters. It blooms a few weeks before leadplant on previous season's wood. Ideally don't prune it at all, but if you feel the need, do so right after bloom or else you'll sacrifice next year's bloom.

Propagation: seed (scarify then stratify) | **Companion plants:** with potentilla for an easy-care planting; with black Samson and snow on the mountain for a meadow planting; to enhance and contrast with midsized bunchgrasses such as blue grama, prairie dropseed, and ruby muhly

Arctostaphylos ×coloradensis

hardy manzanita, mock bearberry

zones 4 or 5–8 • dry slopes, mesas; foothills, pinyon-juniper, shrub steppe, montane • sandy or gritty soils

1–5 ft. × 3–10 ft. • accent, chaparral-inspired planting, hillside plantings, rock gardens, hellstrips

sun, light shade • very low water

Manzanita species are major players in the west coast's chaparral plant communities. This naturally occurring hybrid between greenleaf manzanita and kinnikinnick is one of very few broadleaf evergreen shrubs hardy here. Shiny, coppery bark highlights the gracefully gnarled branches and trunks of mature plants. Forms can be upright, spreading, or cascading. Small white or pink urn-shaped flowers bloom first thing in spring, offering important early food to pollinators. Pea-sized fruit ripens from green to dry reddish brown, lending the plant its name *manzanita* ("little apple" in Spanish). Neat, leathery, oval foliage is typically a warm olive-green; may suffer from winter burn in intensely cold, dry, windy conditions. Plant early or late; sensitive to root rot if watered for establishment during the heat of summer.

Thanks to plantspeople Betsy Baldwin, Scott Skogerboe, Kelly Grummons, Kenton Seth, Robb Smith, Nich Boynton-Steele, and the late Allan Taylor, who have selected wild plants and cracked the code on propagating these shrubs, we now have exceptional plants available: large, vigorous 'Chieftain'; finer-textured, zone-4-hardy 'Panchito'; and 'Cascade'. Deer love to eat new growth; use plastic netting or wire mesh to protect it until well-established.

Propagation: best to buy | **Companion plants:** fringed sage, winterfat, yuccas

Artemisia cana

silver sagebrush

zones 3–7 • dry grassland, hillsides, mountain valleys; plains, foothills, pinyon-juniper, shrub steppe, montane • sandy or gritty soils

2–3 ft. × 2–3 ft. and wider, forming colonies over time • shrub companion in meadow planting, chaparral-inspired planting, accent

sun • very low to low water

This evergreen, extremely hardy, small shrub has narrow gray leaves that shimmer in the sun and glimmer on gloomy days. If it weren't for its running roots and dislike of heavy clay soils, it would probably be one of the most popular of the region's natives for gardens and landscapes. That said, there are still many places to plant this pale beauty.

Like most of our native sagebrush species, it is aromatic when brushed or rained upon. It has a wild, romantic character at maturity when its stems grow thick, gnarled, and picturesque. Spring removal of the remnants of last year's flower panicles and any twiggy dieback keeps the shrub bushier and fresher-looking. Silver sagebrush spreads by rhizomes and forms colonies over time. It is prone to dieback and rotting in heavy and/or moist soils, especially in summer months.

Propagation: seed (stratify, light); suckers | **Companion plants:** Apache plume, fernbush; little bluestem, blue grama, or alkali sacaton; winecup, aromatic aster, and stiff goldenrod; wild blue flax, annual blanketflower, and prairie coneflower; in front of junipers and pines

Artemisia filifolia

threadleaf sage, sand sagebrush

zones 4–7 • dry prairie; plains, foothills • sandy or gritty soils

3–5 ft. × 3–4 ft. • accent, chaparral-inspired planting, backdrop to unwatered flower garden

sun • very low to low water

This evergreen (or ever-silver) aromatic shrub's common name describes its wispy, almost-white foliage. The plant's overall look is feathery and especially beautiful when backlit. As with most sagebrush species, its tiny yellowish tan flowers are arranged in a panicle, but this plant's miniscule blossoms are encased in silvery bracts, creating attractive pale sprays at the tips of the branches. It is truly one of the most striking of our native shrubs.

Growth is open, upright, and arching. Spring removal of the remnants of last year's flower panicles and any weak or dead twiggy wood keeps the shrub bushier and fresher. Threadleaf sage self-sows mildly and combines well with almost any plant.

Propagation: seed (stratify, light) | **Companion plants:** winecup, angel's trumpet, snow on the mountain, ruby muhly grass, plains gayfeather, prickly poppy, desert four o'clock, and any of the larger penstemons; yuccas, manzanita, littleleaf mountain mahogany, desert holly, fernbush, compact forms of pinyon pine, hardy deer muhly grass, and giant sacaton

Artemisia tridentata

big sagebrush

zones 2–8 • intermountain parks, valleys, exposed areas of well-drained soils; foothills, shrub steppe, montane, subalpine • most well-drained soils

3–6 ft. × 3–6 ft. • accent, screening, windbreak planting, chaparral-inspired planting

sun • low to moderate water

Among the most iconic plant groups of our continent, this genus is the keystone for the largest contiguous ecotype of the continental United States, the sagebrush steppe. With a bevy of unique adaptations to its harsh surroundings—including oddities like both evergreen and deciduous leaves and a two-part root system that extends more than ten feet deep—this species is exquisitely adapted to our region. Several animal species (including sage grouse) are sagebrush obligates, unable to survive without the plant, which is also a crucial larval-host plant.

In the wild, these plants form a visual sea, undulating with grasses and wildflowers on rolling terrain between snowcapped peaks. In a smaller space, this effect can be overwhelming, but one or a few plants as accents with their moody, dark, exfoliating bark and dramatic form are wonderful. Hard pruning is often required, as it can prove vigorous on moister and more nutrient-rich garden soils. *Artemisia arbuscula* and *Artemisia nova* are similar but smaller relatives that can make easier-to-manage garden plants.

Propagation: seed (stratify, light) | **Companion plants:** chaparral-inspired: mountain mahoganies, yuccas, junipers, pines, and desert blue holly; floral: scarlet gilia, prickly poppy, bushy buckwheat, broomweed, desert four o'clock, and bush morning-glory; buffalo gourd

Atriplex canescens

four-wing saltbush

zones 4–8 • salt flats, dry grassland, desert; plains, foothills, pinyon-juniper, shrub steppe, montane • sandy or gritty soils

3–6 ft. × 4–6 ft. • accent shrub, chaparral-inspired planting, shelterbelt

sun • very low water

This upright, spreading shrub is technically evergreen, but the tiny, narrow, sparse gray-green leaves make little impact. What sets this plant apart is its fine, twiggy, dense, scratchy texture, making it an excellent wildlife shelter. Male and female plants are separate, and the females sport chartreuse, papery "winged" fruits in mid- to late summer; they often turn rosy in fall and then dry to blonde and persist into winter. These unusual structures are beautiful when backlit, so situate the plant where the sun can shine through it. Male plants are less interesting; good nurseries offer sexed plants grown from cuttings, not seed.

Thrives in the poorest soils and is often browsed by deer, but is so twiggy that damage quickly disappears behind new growth. There are three closely related smaller species of attractive *Atriplex* native to the region that are more difficult to find in nurseries. These have much less showy bracts but more attractive, truly gray or even silver foliage: *Atriplex gardneri*; the very small, silver *Atriplex corrugata*; and *Atriplex confertifolia*, with tidy little rounded gray leaves.

Propagation: best to buy | **Companion plants:** yuccas, pricklypear cacti, crispleaf buckwheat, desert four o'clock, Palmer's penstmon, and angel's trumpet

Berberis aquifolium (Mahonia aquifolium)

Oregon grapeholly

zones 5–8 • woodland clearings, streamsides, canyons; foothills, montane • most well-drained soils

3–6 ft. × 3–6 ft. • shade plantings

light shade to shade • low to moderate water

Unusual because it prefers shade, this plant is perhaps the most polished-looking of our native shrubs and one of few broadleaf evergreens. More common farther west in moister, cloudier regions, grows occasionally in draws and sheltered woodland spots here. Its lush-looking, leathery, glossy green leaves have prickly tips. Slow-growing and suckers a bit over time. When grown in intense sun or exposed to strong winds, the foliage burns badly; better to site this in a sheltered spot, such as on the shaded side of an evergreen, a building, or a wall.

In early spring, clusters of little daffodil-like, honey-scented yellow flowers open. These ripen to jewel-like, rounded, powdery blue berries, more profuse if multiple shrubs are planted for cross-pollination. Foliage turns bronzy or purplish maroon hues in winter (any sunburned foliage will be a dead-looking tan or brown).

'Compacta' is a smaller selection, about one-third the size. Likely not originally from a regional source, but creatures that benefit from the species (including mammals that eat the berries) will benefit from this selection too.

Propagation: seed (stratify); suckers | **Companion plants:** common juniper, boulder raspberry; Colorado spruce, white fir, or bristlecone pine; aspen, alder, or birch with golden banner, golden and blue columbines, and Parry's gentian

Berberis fremontii (Mahonia fremontii)

desert holly

zones 4–8 • rocky slopes, canyons; plains, foothills, pinyon-juniper • sandy or gritty soils

3–10 ft. × 3–6 ft. • chaparral-inspired plantings, perimeter plantings

sun • low water

A picturesque, semi-evergreen, vase-shaped shrub with upright yet crooked, coarse trunks and branches lined with blue-green, prickly foliage shaped like small holly leaves. New foliage emerges a rusty orange color before turning blue-green and leathery. Cold- or wind-burned foliage turns tan. But ample new foliage dependably emerges just before clusters of small daffodil-like, honey-scented yellow flowers open in late spring. These ripen to gold or orange-red rounded berries (valuable to mammals), more dependably profuse if multiple shrubs are planted for cross-pollination.

Despite being semi-evergreen, plants do drop older foliage, which gets pricklier as it dries and is no fun to handle. It's wise to plant this somewhere you don't plan to garden intensely, and mulch well to keep the need for weeding to a minimum.

Red-berry desert holly (*Berberis haematocarpa*) is a slightly wider, coarser, and faster-growing plant with foliage similarly spiny but not quite as blue. It has a more profuse bloom and berry production and red berries. It is slightly less hardy, so more susceptible to winter leafburn and tip dieback, but also grows back more quickly.

Propagation: seed (stratify) | **Companion plants:** pines, junipers, desert olive, Gambel oak, littleleaf mountain mahogany, threeleaf sumac, and Apache plume

Ceanothus herbaceus

redroot, buckbrush

zones 3–7 • open forests and slopes; foothills, montane • most well-drained soils

3–6 ft. × 3–6 ft. • accent shrub, chaparral-inspired planting, backdrop to unwatered flower garden

sun, light shade, shade • very low to low water

Good-sized, glossy, oval leaves give this plant a lush, almost-exotic look and are aromatic when rubbed or crushed. Tiny, starry, pure white flowers open in lacy clusters at the branch tips in late spring and early summer. In full bloom, the bush looks as if flocked by snow. Unlike most of our native shrubs, thrives in shade as well as full sun (if not too hot). Of exceptional value to wildlife, including mammals.

Often accumulates dead twigs and branches; cleanup pruning will keep it attractive. A close relative of blue California lilacs and similarly flammable (plants with aromatic foliage are not ideal in fire-prone sites due to their combustible volatile oils).

Fendler's buckbrush (*Ceanothus fendleri*) is similar except in habit: it forms a much shorter, one- to two-foot spiny groundcover, spreading into dense, woody patches. In cooler areas, makes a simple planting for a slope or in light shade under trees. Flower clusters are smaller than redroot's, and foliage is smaller, narrower, and gray-green. Grow from divisions of the shallow, spreading roots.

Propagation: best to buy | **Companion plants:** common juniper in shade; with mock orange, snowberry, and golden currant in front of pines and spruce in sun

Cercocarpus intricatus

littleleaf mountain mahogany

zones 4–8 • dry hillsides, canyons, rocky flats; plains, foothills, pinyon-juniper • sandy or gritty soil

3–6 ft. × 3–5 ft. • accent shrub, chaparral-inspired planting, hedge or screen

sun • very low to low water

This slow-growing plant is well worth the wait and one of our region's most striking shrubs. Its finely textured, semi-evergreen foliage is short, linear, leathery—much like rosemary without the aroma. Twiggy branch tracery and soft gray bark enhance the lovely foliage, providing year-round elegance and interest. As with all mountain mahogany species, tiny, inconspicuous greenish yellow flowers ripen to seeds with wispy silver tails that transform the plant into a pale, feathery cloud when backlit.

Closely related and much more widespread here, deciduous mountain mahogany (*Cercocarpus montanus*) is even hardier (to zone 2), similar in size, and coarser-textured. It has larger, gray-green, wedge-shaped leaves with prominent veins; its inconspicuous flowers have longer and more persistent seed plumes, the most dramatic aspect of this plant. Fall foliage sometimes takes on muted rusty hues before dropping, but not dependably. Stems and bark are rough and dark gray, almost purple in certain light during the offseason. As with littleleaf mountain mahogany, both mammals and birds eat the seeds and it is a favorite for wildlife shelter and deer browsing.

Propagation: best to buy | **Companion plants:** threadleaf sage, winterfat, Apache plume, desert holly, yuccas, pinyon pine and larger grasses; desert four o'clock and yuccas

Chamaebatiaria millefolium

fernbush

zones 4–7 • dry hillsides, woodland clearings, canyons; foothills, pinyon-juniper, shrub steppe, montane • most well-drained soils

3–5 ft. × 3–6 ft. • accent shrub, chaparral-inspired planting, backdrop to unwatered flower garden

sun • very low to low water

This semi-evergreen shrub has pine-scented, fresh-green, fern-shaped leaves, hence the common name. The overall look is lush for a dryland shrub. Small creamy white flowers open in large, dense, triangular panicles that look reminiscent of a lilac and attract loads of bees for several weeks in midsummer.

The dried reddish brown seedheads are quite pretty in the offseason but as is the case of many dried plant parts that offer interest during fall and winter, those same structures detract against the lacy new greens of spring and fernbush's pale summer-flower trusses, so trim the old ones off before growth unfurls the next spring.

Relatively fast-growing compared to most dryland shrubs and deer-resistant to boot; makes a nice informal hedge or perimeter planting, either mixed with other large shrubs or not. Often self-sows mildly on-site.

Propagation: seed | **Companion plants:** threadleaf sage, yuccas, Apache plume, rabbitbrush; giant sacaton, little bluestem, alkali sacaton, and hardy deer muhly; desert four o'clock and silver prairie sage; butterfly weed and scarlet bugler penstemon

Cornus sericea (Cornus stolonifera)

red-twig dogwood, red osier dogwood

zones 3–7 • moist or wet meadows, streambanks; foothills, montane, subalpine • most moist soils

2–8 ft. × 3–6 ft. • shrub plantings in moist spots, accents in moist meadows, rain gardens

sun, light shade • moderate water to moist

Come late fall and early winter in the mountains, masses of this shrub and willows paint otherwise-muted scenes with their rich orange, yellow, red, and russet stems. Deciduous with sizeable fresh-green, oval leaves; has small, creamy white flowers that open in flatheaded clusters in late spring and early summer, ripening quickly to white berries held in red-stemmed clusters.

Fall foliage can be yellow, orange, or deep maroon; after leaves drop the red stems truly shine, especially once snow blankets the ground.

Quite fast-growing; spreads by underground stems. Dislikes heat. In warmer areas, best on north side of a building, perhaps in a swale that receives rainwater from the roof. Older wood loses its bright coloration, so prune wood that's three or more years old down to the ground annually in late winter or early spring to promote sprouting of new stems. Deer often browse stems so may do the pruning for you.

'Isanti' and Arctic Fire® are excellent selections for rich stem color and more compact size (five feet or shorter). Both have excellent vigor, with less sunscald on twigs in winter. Plant in sites where soil stays moist.

Propagation: seed (stratify); cuttings; suckers | **Companion plants:** willow, aspen, birch, and Colorado spruce

Dasiphora fruticosa (Potentilla fruticosa)

shrubby potentilla

zones 2–7 • moist meadows, along watercourses, forest clearings; foothills, shrub steppe, montane, subalpine, alpine • most soils

2–4 ft. × 2–4 ft. • mixed hedges, accent in moist meadow plantings, mixed borders, rock gardens

sun, light shade • moderate water to moist

Among our most versatile native landscape shrubs, this plant thrives in a variety of spaces, soil textures, and moisture regimes. It blooms reliably in late spring and early summer, cloaking itself in a profusion of quarter-sized, bright yellow flowers with round petals, and features modest rebloom later. This small shrub has attractive, fine-textured foliage, a mounding to arching shape, and rugged, cinnamon-brown peeling bark that is visible in the offseason. Since this species is native to many cooler regions, its appearance and size can vary; many plants in commerce hail from European and Asian collections. They're generally larger and more upright than the smaller, mounded forms growing native in the Rockies.

These unfussy shrubs tolerate light shade as well as sun, though have fullest form and heaviest bloom where all-day sun can be provided. A periodic thinning—pruning the oldest stems right to the ground—can help maintain vigor and fullness. Do this right after bloom or you risk losing next year's flowers, as this shrub blooms on last year's wood.

Propagation: seed (stratify); cuttings | **Companion plants:** Rocky Mountain iris and prairie smoke; Colorado spruce or larger shrubs, such as mock orange and elderberry

Elaeagnus commutata

silverberry

zones 3–7 • grassland, open woods, streamsides, dry slopes; plains, foothills • sandy or gritty soils

6–12 ft. × 8–12 ft. and wider • perimeter planting, hedge, shelterbelts

sun • low water

Silverberry's almost-blindingly-silver, wavy-edged oval foliage shimmers from a distance. If it didn't sucker so much, everyone would grow it. In late spring, masses of small, tubular, yellow flowers open, wafting a permeating lemony fragrance. The early-autumn fruits are also a metallic silver color, like little spray-painted olives. Thrives in moist or dry sites but performs poorly in heavy clay.

Silverberry crossed with the nonnative tree Russian olive (*Elaeagnus angustifolia*), and the resulting plant, 'Quicksilver', is popular in gardens in England and the Pacific Northwest. It has a more refined leaf and form than either parent but is only half native. It's unclear at this point whether its fruits are as tasty to birds and large mammals as those of its nonnative parent, or if it would cross with silverberries nearby. Birds have spread Russian olive all over the region and its fruits also float along watercourses. It has invaded much of the Rocky Mountain west, especially along rivers, ditches, and streams, so it's best to stick with native silverberry.

Propagation: seed (stratify); cuttings; suckers | **Companion plants:** junipers, spruces, and pines; little bluestem, blue grama, and ruby muhly; desert four o'clock

Ericameria nauseosa

rabbitbrush, chamisa

zones 4–8 • disturbed sites, fields, meadows, drainages, and open, rocky soils; plains, foothills, pinyon-juniper, shrub steppe, montane • most soils

1–6 ft. × 2–6 ft. • accent, hedgerow, chaparral-inspired gardens, backdrop in unwatered flower gardens

sun • low to moderate water

For Colorado's Front Range, few natural events mark the arrival of late summer so emphatically or consistently as this plant's bloom. With its billowing form and swaying clouds of glowing, golden flowers, these substantial plants envelop grassland, trails, and roadsides by September. Pollinators swarm to what might be described as the "golden arches" of the Rocky Mountain insect world: a widespread, consistent, and convenient food source with great branding. The bloom of this species coincides with the mass-migration of painted lady butterflies to Mexico, and the plant is an important food source for mammals and host plant for juvenile insects, including iridescent blue-green rabbitbrush beetle larvae.

Occasional hard spring pruning keeps this soft-wooded, vigorous shrub from splaying open, as does reducing irrigation. Can seed aggressively on irrigated and disturbed soils. Spare yourself pulling hundreds of deep-rooted seedlings by planting the less-seedy Plant Select 'Baby Blue', a naturally occurring dwarf form that stays one to two feet high and wide. Both green- and silver-leaf selections of the full-sized form can also be found.

Propagation: seed (stratify, light) | **Companion plants:** Gambel oak, sand cherry, desert olive, and sumacs; yuccas and angel's trumpet; azure sage, red hummingbird trumpet, and purple asters

Fallugia paradoxa

Apache plume, feather rose

zones 4–8 • arroyos, rocky slopes, forest clearings, roadsides; plains, foothills, pinyon-juniper, montane • most well-drained soils

3–5 ft. × 4–6 ft. • accent, chaparral-inspired plantings, backdrop to unwatered flower plantings

sun • very low to low water

When in full seed and backlit by the sun, will stop even the most disinterested soul in their tracks. Even without its stunning seedhead display, its overall effect is appealingly airy and wild. This semi-evergreen shrub has tiny, cleft, olive-green leaves and slender, almost-white stems, giving it some of the finest texture of any of our native shrubs. Grows quite quickly into a casual, densely twiggy plant. White, inch-and-a-half, five-petaled flowers bloom most profusely in late spring but continue sputter blooming into early fall when there is enough moisture. The flowers ripen to seeds with peachy pink, feathery tails in fluffy balls all over the plant; if there isn't much rain, these dried fluffballs persist much of summer until they bleach to white and blow off in the wind.

Often spreads a bit by suckers and low-growing horizontal branches rooting close to the original plant. In the wild, sometimes forms colonies; also self-sows mildly in gravel. Deer- and rabbit-resistant. Make sure to place it where low backlighting occurs either early or late in the day, or you'll miss the extraordinary glowing effect of the feathery pink seedheads.

Propagation: seed (stratify); cuttings | **Companion plants:** yuccas, pricklypears, chollas, pines, and junipers

Fendlera rupicola

cliff fendlerbush

zones 4–8 • rocky hillsides, canyons, rock ledges, woodland clearings; foothills, pinyon-juniper, shrub steppe • sandy or gritty soils

4–6 ft. × 4–5 ft. • accent, chaparral-inspired plantings, backdrop to unwatered flower plantings

sun • very low to low water

At once neat and tailored yet old-looking and picturesque, with stiff, gawky, pale gray branches. The overall effect is of a bonsai mock orange, less lush but with much finer detail. It has a slow, irregular growth habit and tiny, narrowly oval, shiny leaves paired neatly opposite one another in tidy rows. Foliage is occasionally evergreen in wind-protected spots during mild winters, but usually not. Eventually this tough dryland shrub matures into an irregular, somewhat vase-shaped plant.

Pure white, four-petaled flowers open in late spring and early summer, ranging from half an inch to an inch and a half in diameter. They are very profuse and sometimes have a touch of pink in the petals. The petals are pinched at the base and form a squarish cross, crisp and tidy-looking like the foliage, giving the plant a quaint charm. The blossoms are lightly fragrant, especially in the evening.

Cliff fendlerbush needs a berm or a slope where the soil is heavy and clayey.

Propagation: seed (scarify then stratify); cuttings | **Companion plants:** pines, tree-form junipers, manzanita, and silver sagebrush; silvery lupine, rice grass, and white evening primrose

Holodiscus discolor var. *dumosus* (*Holodiscus dumosus*)

rockspray

zones 3–7 • dry rocky slopes, canyons, rock ledges; foothills, pinyon-juniper, montane • sandy or gritty soils

4–6 ft. × 4–6 ft. • accent, chaparral-inspired plantings, hillside plantings

sun, light shade • low to moderate water

This deciduous shrub has small, oval, toothed leaves that smell peppery when rubbed; it grows into a casual, upright, arching plant. Small, lightly fragrant, ivory-white flowers open in showy, loose, pointed clusters in midsummer, turning peachy pink and then a warm rusty brown as they dry and persist well into winter. Fall-foliage color can be a muted brownish red. The overall effect is airy, fine-textured, and wild—lacy and a bit disheveled. Relatively fast-growing and water-thrifty, this makes an excellent plant choice for partly shaded, dry slopes or near greedy-rooted trees.

Close relative cream bush (*Holodiscus discolor* var. *discolor*) has larger, denser, all-around more beautiful flower clusters but unfortunately needs much more consistent moisture than mountain spray to thrive. It is native farther north and west in our region. If ample moisture is available, it is a top selection for planting.

Propagation: seed (stratify); cuttings | **Companion plants:** spruce, maple, cottonwood, poplar, and willow; Rocky Mountain juniper, white fir, and bristlecone pine

Jamesia americana

waxflower, five-petal cliffbush, cliff jamesia

zones 3–8 • coniferous woods, rocky north slopes, cool ravines; foothills, pinyon-juniper, montane • sandy or gritty soils

2–6 ft. × 2–4 ft. • accent shrub in shaded planting, hillside plantings, shaded rock gardens

sun, light, full shade • low to moderate water

Has a quirky, sweet appeal; often the only thing conspicuously blooming in the mountain-forest shade. In late spring, clusters of waxy, white (or, rarely, pink) flowers open, their pale color and lovely scent helping insects find them. The dry, dark brown fruit has less visual appeal but is eaten by birds and small mammals. Stiffly upright branches have ruddy, peeling bark and are clothed in thick, rounded, rich green, pleated foliage that's strikingly pale underneath. In fall the leaves turn orange, ruddy red, and sometimes even pink before they drop.

Sadly, tends to sulk and get root rot in a pot under nursery culture, so plants aren't easy to find. Attempts to transplant from the wild promise almost-certain failure. Nurseries specializing in native plants are more likely to have a few; grab one as soon as you see it. Don't disturb the root ball when planting, and don't overwater; it can be fussy, hates clay, and prefers the coarse, open, rocky soil and swift drainage of slopes and ravines. Plant it in a cool, well-drained spot—full sun or light shade in cool-summer climates, shade in hotter sites.

Propagation: seed (light); cuttings | **Companion plants:** columbines and common juniper

Juniperus communis var. *depressa*

common juniper

zones 3–6 • slopes, understory in dry coniferous woods, pine savanna; foothills, montane, subalpine • most well-drained soils

1–3 ft. × 4–8 ft. • accent evergreen shrub under trees, hillside plantings, with boulders, shaded hellstrips

light shade • low to moderate water

This evergreen plant—including tree, shrubby, and ground-covering forms—is aptly named *communis*, as it grows more widely than almost any other tree or shrub on the entire planet. Our form is a wide-spreading, low evergreen shrub found at higher elevations. Horizontal sprays of feathery but prickly green foliage create a graceful, near-weeping shape. Resembles pines more than other junipers with its color and needlelike texture.

Many nursery selections are from other regions and are not well adapted to the climate or the drier, often more alkaline soil conditions common here. Look for (sometimes hard-to-find) selections such as Blueberry Delight® from western North Dakota or Alpine Carpet® from Utah; these true natives have much better adaptability here and even thrive in hotter, drier lower elevations when planted in shade.

Unlike junipers that turn bronze in winter, most of these regional introductions stay greener, especially when grown in winter shade. Soft new growth, a luminous chartreuse, emerges in spring. Dark blue fruits produced late summer on female plants are eaten by birds and other wildlife and used to flavor gin. Provides important shelter for nesting and winter survival for both birds and small mammals.

Propagation: cuttings | **Companion plants:** creeping grapeholly, columbines

Juniperus horizontalis

creeping juniper

zones 3–8 • rocky slopes, ledges, forest clearings; plains, foothills, montane • most well-drained soils

2–24 in. × 6–10 ft. and unlimited spread • chaparral-inspired plantings, groundcover, hillside plantings, hellstrips

sun, light shade • very low to low water

Often considered a boring cliché, but plants have their own presence and value irrespective of our interest. This evergreen, low, groundcovering shrub is native to much of the continent and grown in plantings nationwide thanks to its beauty, ease of care, and rugged adaptability.

Tiny, aromatic leaves grow in shaggy clusters, creating a feathery texture. Foliage is green to silvery blue and takes on purple hues in winter. Plants are separately male and female; females make small blue fruits. Spreads by horizontal branches rooting along ground; cuttings taken in late winter root best using rooting hormone. Grow this on slopes, among rocks, or as a groundcover for year-round interest.

Most nursery selections originate much farther east and don't have as much tolerance for dry, alkaline soil as those from our region. Recently available from Kelly Grummons via Plant Select is 'Guernsey Green', which he found in southeastern Wyoming. It stays extremely low at about three inches in height; has a lacy, fresh-green look; and is female. It's about as heat-, cold-, and wind-tolerant as our natives get and thrives in sun or light, dry shade.

Propagation: cuttings | **Companion plants:** Apache plume, littleleaf mountain mahogany, or wavyleaf oak

Krascheninnikovia lanata (*Ceratoides lanata, Eurotia lanata*)

winterfat, white sage

zones 3–8 • dry grassland, rocky flats, mesas, dry hillsides; plains, foothills, pinyon-juniper, shrub steppe, montane • sandy or gritty soils

1–3 ft. × 2–3 ft. • chaparral-inspired plantings, dry meadow plantings, hellstrips

sun • low to moderate water

This unusual-looking, low semi-evergreen shrub has small, narrow leaves and stems covered in pale felt, giving it a grayish silver look. Has a casual, densely twiggy form. Flowers are barely noticeable and separately male and female, in sinuous long spikes. Female blossoms ripen seed with very showy, silky white tufts lining the spike; these persist from summer well into winter. When backlit, the overall effect of the shrub in seed is as if dusted by snow.

Birds and small mammals eat the seeds, and larger mammals browse the highly nourishing plants extensively in winter. Plants resprout vigorously in spring; gardeners do well to cut the plants almost to the base right before growth resumes. If not pruned by gardener or wildlife, eventually looks tired, with many weak, half-dead older branches. Self-sows a bit and is easily grown by sowing ripe seed immediately after collection directly into the ground; seed doesn't store well. If possible, plant it where the white cottony seedheads can get some backlighting.

Propagation: fresh seed | **Companion plants:** yuccas, pricklypears, and chollas; pines and one-seed juniper; rabbitbrush, threeleaf sumac, and manzanita; blue grama and hardy deer muhly; broomweed, plains gayfeather, angel's trumpet, and desert four o'clock

Peraphyllum ramosissimum

wild crab apple, Ute apple

zones 4–8 • meadows, woodland clearings, mesas, hillsides; foothills • most well-drained soils

4–6 ft. × 4–6 ft. • shrub border, chaparral-inspired planting

sun • low water

Mature shrubs in full bloom are a beautiful, somewhat incongruous sight, reminiscent of old-world cottage-garden shrubs and trees in spring. This uncommon gem deserves more attention, combining excellent wildlife (including mammals) and pollinator benefits and a rugged constitution with nostalgic charm. Its habit is upright, twiggy, and stiff, and the shrub has narrowly oval, leathery, dark ashy green foliage in clusters along its gray branches. In mid to late spring the flowers open: five-petaled, blush-pink to white, fragrant blossoms like an apple tree's. Pretty, half-inch, red-cheeked yellow fruits look like a cross between a crab apple fruit and a rose hip.

Seeds will germinate sporadically in warmer temperatures. Expect this to be a long-term project, as this is one of the slowest-growing of our native shrubs.

Propagation: seed (stratify) | **Companion plants:** tree junipers and pinyon pine; silver and gray sagebrushes, fernbush, Apache plume, and desert holly

Philadelphus lewisii

mock orange

zones 4–8 • moist slopes, forest clearings, woodland edges; plains, foothills, shrub steppe, montane • most well-drained soils

6–8 ft. × 6–8 ft. • shrub border, accent, backdrop to flower garden

sun • low to moderate water

This lovely, large, arching deciduous shrub has exceptional wildlife value and is Idaho's state flower. Hardier, denser, and needs less water than nonnative mock oranges, yet offers masses of the same beautiful, sweet-scented, four-petaled white blossoms for a few weeks in early summer. Foliage is neatly, oppositely arranged along the stems.

Cheyenne®, chosen by Plant Select in 2001 thanks to plantsman Scott Skogerboe, was the only mock orange doing more than merely surviving in the ferociously windy, dry, and cold climate of the Cheyenne Horticultural Field Station in the 1990s. 'Blizzard' is a Canadian selection that boasts amazing cold hardiness—zone 3 or warm zone 2. Avoid selections with double flowers, which come at the expense of pollen and nectar production.

Benefits from some pruning every few years, done either in the dormant season or right after flowering. Remove weak, old, and twiggy wood down to the base, and trim gawky shoots that grow way above the arching silhouette. Plant close to paths, windows, or entryways to enjoy the fragrant blossoms in the mornings and evenings, and if possible, set the white flowers against a backdrop of darker evergreens.

Propagation: seed (stratify); cuttings | **Companion plants:** pine or fir trees

Philadelphus microphyllus

littleleaf mock orange

zones 5–9 • scrub, canyons, hillsides; foothills, shrub steppe, pinyon-juniper, montane • sandy or gritty soils

3–5 ft. × 4–6 ft. • shrub border, accent, hillside plantings, chaparral-inspired plantings

sun • low water

This slow-growing deciduous shrub has very small, oblong leaves that give it a neat, fine texture. Lightly fragrant, starry white flowers have petals not as wide or overlapping as those of mock orange but otherwise similar; they bloom in early summer. In the wild, often grows among rock outcrops with a casual, arching habit, its fine texture and delicate countenance contrasting with the solid forms of the boulders, something easily emulated in a garden using either rocks or walls.

Needs less water to bloom well than mock orange. Looks a lot like fendlerbush but with bigger flowers that bloom later, and more arching and less stiffly branched overall.

Forms with larger and more profuse flowers are worth seeking out: They are perfect examples of how sometimes selections, when made in consideration of habits beneficial to wildlife (such as more profuse flowering), can increase the wildlife value of a native plant species. 'Desert Snow' and 'June Bride' are both selections made for floral size and abundance.

Propagation: seed (stratify); cuttings | **Companion plants:** evergreens such as pines and junipers; shrubs like Apache plume, littleleaf mountain mahogany, or silver sagebrush; any early-summer wildflowers, especially wild blue flax, silvery lupine, and blue penstemons

Physocarpus spp.

ninebark species

zones 3–9 • drainages, watercourses, rocky places, cliffs, hillsides; plains, foothills, montane • most soils

4–10 ft. × 4–10 ft. • shrub borders, hedgerows

sun, light shade • low water to moist

A few species of ninebark can be found throughout our region in a variety of habitats, ranging from dry and rocky to moist and forested. The most common and largest of these is mountain ninebark (*Physocarpus monogynus*), which forms a substantial shrub well-cloaked in lush, lobed leaves. In early summer, plants produce a flush of small, white to cream, five-petaled flowers held in dense, rounded clusters all over the plant. In years with favorable moisture (or in cases of particularly vigorous individuals), the show can be arrestingly dramatic. While out-of-leaf, mountain ninebark presents well, with peeling bark and long, arched branches. Grows well in moderate to moist soils and full sun, and can handle quite dry conditions in light shade.

Most other native ninebarks here—including *P. opulifolius* var. *intermedius*, which closely allies with the common or eastern ninebark, and *P. malvaceus*, mallow-leaf ninebark—can be grown in conditions similar to those of mountain ninebark, where they grow to be shrubs of similar or somewhat smaller sizes. Effectively fills large areas of the home landscape and can be used as visual screens and hedgerows.

Propagation: seed (stratify) | **Companion plants:** ponderosa pine; silvery lupine

Prunus americana

American plum, wild plum

zones 3–8 • draws, canyons, slopes, along watercourses; plains, foothills, shrub steppe, montane • most well-drained soils

5–20 ft. × 5–20 ft. • hedgerow, screen, windbreak

sun, light shade • low water to moist

Easily spotted in mid-spring thanks to its striking bloom of pure white, sweet-scented flowers against bare, charcoal-colored branches. By late summer, jewel-like, silver-dollar-sized fruits dangle from the stems, glowing in oranges and soft reds and drawing the interest of wildlife ranging from turkey to deer. In fall, plants dazzle again with brilliant orange and yellow foliage.

Despite all this, not frequently seen in landscapes; most individuals sucker prolifically, eventually creating large thickets of sharply spurred stems. Plant genetics and garden site can significantly affect the vigor of this tendency. Larger, suckering forms are wonderful additions to expansive properties, where they act as veritable apartment complexes for wildlife. Occasionally, non-suckering forms can be purchased that can easily be pruned into small, somewhat short-lived trees. The near-relative *Prunus mexicana* (Mexican plum, originating in the Southern Great Plains) provides many of the same benefits as American plum on a reliably tree-form plant with less cold hardiness (zones 5–9).

Bryan has grown these plums easily using the refrigerator method of cold-moist stratification, bagging the pits as soon as they are cleaned of flesh and still moist.

Propagation: seed (stratify); cuttings; suckers | **Companion plants:** pines, spruces, firs, and junipers

Prunus pumila var. *besseyi*

sand cherry, western sand cherry

zones 3–9 • rocky places, exposed bedrock, sand prairies; plains • most well-drained soils

1–5 ft. × 3–6 ft. • shrub borders, hedgerows, shelterbelts, hellstrips (low forms only)

sun, light shade • low to moderate water

Evolution has created a staggering array of plant shapes and sizes; a regional example of this is western sand cherry. A cherry in every sense, this plant has woody stems, glossy leaves, and abundant, fragrant (albeit tiny), five-petaled, creamy white flowers that precede glistening, carmine cherries loved by birds and mammals. In the eastern portions of its range, it matures into a large, rounded shrub five feet (or more) tall and wide, yet in our region plants remain exceptionally low-growing, probably to hunker down from the whipping, drying winds of the High Plains. These scarcely exceed a foot in height and remain short in garden cultivation, too.

So, it's important to understand how large the sand cherry you're buying may get. 'Boulder Weeping', Jade Parade®, and Pawnee Buttes® typically remain under two feet high in a garden, as do most marked "var. *besseyi*"; other plants may or may not grow much taller. All develop exquisite, glowing crimson fall color.

To propagate from seed, clean and cold-moist stratify pits. Rodents threaten seeds stratified outdoors; consider using the refrigerator method of stratification.

Propagation: seed (stratify); cuttings | **Companion plants:** spreading juniper or skirting leadplant and rabbitbrush; little bluestem, ruby muhly, hardy deer muhly, fringed sage, and aromatic aster

Prunus virginiana var. *melanocarpa*

black chokecherry

zones 2–6 • along watercourses, moist slopes; plains, foothills, montane, subalpine • most soils

8–20 ft. × 8–15 ft., unlimited spread • wildlife shelterbelt, suckering casual hedge or screen

sun, light shade • low to moderate water

This fast-growing, deciduous shrub suckers prolifically, forming dense thickets about eight to ten feet tall that create shelter for and offer food to many species of wildlife. Showy bottlebrushes of small, fragrant creamy white flowers bloom in spring after foliage emerges, followed by shiny, rounded, dark purple (almost black) fruit in summer. Fruits are savored by birds and mammals but unpleasant-tasting to people when eaten raw. Glossy, coarse, dark green leaves turn yellow and orange, sometimes red, in fall.

To grow from seed, clean ripe fruit and sow, keeping moist through the rest of the season, and then let the seed receive a winter's worth of cold-moist stratification.

'Yellow Bird' is a selection originally found in Wyoming with flashy, bright yellow fruits rather than the less-visible dark purple ones typical of the species. If you have room, this is an exceptionally valuable wildlife plant to include in your gardens.

Propagation: seed (stratify); suckers | **Companion plants:** grasses, prairie sage

Purshia tridentata

antelope bitterbrush

zones 4–8 • dry hillsides, grassland, rocky woodland clearings; plains, foothills, pinyon-juniper, shrub steppe, montane • sandy or gritty soils

3–7 ft. × 3–4 ft. • hillside plantings, chaparral-inspired plantings, backdrop to unwatered flower garden

sun • very low to low water

When not in bloom, this gawky shrub resembles mountain mahoganies in its dense, twiggy, irregular habit; small foliage; and gray bark. Lacks their plumed seedheads but has much showier flowers. In late spring and early summer, fragrant cream to pale yellow, starry, five-petaled flowers bloom. Has small, semi-evergreen, leathery, wedge-shaped, gray-green leaves. The plant's gnarled look is one of charming, wild refinement; it's ideal among boulders. Offers excellent wildlife cover and food for mammals (deer love it!), birds, and insects.

Close cousin cliffrose, *P. stansburiana*, is a true desert shrub: needs hot summers to thrive and resents long periods of snow cover, so has less potential regionally. Similar in size, it often grows sideways and downward with age, with dark, shaggy bark on older trunks. The tiny evergreen leaves are much prettier than this plant's—scalloped, dark gray-green, and with a fresh medicinal aroma. Flowers are larger with wider petals and have a sweet, musky fragrance. The late-spring bloom absolutely covers the plant; some sputter bloom occurs through summer and into fall. Cliffrose seeds have noticeable plumes.

Propagation: seed (scarify then stratify) | **Companion plants:** threadleaf sage, juniper, pinyon pine, and other dryland shrubs and trees

Quercus gambelii

Gambel oak, scrub oak

zones 4–8 • dry slopes, canyons, streamsides; foothills, montane • most well-drained soils

5–30 ft. × 6–20 ft. and eventually wider when it suckers • mixed shrub and tree borders, hillside plantings

sun • very low to low water

One of our region's most iconic woody plants; can be a suckering shrub or (less commonly) a small tree. In some areas, carpets entire hillsides and fills valleys with groves. Habit is open and irregular, eventually forming a rounded crown. Flowers are long, yellow-tan, tassel-like catkins and bloom in spring just as foliage unfurls. Foliage is deciduous, deeply lobed, and varies in size and shape, sometimes even on one plant. In summer, leaves are a lustrous medium green, turning amber or sometimes orange, red, or russet in fall. Acorns are small, hard, tan, and oval, ripening in mid- to late summer. Slow-growing, so won't become a thicket for quite some time. Exceptionally valuable to wildlife, including mammals.

Large, tree-form Gambel oaks (such as 'Gila Monster'), perhaps relics of ice-age hybridization with larger oak species, have been found in southern Colorado and western New Mexico and introduced to the regional nursery trade. Naturally occurring, highly variable, shrubby crosses between shrub live oak (*Quercus turbinella*) and Gambel oak are called wavyleaf oak.

Propagation: fresh acorns (stratify) | **Companion plants:** perimeter planting with pines and junipers; dry hillside or meadow planting with blue grama, prairie sage, and western yarrow

Quercus ×pauciloba (Quercus undulata)

wavyleaf oak

zones 4–8 • dry slopes; foothills, montane • most well-drained soils

6–12 ft. × 6–8 ft. • accent or grouping, hedge, wildlife shelterbelt, chaparral-inspired planting

sun • very low water

This irregularly branched large shrub or small multi-stemmed tree is a naturally occurring hybrid between two compact oaks that need very little water to thrive: deciduous Gambel oak (*Quercus gambelii*) and the less-hardy, evergreen shrub live oak (*Quercus turbinella*). Foliage varies widely, as is the case with many hybrid plants from parents that have differing attributes. The leaves range from evergreen to semi-evergreen to entirely deciduous, from rather large with a few rounded lobes to small with many points (almost like a holly), and all sizes and shapes in between. The smaller, gray-blue, prickly holly-like leaves tend to have less fall color but are more evergreen, and the more green, wavy-leaved, larger-leaved plants often develop better fall color—from yellow to orange to red—before dropping their foliage.

Most are finer-textured than Gambel oak, even slower-growing, and not as suckering (if at all), but with better cold hardiness than the shrub live oak. The shrub, valuable to mammals for its acorns, grows slowly and is best in a casual planting with other dryland small trees and shrubs or as part of a low screen.

Propagation: fresh acorns (stratify) | **Companion plants:** juniper, pinyon, Apache plume, fernbush, and sages

Rhamnus smithii

Smith's buckthorn

zones 4–8 • meadows, draws, woodland clearings, moist slopes; foothills • most well-drained soils

6–10 ft. × 6–10 ft. • mixed shrub borders, chaparral-inspired plantings

sun • low to moderate water

Grows into large, broad, multi-stemmed deciduous shrub or small tree. It has a lush look rarely seen in our region's native woody plants. You can train it to be single-trunked, but it will need regular policing and repruning to remain so. Better to choose a few branches low on the trunk and keep them open as they grow to show off the pretty, pale bark, or just leave it alone and let it grow into a full, bushy plant.

This shrub has shiny, rich green, oval foliage with wavy edges, giving it a playful, lively look. The pale gray bark of branches and trunks contrasts nicely with the foliage. In spring, tiny, starry, fragrant, greenish yellow flowers open briefly, attracting myriad pollinators. Later in summer loads of black, pea-sized fruit ripen and are very popular with birds and small mammals (this plant has exceptional wildlife value). The foliage turns yellow in fall before dropping.

Propagation: seed (stratify) | **Companion plants:** Rocky Mountain juniper and white fir; rabbitbrush and smooth sumac

Rhus glabra

smooth sumac

zones 3–8 • woodland clearings, slopes, gulches, roadsides; plains, foothills • most well-drained soils

2–10 ft. × 6–10 ft. (wider over time) • hillside plantings, perimeter plantings

sun • low to moderate water

Has a lush, almost-tropical appearance not typically seen in our region's native woody plants. Its rich green, ferny foliage make it easily recognizable in the wild. This large, suckering, deciduous shrub's coarse, sinuous branches carry the bright green foliage on their upper parts.

Come late spring, tiny, creamy green flowers open in stout pyramidal clusters on the tips of all the branches. Later in summer these ripen to small, reddish, felted fruit, held in the same conical shape but transformed to red flames or cockscombs over the top of the shrub. These persist handsomely in winter with now a more rusty, red-brown hue. Foliage turns briefly but extravagantly orange or red in fall before dropping. Small mammals eat the fruit, and this plant is especially valuable to wildlife.

A regional variant, sometimes known as var. *cismontana* and commonly called Rocky Mountain smooth sumac, is identical except much shorter, staying typically three to four feet in height.

Propagation: seed (scarify); suckers | **Companion plants:** white fir and Rocky Mountain juniper; larger grasses such as giant sacaton, switchgrass, and golden feather grass; rabbitbrush

Rhus trilobata (*Rhus aromatica* ssp. *trilobata*)

threeleaf sumac, skunkbush

zones 3–8 • grassland, mesas, dry slopes; plains, foothills • most well-drained soils

3–7 ft. × 6–8 ft. • chaparral-inspired plantings, hillside plantings, hedge

sun • low water

One of our best native woody plants for fall color; turns hillsides, ravines, and roadsides striking gold, amber, orange, and red shades before the dormant season sets in. This multi-stemmed, suckering, deciduous shrub is usually quite low-growing unless sited in moist, rich soil where it can quickly become a large shrub. The shiny, rich green, three-parted, lobed foliage is pungently aromatic when crushed.

In early spring tiny, fragrant, clustered yellow flowers open briefly, giving the still-bare branch tracery a quiet, pale yellow haze. Later in summer, ripe clusters of translucent, sticky, furry orange-red fruit form on female plants. They're eaten by birds and mammals, especially bears, and can be made into a tangy lemonade.

One of the faster-growing of our native shrubs, it responds well to shearing and can be used as a good-sized hedge in moister sites. 'Autumn Amber' is a prostrate-growing selection—lovely on a slope, over a wall, and around boulders—and is hardy to zone 4.

Propagation: cuttings; seed (scarify then stratify); suckers | **Companion plants:** junipers, pines; silver shrubs such as rabbitbrush, winterfat, leadplant, or sagebrush; prairie sage; aster, blue grama, and ruby muhly

Ribes aureum

golden currant, buffalo currant, clove currant

zones 4–7 • draws, moist slopes and canyons, woodland clearings, streamsides; plains, foothills, shrub steppe, montane • most well-drained soils

4–6 ft. × 5–6 ft. • accent, wildlife shelterbelt, mixed shrub and tree planting, casual hedge or screen

sun, light shade • low to moderate water

In the northern Colorado foothills, this plant's sunny yellow bloom synchronizes with the springtime reappearance of migratory broad-tailed hummingbirds. Sweetly clove-scented, the long-lasting tubular blossoms flower in clusters and are often red-tinged as they mature.

Grows quickly into an irregular, coarsely rounded, open shrub. Adapts well to both sun and some shade, so is good for light, dry shade conditions where not many plants thrive. Give it a bit more water in full sun. Small, three-lobed leaves have toothed edges and are light green or gray-green, turning ruddy tones in autumn, sometimes brilliant red. Large, edible, rounded fruit (beloved by mammals, including humans!) ripens in mid- to late summer and varies from shiny black to reddish brown to amber or gold. Fruit is tart-sweet; flavor varies considerably from shrub to shrub. Plants only bear fruit heavily with other individuals nearby.

Golden currants sucker in moist conditions, and suckers can be cut belowground and transplanted in spring or fall. Plants often seed around a bit, and seedlings move readily.

Propagation: cuttings; seed (stratify) | **Companion plants:** with boulder raspberry in the dappled shade of aspen, alder, or birches; with blue juniper, spruce, or fir in sun; prairie smoke

Ribes cereum

wax currant

zones 4–7 • woodland clearings, draws, slopes, canyons; most life zones • sandy or gritty soils

2–5 ft. × 2–5 ft. • mixed shrub border, shaded garden

sun, light shade • low to moderate water

A fine-textured, small to midsized deciduous shrub with quiet appeal. Despite its delicate looks, it's tough as nails. Small, rounded, pale lime-green foliage is lobed—almost scalloped, giving the shrub a ruffled look. In late spring, clusters of demure, lightly fragrant, baby-pink tubular flowers dangle from the branches and are popular with all sorts of pollinators. Later in summer glassy, rounded vermilion fruit ripens, dressing up the shrub and feeding many creatures.

In hotter, lower-elevation sites, does best in light, dry shade; otherwise thrives in full sun.

Propagation: seed (stratify); cuttings | **Companion plants:** in moist sites, potentilla and mock orange; in drier sites, Apache plume; in dappled shade, bigtooth maple, honey locust, or hackberry; in front of pines; with harebell and columbines in part-day sun; with sulfur flower, silvery lupine, and blue penstemons on a sunny slope in a cooler area

Rubus deliciosus

boulder raspberry

zones 4–8 • rocky places, slopes, ponderosa pine woods, along waterways; plains, foothills, montane • most well-drained soils

3–4 ft. × 4–6 ft. • accent shrub, hedgerow, chaparral-inspired planting

sun, light shade • low to moderate water

This striking member of the rose family can be spotted on moderate- to low-elevation slopes and growing among rocks, often in afternoon shade. With unique, rounded, deeply wrinkled leaves that emerge just before its showy, five-petaled, two-to-three-inch white flowers, it's easy to identify. Plants range from graceful, vase-shaped, and arching to more amorphous. All respond well to pruning: cut out the oldest canes to the base every few years to maintain vigor and promote better form.

The fruits are relished by many bird species. When first encountering this plant in his youth, Bryan assumed the berries would taste sweet rather than somehow combining "berry" and "jerky" into one pithy fruit. Perhaps the epithet *deliciosus* was literally for the birds (though some mammals like them).

In winter, plants remain attractive thanks to distinctive reddish brown, peeling bark. Plants perform best with protection from sun during the hottest period of summer days, along with occasional deep watering. One of our region's best offerings for dry shade, further setting this beautiful and functional plant apart from most shrubs.

Propagation: cuttings; seed (stratify) | **Companion plants:** aspen, bigtooth maple, alder, or birch; common juniper and Oregon grapeholly; columbines, harebells, and prairie smoke

Sambucus racemosa (var. *melanocarpa* and var. *microbotrys*)

red elderberry, black elderberry, Rocky Mountain elderberry

zones 3–7 • streamsides, moist slopes; foothills, shrub steppe, montane, subalpine • most moist soils

8–12 ft. × 8–12 ft., can form thickets (uncommon) • screening, windbreaks, shrub borders

sun to part shade • moderate water to moist

Features large, lush leaves—an unusual look in our region—and combines this unique offering with fragrant (some might say smelly), cream-colored flower clusters in late spring and early summer. These flowers are followed by substantial clusters of berries so intensely red they look freshly painted. Autumn, however, is this plant's finest season: elderberry sets itself ablaze with hot orange and searing red foliage, coloring hillsides in the high country.

One of three elderberries native here and the most cold-hardy, making its way along streamsides all the way into the frigid subalpine biome. Not all forms run, but those that do attain size even greater than clumping forms (large to begin with). These vigorous plants are an important food source for native insects and larger animals, providing nectar and pollen for insects and vegetative forage for large herbivores. Prodigious quantities of juicy, orange-red (var. *microbotrys*) or black (var. *melanocarpa*) berries follow, adored by birds. Stems serve as nesting sites for native bees. Despite its high-elevation origin, plants perform respectably at lower elevations with irrigation and moisture-conserving, root-cooling mulch.

Propagation: cuttings; seed (stratify) | **Companion plants:** white fir, Colorado spruce, Douglas fir, alder, birch, or peachleaf willow

Shepherdia argentea

silver buffaloberry

zones 2–8 • streamsides, ravines, ditches, slopes; plains, foothills • most well-drained soils

8–15 ft. × 8–12 ft. (wider over time) • hedges, perimeter plantings, shelterbelts

sun • low to moderate water

This deciduous shrub suckers to form thickets. It sports narrowly oval, sage-green foliage that makes a great backdrop for wildflowers. The dense twigs are spine-tipped and roots sucker widely; definitely a plant for the back forty.

In early spring, tiny, fragrant yellow flowers open briefly, followed in summer by multitudes of bright orange-red fruit on female plants. You only need one male, any number of females, and pollinating insects to make berries happen.

'Totem', a columnar selection from Plant Select, is female and only two to three feet wide but may also sucker.

Smaller cousin *S. canadensis* has dull green leaves and darker red fruit; not as handsome but suckers less. Spectacular silver *S. rotundifolia* needs dry desert soils, often struggles in cultivation. It crosses with silver buffaloberry, and these hybrids are being tested for future landscape use. Their silver foliage is undeniably gorgeous; hopefully, some will sucker less aggressively or not at all while retaining this plant's many wildlife benefits.

Propagation: seed (stratify); cuttings | **Companion plants:** junipers, spruces, and pines; grasses such as little bluestem and ruby muhly; rabbitbrush, Apache plume, and golden currant; Maximilian sunflower, horsemint, and aromatic aster; prickly poppy, Rocky Mountain beeplant, snow on the mountain, cowpen daisy, and sunflowers

Symphoricarpos spp.

common snowberry, western snowberry, mountain snowberry

zones 3–8 • meadows, slopes, mesas, woodland, roadsides, near streams and lakes; plains, foothills, shrub steppe, montane • most well-drained soils

1.5–5 ft. × 6–8 ft. and wider • chaparral-inspired planting, hillside planting, casual perimeter hedge

sun, light shade • low to moderate water

A handful of snowberry species are native here; all are arching, graceful deciduous shrubs that spread by suckering roots and make low thickets over time. Soft green to blue-green, rounded to oval leaves grow in pairs along stems. In late spring or early summer depending on altitude and latitude, small, bell-shaped, fragrant white or pink flowers open in clusters and later ripen into showy, white, oval to rounded fruits (quite valuable to wildlife) by late summer. Fruits often persist into winter.

One of the faster-growing of our shrubs, thrives in shade as well as sun. In light shade they are quite water-thrifty and the white fruits show up best. Most commonly available are: common snowberry (*Symphoricarpos albus*); western snowberry (*S. occidentalis*), which has slightly larger, thicker, more blue gray-green foliage, spreads the most rapidly, and has less persistent, not as bright fruit; and mountain snowberry (*S. rotundifolius*, formerly *S. oreophilus*), which thrives best in cooler conditions and is lower-growing. It also grows a bit less rambunctiously; flowers are shapelier and bell-like. *S. longiflorus* has the prettiest flowers, is most xeric, but is picky about site.

Great used alone as a loose, naturalistic planting among trees or on banks and hillsides.

Propagation: cuttings; suckers | **Companion plants:** junipers, pines, and white fir; aspen or birch

Trees

On an individual basis, trees are perhaps our most precious wild plants. Longer-lived than most other plants, with aboveground structure that gives protection and places for rearing young, they are natural homes and waystations for all sorts of animals. Their size and large root systems allow them to tap into and store water and soil-nutrient reserves to produce an enormous amount of biomass each year in the form of foliage, flowers, fruits, and seed. Untold numbers of insects depend on these tree parts as food and places to reproduce. This forms the basis of the animal food chain, as entomologist, author, and pioneering ecologist Doug Tallamy describes so evocatively in his groundbreaking books *Bringing Nature Home* and *Nature's Best Hope*. Without trees and the insects they support, the web of life loses a huge and essential resource. Our region is also home to many shrubs, grasses, and wildflowers that perform similar functions, but in terms of what one person can do, planting one native tree that will thrive on your site has a larger long-term effect than planting one or even numerous other types of native plants.

The Rocky Mountain region encompasses large wild areas that have natural forest ecosystems, for the most part dominated by evergreen needled trees, known as conifers, with patches of leafy deciduous trees interspersed and along watercourses. At lower elevations and in drier areas where most people in our part of the world have settled and live, most trees can't and don't exist unless they root along a year-round water source or into an unusually high water table, either natural or due to human intervention. With fewer native choices of tree species, large shrubs that can easily be trained into vase-shaped, multi-trunked specimens can be and are often pressed into tree service and are included here.

So unless you live at quite high elevation or in an unusually moist spot, if you want to grow trees you'll most likely need to provide additional water to keep your tree(s) alive and thriving. This is true of the majority of native trees we recommend in the following pages. In nature most of these plants either grow at higher, moister elevations, in mountain ravines, or along watercourses in the lower, flatter parts of the region. A few species need very little extra water once established, others need additional water regularly throughout their existence, and all require diligent watering during the first few years of establishment, including monthly in winter when temperatures allow. Make sure you water an area on the ground the same diameter or wider than the height of the tree. This encourages wide rooting, stabilizing the tree and giving it better ability to mine for moisture when it receives less help from the hose or spigot as it matures. Many trees struggle in dense lawns that are irrigated frequently but shallowly. Water trees separately, less often, and more deeply, and put mulch or plant shade-tolerant wildflowers such as columbines in their shadows, not turf.

Trees provide much-needed shade in this sunny, often hot part of the world and can buffer and divert strong winds that blow across the backbone and roof of the continent that we call home. Instead of relying on air conditioning and huddling indoors during the sunniest, hottest parts of the day and year, it makes more sense to plant one or several well-adapted native deciduous shade trees on the east, south, and/or especially the west side of the home, blocking sunlight during summer months but allowing the sun to warm and light the home in winter. Conifers are good on the north side to protect the home from prevailing cold winds, but if you live in a fire-prone area, it's best to keep these more-flammable trees at least thirty feet or more from the house and to clean up and remove dry, fallen needles regularly.

In areas that deer, elk, or moose frequent, you'll need to cage or fence young trees until they reach a height that the animals won't be able to browse into oblivion. Putting wire cages around young trunks protects the trees from animals' rubbing.

Propagation of the following trees is only discussed if the species is very fast-growing and/or is difficult to find in the trade. For most residential purposes it makes little sense to start trees from seed or cuttings, because of the length of time it takes to reach a decent-sized specimen and the amount of care a young, recently propagated and potted tree needs over the several years before it is ready to go into the ground.

Abies concolor

white fir

zones 3 or 4–7 • ravines, canyons, along rocky streambanks; foothills, montane • sandy or gritty soils

30–50 ft. × 15–30 ft. • accent evergreen or small grouping

sun, light shade • moderate water

Seeing a mountain slope spangled with white fir is magical, like from a fairytale. This softly elegant evergreen's Christmas-tree shape and shimmering gray-green or blue-green needles give it year-round appeal. Similar Colorado spruce has stiffer, shorter, prickly needles and often becomes straggly over time. White fir grows more slowly but remains beautiful at any age, often sporting striking, upward-held purple cones in early summer. Small mammals eat the seeds from this tree.

Provide mulch and extra water during drought periods, especially in spring and fall. If planted in full year-round sun, site it away from strong prevailing winter winds. Be aware that the tree may be browsed by deer, especially when young.

Bright, silvery blue selections exist, as do less common compact and dwarf forms. Subalpine fir (*Abies lasiocarpa*) is similar to white fir but needs cooler summer temperatures and more dependable year-round moisture to thrive.

Propagation: best to buy | **Companion plants:** bigtooth maple and smooth sumac

Acer grandidentatum (*Acer saccharum* ssp. *grandidentatum*)

bigtooth maple, Wasatch maple

zones 3–8 • slopes, canyons, streamsides; foothills, montane • most well-drained soils

20–40 ft. × 15–30 ft. • accent or grove, perimeter screening, mixed with evergreen trees

sun, light shade • low to moderate water

Our native shade-tree options without aggressive root systems, weak wood, or a need for significant extra water are few. This maple thrives on our alkaline soils and needs much less additional water than many of our native deciduous trees. Strong branches and sturdy structure rarely suffer breakage in wind or snow, making them popular trees for nesting. Birds also sometimes eat the small, lime-green early flowers.

One of the latest trees to leaf out, this maple avoids damage by late-spring snows or freezes. The medium-green, five-lobed leaves unfurl in late spring. These are tough, taking little wind or hail damage, yet still transmit light to the ground below. This makes it possible to grow plants beneath a grove.

Winged seeds in pairs, called samaras, dangle on the tree in summer before drying and dropping. Fall color is often dramatic orange or crimson, and selections have been made for such: upright oval Mesa Glow® (for narrower spaces and groves), and extra large and wide Rocky Mountain Glow® (a solitary shade tree).

Easy to transplant and establish. In hotter areas, plant on the north or east side of a building.

Propagation: best to buy | **Companion plants:** pines, spruces, or junipers

Alnus incana ssp. *tenuifolia*

thinleaf alder

15–30 ft. × 12–20 ft. • along watercourses; plains, foothills, montane • most moist soils

zones 2–7 • groupings/groves, tall hedges

sun, light shade • moderate water to moist

Grows naturally into a small, multi-stemmed oval tree with smooth gray bark but can be easily pruned and trained to have only one trunk. An ideal well-behaved tree for moist spots and a great substitute for aspen where the latter's suckering is problematic or in hot-summer regions where aspen suffer from stress and disease.

Pleated leaves are tidy but unremarkable until autumn, when they turn a rich, warm gold before dropping. In early spring, small, clustered yellow- and ruddy-colored catkins bloom. Some of these (the female catkins) mature to petite, dark brown, cone-like fruits with seeds that birds relish. The fruits' tracery at the ends of the twigs persists all winter, giving the tree a textural outline during the dormant season, especially against a blanket of snow.

Grows quite quickly and deserves to be chosen for consistently moist or sometimes-swampy conditions where willows and nonnative oaks, maples, and hybrid selections are often planted. Willows are weak-wooded, and the other trees mentioned often show chlorosis (summer leaf yellowing, reduced vigor) in our region's soils. This small tree performs without any of those drawbacks.

Propagation: seed (stratify) | **Companion plants:** Colorado spruce

Betula occidentalis (*Betula fontinalis*)

western birch, water birch

zones 3–6 • moist mountain valleys and hillsides; plains, foothills, montane • most moist soils

15–35 ft. × 10–25 ft. • casual grouping, hedgerow for moist or wet spots

sun, light shade • moderate water to moist

This graceful, small shrubby tree should be left to develop into its natural multi-stemmed form (i.e., don't try to train it to grow with a single trunk). Its casual habit and pliable trunks and limbs don't lend themselves to growing in the straight manner a single trunk calls for, and the tree will continually sprout new shoots from the base. For a native birch that does well with a single trunk, choose paper birch (*Betula papyrifera*) instead.

Grows faster than most native trees here, yet unlike some other speedy species, it rarely breaks in strong wind or from ice or heavy snow loads. Even when bent almost to the ground, it will bounce back up once released from the weight. Gets quite full and broad, yet still appears light and airy thanks to slender, arching branches and small, delicately toothed, fresh-green foliage. Leaves turn a pretty, warm yellow in fall. Beautiful shiny, coppery bark with pale dots and lines accentuates the tree's sprightly silhouette after the leaves have dropped and shimmers in winter sun with a backdrop of snow.

Propagation: best to buy | **Companion plants:** compact Colorado spruce selections; common juniper

Betula papyrifera

paper birch, white birch

zones 2–6 • along watercourses; plains, foothills, montane • most moist soils

50–70 ft. × 15–25 ft. • accent tree, grouping or grove for moist spots

sun, light shade • moderate water to moist

Has one of the most stunning barks of any tree—pure white, peeling in paper-like strips, with unique black horizontal markings on the trunks and main branches of maturing trees. Whether you decide to train the tree to grow with a single trunk or allow it to have several, these year-round, stunning pale vertical accents make this birch worth planting in any site that offers a cool, moist root run. Pruning to remove the lowest branches uncovers the trunk(s) and heightens the color and vertical drama. Small mammals eat the tree's seeds.

Grows quickly into an oval-crowned, large tree, so give it room. Soft yellow catkins bloom in early spring with a much less subtle yellow reprise come fall, when the entire tree becomes a luminescent beacon before dropping its leaves for winter. Trunk, catkins, and fall foliage of paper birch all call out for a darker background to show them off—either from a dark-hued building facade or from evergreens.

Propagation: best to buy | **Companion plants:** Douglas fir or green-needled Colorado spruce

Celtis occidentalis

western hackberry

zones 3–9 • grassland, savanna, watercourse margins, bluffs; plains • most soils

40–60 ft. × 40–60 ft. • shade tree, street tree, living windbreak

sun, light shade • low water to moist

Spectacularly average at a glance, but redeems itself as a superb larval host that produces berries enjoyed by many creatures—even its galls provide morsels for birds. A dull green-lollipop during growing season without mentionable bloom or colorful fall display. With a twiggy form and propensity to develop nipple gall (odd, raised growths on leaves) and "witches' brooms" (dense clusters of twiggy growth), it can be downright homely.

Also stands out for best-in-class durability, enduring drought, cold, heat, and wind with aplomb and requiring little water after establishment. Does best with a warm growing season and may not thrive in cool mountain areas.

Netleaf hackberry (*C. reticulata*) is a smaller native tree better adapted to a shorter season. Grows slowly, with arching branches and leaves arranged in a zigzag pattern. Offers similar wildlife benefit but is even more drought-tolerant and attains only half the size. Requires well-drained soils; less prone to brooms and galls. (While they typically cause no decline in vigor, both brooms and galls can be selected against by choosing resistant cultivars.)

Propagation: seed (stratify) | **Companion plants:** junipers and pines; among shrubs with similarly excellent wildlife benefits, such as silver buffaloberry, silverberry, American plum, and sumac

Cercocarpus ledifolius

curl-leaf mountain mahogany

zones 4–8 • dry slopes, rocky sites; foothills, pinyon-juniper • most well-drained soils

10–20 ft. × 8–12 ft. • accent, chaparral-inspired planting, hedge, backdrop to unwatered flower garden

sun • very low to low water

Taller and faster-growing than its cousin littleleaf mountain mahogany, this small tree or large shrub is similarly semi-evergreen but prone to winter burn. Leaves are narrowly oval, glossy rich green, pale underneath, and roll under. Tiny, inconspicuous, creamy flowers produce seeds with long, pale, feathery tails that capture low light in a surprising and beautiful way, transforming the plant.

Gives scale to a space and planting and creates a sense of age; also makes an excellent wildlife shelter with its tall, twiggy, dense growth offering hiding, resting, and nesting opportunities out of reach of most predators.

With patience and pruning, can be trained to have no lower branches or foliage. Can also be sheared if desired; otherwise it will develop a picturesque, irregular habit and crown. Has an upright, multi-trunked habit that opens up and becomes more billowing over time. Deer like to browse this plant, and other mammals eat its seeds.

Can be pruned regularly for more formality of shape if that look is desired.

Propagation: best to buy; seed (scarify then stratify) | **Companion plants:** junipers, sagebrush, rabbitbrush, winterfat, and shepherdia; giant sacaton

Chilopsis linearis

desert willow

zones 5–8 • arroyos at lower elevations in southernmost parts of region; plains • sandy or gritty soils

10–20 ft. × 10–20 ft. • accent tree for patio, near building

sun • low water

A beautiful small tree, native only to a few warm spots regionally. Hardy selections have come through -30°F, so it's worth growing in areas with hot summers. Willow-like, narrow green foliage emerges late in spring, avoiding most late frosts. From early summer well into fall, large, ruffled, foxglove-like blossoms continue to open. These can be pink, burgundy, white, or bicolored, often have freckled throats, and are softly fragrant.

Leave it to grow multi-stemmed (more options for resprouting after a harsh winter). Becomes hardier as it matures—dieback to the ground is more likely for a young specimen. Don't think it's dead if this happens; given until midsummer to send up new shoots, it usually will. Should be spring-planted in our region; is deer-resistant. Discontinue irrigation from early fall onward to harden it off for winter. Needs a bit of cleanup in spring of winter tip dieback and persistent seedpod clusters.

Hardy selections include white-flowered 'Hope', pink 'Paradise', and Santa Fe plantsman David Salman's 'Conchas Dam Pink' and seedless 'Everpink' (which blooms more profusely into fall and forms no seedpods). Give desert willows reflected heat from walls, stone or gravel patios, or driveways.

Propagation: seed; cuttings | **Companion plants:** angel's trumpet

Forestiera pubescens var. *pubescens*
(*Forestiera neomexicana*)

desert olive, New Mexican privet

zones 4–8 • lower elevations, hillsides, mesas, moist valleys, both dry and riparian sites; plains, foothills • most well-drained soils

10–15 ft. × 8–10 ft. • shelterbelts, hedges, casual accent for patio or near house

sun • low water

In early spring while still leafless, this small, vase-shaped, multi-stemmed tree is enveloped in a bee-filled haze of tiny yellow flowers. Then small lime-green leaves unfurl, a refreshing contrast to the muted greens and grays of low-water plantings. In summer, female plants bear loads of bird-beloved, blueberry-like fruits when a male plant grows nearby. Plant several individuals to ensure having both sexes, or look for the sexed selections 'Happy Boy' and 'Berry Girl'. Larger nursery-grown female plants often bear fruit while in their pots in late summer, which is helpful when shopping. This tree is especially valuable to wildlife.

Come fall, leaves change to luminescent yellow. Many but not all of these trees have lovely pale bark, especially noticeable in winter. Large branches may flop in heavy snow but rarely break, and they spring back if snow is removed within a day or two. Thoughtful, role-specific pruning helps this fast-growing small tree adapt to being either a specimen tree or part of a hedge. It is quick and easy to establish with regular additional water to start.

Propagation: seed (stratify); cuttings | **Companion plants:** junipers and pines

Gleditsia triacanthos

honey locust

zones 3 or 4–9 • savannas, drainages, watercourses; plains • most soils

60+ ft. × 40 ft. • shade tree, specimen tree, street tree, allées

sun • low water to moist

Against the horizon on the plains, looks like it would be more at home on the African savanna than the North American prairie. This is no accident; it coevolved with large mammals like those still found in Africa and has three-inch-long spines—which prevent browsing—to prove it. Available selections are bred to be thornless. Many are also seedless, a debatable improvement; while patios and sidewalks stay cleaner, the large seeds feed many animals.

Blooms in late spring with sweet-scented but drab flower spikes that nevertheless brim with nectar. Transplants well and is quite drought-tolerant once established, offering light, dappled shade. Can struggle in a lawn unless it's watered separately, less often, and more deeply than lawns typically are.

In the mountains or colder areas, plant in locations with radiant and reflected heat (such as near stone or pavement). Avoids spring frosts by pushing foliage quite late, up to a month after other trees. Displays rich gold fall color and drops its leaves a bit earlier than many trees. This trait, combined with wide-angled branch architecture and late-spring bud, helps it resist breakage in heavy snows.

Propagation: best to buy | **Companion plants:** white fir or Colorado spruce; bigtooth maple

Juniperus monosperma

one-seed juniper

zones 4–7 • desert scrub; plains, foothills, pinyon-juniper • most well-drained soils

8–20 ft. × 8–15 ft. • year-round screening, chaparral-type planting

sun • very low water

Grows quickly into an irregular, rounded shape that looks aged and picturesque in very little time. Typically multi-trunked with reddish brown bark, it stays shorter and grows wider than its cousin Rocky Mountain juniper and is olive-green rather than a blue or gray-green hue. The textural, spreading branches turn upward at their ends, giving some individuals an almost flame-like appearance. The plant's warm green color lends a richness to the dusty greens and grays of many other dryland plants.

Female plants produce round, blue, one-seeded fruits that turn coppery tan as they dry. The mature scaled foliage is prickly to the touch, making it unpleasant to work under and to prune (which it rarely needs).

This is an ideal evergreen tree for the harshest and driest sites, providing food and shelter to birds and small mammals and serving as a windbreak and beautifier for properties.

Propagation: best to buy | **Companion plants:** wavyleaf oak, pinyon, sagebrush, winterfat, and littleleaf mountain mahogany

Juniperus scopulorum

Rocky Mountain juniper

zones 3–7 • draws and canyons, lower-elevation mesas; montane; foothills, pinyon-juniper • most well-drained soils

10–30 ft. × 10–15 ft. • year-round screening, wildlife shelterbelt, evergreen accent tree

sun • low water

Grows slowly into a pyramidal to upright, rounded small tree, either single-trunked or multi-stemmed—symmetrical, yet not as formal as triangular firs and spruces. It outdoes those trees in tolerance for a wider range of soils and moisture regimes. (Newly planted specimens still need supplemental watering for a couple years.)

Scaly, evergreen foliage sprays vary from dark green to silvery blue and may take on plum, lavender, or coppery hues in winter. The slender, pliable younger growth gives the tree a soft, almost-fuzzy outline. Female junipers bear round, pale blue fruits, popular among wildlife.

If a uniquely narrow look is warranted, try 'Woodward' (splays less in heavy snow than other selections). Junipers rarely break, but bent branches don't spring back and require tedious tucking back or even tying. Grow in lean, dry conditions to promote a stronger branching framework with denser wood that's less prone to splaying.

Utah juniper, *J. osteosperma*, similar to one-seed juniper, makes a better choice for sites that are very hot and dry. It's a rich, warm green, grows wider than tall, and has much larger fruit.

Propagation: best to buy | **Companion plants:** desert olive and bigtooth maple; chokecherry, sand cherry, American plum, and golden currant

Picea glauca 'Densata' (*Picea glauca* var. *densata*)

Black Hills spruce, white spruce

zones 2–6 • streamsides, seasonally moist slopes; foothills, montane • most moist soils

30 ft. × 15 ft. • specimen tree, windbreaks, screening

sun, light shade • moderate water to moist

Named *glauca* for the attractive, smooth, whitish or blue-green cast on the needles of mature specimens, this plant is considered the most garden-worthy form of the broadly distributed white spruce. Formerly considered a botanical variety called *Picea glauca* var. *densata*, Black Hills spruce is sold both under that old name as well as the name *Picea glauca* 'Densata'. Regardless of how it is classified, this white spruce, originating as an isolated population in the Black Hills, grows slowly to moderately, producing an unusually dense, fine-textured, and naturally compact spruce tree with symmetrical form. In landscapes, these picturesque, blue-green trees make ideal living specimens for holiday lights, especially when sited where they can be enjoyed from indoors.

In nature, Black Hills spruce thrives in wetter locations such as drainages and on slopes that hold significant snow cover. In the landscape, trees are adaptable but suffer in hot or dry sites, as this species is well-suited to cooler portions of our region.

Propagation: seed (stratify) | **Companion plants:** birch, aspen, or alder; red-twig dogwood, snowberry, and wax currant

Picea pungens

Colorado spruce, blue spruce

30–60 ft. × 10–20 ft., taller in the wild • moist slopes, ravines, along streams; foothills, montane • most moist soils

zones 2–7 • accent tree, screening, windbreak in cool regions

sun • moderate water to moist

This grand plant is the state tree of Colorado and probably the western native most planted elsewhere. Thrives in cool conditions, so in hotter, drier sites plant on the north or east side of a building. Stiff, prickly needles radiate around the stout twigs, and large, light brown cones hang from upper branches.

This eventually gargantuan tree overwhelms many front yards. Give it space, as its symmetrical, dense, pyramidal form and often-icy-blue color make it overwhelmingly dominant. Thankfully, there are dozens of compact and dwarf selections—flat-topped, conical, columnar, rounded, weeping, green, gray, and blue.

Can get sparse and scraggly with age, especially if grown dry or in excessive shade. Don't remove the skirt of lower branches; very little will grow around the tree's base, and such limbing-up ruins the tree's shape and removes its natural self-shading and self-mulching habit.

Green forms deserve more use, as they lend a natural freshness to the year-round landscape—pick green trees from seedling nursery plants. Water consistently and broadly the first few years after planting to nurture the wide-spreading fibrous root system.

Propagation: best to buy | **Companion plants:** thinleaf alder, birches, or aspen; rockspray, elderberry, mock orange, or Oregon grapeholly

Pinus aristata

bristlecone pine, foxtail pine

zones 2–6 • exposed ridges, slopes; montane, subalpine • most well-drained soils

20–30 ft. × 15–20 ft., extremely slow-growing; 8–12 ft. × 6–10 ft. in landscapes • accent plant, rock gardens, evergreen grouping for wildlife shelter

sun • low to moderate water

Just below or at treeline in many western mountain ranges, twisted and gnarled bristlecone pines—among the earth's most ancient beings—cling to life, some several thousand years old. This striking medium-sized evergreen grows slowly and irregularly—lush, full, yet picturesque. Keeps its dense, dark green needles along the length of the branches, giving it a furry look. Shrub-like when young, its irregular branching gives a landscape a settled, romantic feel. Some individuals exude droplets of white resin along their needles, with an almost-frosty effect. Egg-shaped, shiny brown cones become prickly when ripe and dry.

In heavy soils, give it a berm or slope to help drainage. In hot locations, a north or east exposure and mulching of the root zone help keep the tree's roots cooler. Resents root disturbance, so established container-grown plants or those grown in root-control bags in nursery fields establish more dependably than balled and burlapped nursery trees. Buy small and enjoy this unique pine without expecting great size in your lifetime. In some ways it's ideal to leave bristlecone unpaired, so its unique growth habit and texture can be allowed to shine solo.

Propagation: best to buy | **Companion plants:** bigtooth maple; Rocky Mountain juniper

Pinus contorta var. *latifolia* 'Taylor's Sunburst'

Taylor's Sunburst lodgepole pine

zones 3–7 • dry slopes; foothills, montane, subalpine • most well-drained soils

12–15 ft. × 8–10 ft. • accent tree

sun • low to moderate water

Lodgepole pines typically grow quite tall with a rangy, open, gawky-teenager habit. By contrast, the compact selection 'Taylor's Sunburst', with stunning yellow new growth, merits pride of place where it can shine. Discovered in the Colorado mountains by the late plantsman Allan Taylor, this special tree grows at medium speed, maturing to a dense, upright oval shape. Small, tan, egg-shaped seed cones persist for years, and in spring lipstick-red pollen cones decorate the upper part of the tree, which by late summer becomes uniformly green. Irregular, stout branches, densely clothed in short, twisted, paired needles, give the plant character even when young.

Does best in full sun except in very hot, dry sites, where the north or east side of a building with some shade and more moisture retention is preferred. Not much will grow at its base; don't remove the lower branches unless they have died off. The skirt of lower branches naturally shades the tree's roots, conserves moisture, and reduces stress.

Colorful native plants don't blend so well with this bold showstopper; best with woody plants and grasses.

Propagation: best to buy | **Companion plants:** Gambel oak, currants, or sumacs; compact blue forms of white fir or Colorado spruce

Pinus edulis (*Pinus cembroides* var. *edulis*)

pinyon pine

zones 4–8 • dry grassland, dry mesas, hillsides; foothills, pinyon-juniper, montane • most well-drained soils

12–20 ft. × 12–15 ft. • casual grouping, evergreen accent, wildlife shelter planting

sun • very low water

This iconic southern Rocky Mountain native offers greenness, shade, shelter, and when in season, delicious pine nuts in the harsh, dry, rocky wild places it inhabits. Grows slowly into a shrubby, irregularly rounded evergreen tree. Round reddish brown cones produce the edible seeds. The disjunct northern pinyon population in Owl Canyon north of Fort Collins—steep, rocky hillsides crowded with these pines—is a lovely and mysterious surprise for anyone driving toward the Wyoming border.

Selections 'Farmy' and 'Trinidad' are two very dwarf brooms found by Colorado conifer expert Jerry Morris and grafted and grown by Fort Collins nurseryman Kirk Fieseler as part of the regional Plant Select program. These look mature almost immediately with their dense, extremely slow growth habit, making them ideal choices for small spaces and rock gardens.

Wild-dug and balled and burlapped pinyons are common; wild-dug should always be avoided and discouraged. Both often struggle to establish; look for plants grown in root-control bags in nursery fields, seedlings grown in containers for at least a year, or several-year-old container-grown seedlings.

Propagation: seed (stratify) | **Companion plants:** any waterwise plant

Pinus flexilis

limber pine

zones 3–7 • slopes, rocky ledges, exposed ridges; foothills, montane, subalpine • most well-drained soils

30–50 ft. × 15–35 ft. • casual grouping, picturesque evergreen accent, wildlife shelter plantings

sun • low water

This slow-growing evergreen tree deserves more attention for its adaptability and beautiful soft green, sometimes blue-green, often-twisted needles. Branches bend with snow loads, then spring back up and are so flexible they can be tied into knots. Has a picturesque upright yet irregular and open form and a variable habit. Its windswept look adds character and age to a planting.

Sometimes a particular selection of a plant can unfortunately dominate the market—in this case, the popular 'Vanderwolf's Pyramid'. This uncharacteristically symmetrical, fast-growing, and not particularly water-thrifty selection is often the only limber pine to be had. Though beautiful, it doesn't have the wild, natural look or toughness of seedling species from the harsher, more interior parts of the species' range, and its full, fluffy, more formal look blends best in more lush, traditional plantings.

Dwarf selections from brooms, including some found by Colorado conifer expert Jerry Morris, look mature even when small and are very slow-growing. Compact, narrow, and weeping forms are also available.

Propagation: seed (stratify) | **Companion plants:** bigtooth maple, sumac, or sand cherry

Pinus ponderosa

ponderosa pine, western yellow pine

zones 3–7 • dry slopes, mesas; foothills, montane • sandy or gritty soils

50–60 ft. × 20–30 ft. • large-specimen evergreen, shade tree, wildlife shelter planting, windbreaks

sun • very low water

Grows in open groupings in the wild, especially in dry, hilly terrain, creating the classic pine savanna. Long, coarse needles cluster in stiff bushy bundles and are a medium green, giving the trees' sunny, open haunts a cheerful feeling. Grows slowly without access to extra moisture, developing an irregular, open, rounded crown over time.

Trees lose their lower limbs with age, making this one of the best evergreens for sitting under. Attractive, large, rounded prickly cones litter and persist on the ground beneath mature trees, so a seat or pillow helps. On warm, wind-still days the lovely, thick, flaking orange and tan bark smells like vanilla to some (butterscotch to others).

Vigilant extra watering for at least two years after planting is vital for establishment. Wild- or field-dug plants often struggle to reestablish because their sparse root system has been disturbed; container-grown plants establish much more successfully. This tree dislikes competition from other trees and is flammable, so give it pride of place away from the house, with plenty of space and no tree or large shrub companions—just a nice bench at its base once it grows tall enough to sit beneath.

Propagation: seed (stratify) | **Companion plants:** none

Pinus strobiformis

southwestern white pine

zones 5–7 • ravines, streamsides, cool sites with seasonal moisture; foothills, montane, subalpine • most well-drained soils

30–50 ft. × 20–30 ft. • large-specimen evergreen, screening, wildlife shelter planting

sun • low water

One of our region's most beautiful and underused evergreens. Its pyramidal shape becomes more rounded with age and has a full, soft look. Closely related to limber pine and shares many of its characteristics: soft needles, elongated cones, and very flexible twigs and branches. A few experts consider the hardier form of this plant an intermediate between the two species and call it *Pinus reflexa*; it is suited to the winter rigors of our region.

Protection from strong winds, especially in winter, is important as the needles can burn in exposed sites. Anecdotal experience suggests that keeping this pine drier during the latter part of the growing season (after the new growth has fully expanded) may help it harden off sooner for winter and be less vulnerable to foliage damage. However, during a drought, no plant should be left entirely to its own devices—trees weakened by drought will succumb to damage from extreme weather or insects.

Other forms available include the compact, very blue 'Loma Linda'; 'Coronado', a true dwarf that makes an irregular, almost horizontally growing specimen; and, occasionally, truly prostrate forms.

Propagation: seed (stratify) | **Companion plants:** bigtooth maple, desert olive, and sumac

Populus angustifolia

narrowleaf cottonwood

zones 3–7 • watercourses, drainages, areas with seasonally raised water tables; plains, foothills, shrub steppe, montane • most moist soils

60 ft. × unlimited spread • windbreak, wildlife shelterbelt; tough-as-nails landscape tree where there is room

sun • moderate water to moist

Some might wonder why this book includes this species, unsuitable as it is for smaller properties due to its soft, brittle wood and suckering. While not flashy (it's like a narrower, more reserved-looking version of plains cottonwood), this tree is among the most resilient in our region, unfazed by poor soils and only made longer-lived by wind toughening its vigorous growth. In extraordinarily harsh intermountain parks such as the Bighorn Basin, it makes welcome windbreaks for houses and critters.

Easily picked out in those haunts, it rises above streams and low, grassy meadows, among the only trees to be found. Makes premiere nesting and perching spots for birds; it's also an exceptional larval host, a good food source for adult insects, and shelter and forage for birds and mammals.

Hybridizes freely with other native cottonwoods. For the coldest, harshest sites, consider Balsam poplar (*Populus balsamifera*) and its hybrids, which are even more cold-hardy than this tree but with a less attractive form.

Suckers vigorously to form loose woods or thickets; this can be controlled by mowing or grazing and is less vigorous in harsher sites. Tolerates periodic drought and flooding once established.

Propagation: suckers; cuttings; fresh seed (light) | **Companion plants:** none

Populus deltoides (*Populus sargentii*)

plains cottonwood

zones 3–8 • along watercourses and in floodplains; plains, foothills • most moist soils, soils with high water tables

60–90 ft. × 40–60 ft. • specimen shade tree, wildlife tree

sun • moderate water to moist

Arguably the grandest of our deciduous native trees. Serves as a massive hotel and smorgasbord, offering shelter and nesting sites to waterfowl, raptors (including owls), many other birds, and squirrels. Early spring-blooming catkins feed birds, and the foliage and bark feed many insects in both adult and larval phases (including butterfly larvae), which in turn feed birds and their young. Meanwhile, deer browse the foliage.

Grows quickly, developing large, coarse trunks and scaffold branches with fissured, sculptural, dark gray bark. Shiny, triangular fresh-green foliage rustles in breezes and turns a rich bright gold early in fall.

Keep this tree away from buildings; it often loses large older limbs. It's messy, dropping loads of springtime catkins, twigs after every wind, leaves in fall, and even sappy insect exudates. Some town ordinances allow planting of only male trees because of the fluffy white "cotton" that female trees release to the wind in early summer. Not just messy, the cotton can irritate people's respiratory tracts. Despite all this, a wonderful specimen for the back forty if you have a moist spot, a high water table, or water (such as a creek) on your property.

Propagation: suckers; cuttings; fresh seed (light)
Companion plants: none

Populus tremuloides

aspen, quaking aspen

zones 2–6 • moist slopes, cool ravines, along streams; foothills, montane, subalpine • most moist soils

20–50 ft. × unlimited spread

sun, light shade • moderate water

This icon of the high country, the most widespread tree in North America, supports a large web of life year-round, even offering browse in harsh winters. At lower elevations with hotter summers, the warmer, heavier soils and drier conditions weaken aspen, making them prone to disease and insect attack. Planting on the cooler north or east sides of a building, preferably with access to rain run-off, helps a great deal. Even in the wild, trees grow quickly but are short-lived, typically replaced after twenty to thirty years by their own suckers. These colonies are some of Earth's largest single organisms, often centuries old.

In spring before leaves emerge, silvery catkins hang like tinsel. Then small, rounded, light green foliage expands, rustling in breezes. In autumn, bright yellow (less commonly orange-red) fall color lures leaf-peeping drivers. Come winter, the white bark with black branch scars takes center stage.

Be prepared to continually cut back or mow suckers if you want a single trunk or just a small clump. Or leave aspen to ramble and become visual screens; the rustling foliage helps drown out unwanted noise.

Propagation: suckers; fresh seed (light); cuttings | **Companion plants:** columbines, harebell, wood lily, horsemint, and golden banner

Pseudotsuga menziesii var. *glauca*

Rocky Mountain Douglas fir

zones 3–7 • moist slopes, valleys, waterway edges; foothills, montane, subalpine • most moist soils

80 ft. × 40 ft. • accent tree, windbreak, screening tree

sun, light shade • moderate water

With a scientific name meaning "Menzies' false hemlock" and a common name that was originally "Douglas' spruce," this tree may be our top pick for most likely to have an identity crisis. Laughably, it isn't a true fir either, as the current common name suggests, but has a genus of its own. Ironically, it is among the easiest of our native conifers to identify—simply look for half-inch-long "mouse tails" protruding from the cone scales.

A beautiful conifer, with fine-textured, short needles and a clean, conical shape. Bark is handsome and rugged, cracking into large, geometric shapes and developing a warm, reddish brown color with age. Foliage varies from a forest-green to a dusty blue. A widespread species growing throughout the Rockies from Mexico to Canada, inhabits cool microclimates in warmer portions of its range, while thriving in warmer microclimates in cooler portions of the rwegion. At low elevations or in southern portions of the region, thoughtful siting on the north or east side of a building and the use of mulch or living groundcovers benefit this tree.

Propagation: seed (stratify) | **Companion plants:** bigtooth maple; birch and aspen; serviceberry, redroot, rockspray, mock orange, boulder raspberry, and snowberry

Quercus macrocarpa

bur oak, mossy-cup oak

zones 3–8 • savannas, woodland; plains • most soils

50–60 ft. × 40–50 ft. • shade tree, specimen tree

sun • low to moderate water

One of our largest and best shade trees; long-lived, thrifty, and easy to grow things beneath thanks to deep roots. Foliage, bark, and habit are coarser than chinkapin oak's, and this grows more slowly. Looks rugged even at a gawky, young age, but as its scaffold branches develop and grow sinuously outward and even downward, becomes a sculptural character in the landscape.

Large, coarsely lobed, leathery, dark green foliage shows pale undersides in the wind. Fall color is typically a dull yellowish brown. A great kid's tree with its big, fringe-cupped acorns and strong climbing branches. When planted in the open where its venerable, heavy silhouette and corky furrowed bark can be appreciated, it has a fairy-tale or council-tree quality.

Leaves can be ragged from insect damage by late summer, as it hosts a variety of chewers, miners, gall-makers, and other insect larvae and adults, but the tree carries on as a hub for wildlife. Many mammals and large birds eat the acorns; some nest in the strong branches.

Regular additional moisture speeds growth somewhat. This stately tree makes a great natural home cooler on the west side of a house.

Propagation: fresh acorns (stratify) | **Companion plants:** many

Quercus muehlenbergii (Quercus prinoides)

chinquapin oak

zones 5–8 • mesas, canyons, rocky uplands, moist but well-drained bottomlands; plains • most well-drained soils

40–50 ft. × 40–50 ft. • shade tree, specimen tree

sun • low water

Oaks are among the most long-lived and tough trees and rank as our most important wildlife trees, but only a few are well-adapted to our region's dry, cold climate and often alkaline soils. Though native only to the edges of our region, this species thrives here and deserves to help replace the overused ash. A truly low-water shade tree, yet has a medium to fast growth rate depending on water availability. Leathery olive-green foliage is lush yet casual. Often somewhat shiny, toothed, oval leaves are silvery gray or sometimes pale yellow beneath, creating a bicolored, shimmery effect in wind. In spring, tiny yellowish flowers dangle on long stalks.

Fall foliage color varies from brownish gold to orange, red, and deep russet. Holds its leaves late into fall and often through winter, dropping them as the new foliage emerges. 'Fort Collins Select' has good reddish fall color.

This oak's mature shape is not overly regular but still stately and handsome enough for a large-specimen or shade tree; can be pruned to make a good street tree. Its deep, benevolent root system allows all sorts of plantings to thrive in the shade beneath it.

Propagation: fresh acorns (stratify) | **Companion plants:** many

Salix amygdaloides

peachleaf willow

zones 2–7 • along streams and ditches, moist sites; plains, foothills • most soils

40–60 ft. × 40–60 ft. • fast-growing shade tree for moist locations, wildlife tree

sun • moderate water to moist

The only tree-form willow native to our region (the rest are shrubby and often spread aggressively). Willows have high wildlife value and stabilize streambanks with their dense, wide root systems. This species does all that and more: its thick branches and trunk also provide cavity nesting sites for birds.

The deciduous leaves—narrow, pointed, and somewhat glossy—give the tree its common name. They emerge, chartreuse, early in the season, adding to the landscape's lovely lime-green haze as winter gives way to spring. Foliage turns a soft yellow in fall, and the coppery, fine-textured tracery of its bare twigs add warmth to the wintry landscape. Plump, creamy yellow catkins emerge in spring, announcing its arrival, providing great early food for bees, and starting the cycle anew.

Usually a sprawling, multi-stemmed clump, can be trained into a single-trunked specimen with persistence. This willow is a messy, weak-wooded tree like cottonwood, so plant it away from buildings. Consider it a great choice for a fast-growing wildlife tree for the back forty if the site is suitably moist.

Propagation: cuttings; fresh seed (light) | **Companion plants:** none

Resources

Reading

Ackerfield, Jennifer. ***Flora of Colorado***. 2nd ed. Fort Worth, Texas: BRIT Press, Fort Worth Botanic Garden, Botanical Research Institute of Texas, 2022.

American Rock Garden Society, Rocky Mountain Chapter and Denver Botanic Gardens. ***Rocky Mountain Alpines: Choice Rock Garden Plants of the Rocky Mountains in the Wild and in the Garden***. Portland, Oregon: Timber Press, 1986.

Barr, Claude A. ***Jewels of the Plains: Wildflowers of the Great Plains, Grasslands, and Hills***, rev. ed. Edited by James H. Locklear. Minneapolis, Minnesota: University of Minnesota Press, 2015.

Bonnicksen, Thomas M. ***America's Ancient Forests: From the Ice Age to the Age of Discovery***. New York: John Wiley & Sons, Inc., 2000.

Busco, Jan and Nancy R. Morin. ***Native Plants for High-Elevation Western Gardens***. 2nd ed. Lakewood, Colorado: Fulcrum Publishing, 2010.

Denver Botanic Gardens. ***Wildflowers of the Rocky Mountain Region***. Portland, Oregon: Timber Press, 2018.

Kartesz, J.T., The Biota of North America Program (BONAP). 2015. North American Plant Atlas. (http://bonap.net/napa). Chapel Hill, North Carolina: maps generated from Kartesz, J.T. Floristic Synthesis of North America, Version 1.0. Biota of North America Program (BONAP), 2015.

Lady Bird Johnson Wildflower Center—University of Texas at Austin. wildflower.org, 2023.

National Audubon Society. audubon.org, 2024.

Nold, Robert. ***High and Dry: Gardening with Cold-Hardy Dryland Plants***. Portland, Oregon: Timber Press, 2008.

SEINet Portal Network. swbiodiversity.org/seinet/index.php, 2024.

Tallamy, Douglas W. ***Bringing Nature Home: How Native Plants Sustain Wildlife in Our Gardens***. Portland, Oregon: Timber Press, 2007.

United States Department of Agriculture Natural Resources Conservation Service. PLANTS Database, plants.usda.gov/home.

United States Department of Agriculture Plant Hardiness Zone Map, 2023. Agricultural Research Service, United States Department of Agriculture. Accessed from planthardiness.ars.usda.gov.

United States Department of Transportation Federal Highway Administration, Ecoregional Revegetation Application (ERA), accessed 2025. nativerevegetation.org.

United States Geological Survey. ***Climate: Past as Prologue for Ponderosa Pines***. U.S. Department of the Interior, 2022. usgs.gov/news/national-news-release/climate-past-prologue-ponderosa-pines.

Wild Ones Front Range Chapter, ***Germination Guide for Native Seeds***, Jan Midgley, 2024. frontrange.wildones.org/wp-content/images/sites/105/2024/07/Germination-Guide-7924-pdf.pdf.

Xerces Society for Invertebrate Conservation. ***Attracting Native Pollinators: Protecting North America's Bees and Butterflies***. North Adams, Massachusetts: Storey Publishing, 2011.

Xerces Society for Invertebrate Conservation. xerces.org, 2006–2024.

Seed

Many states have their own native plant societies that act as hubs for sharing information as well as seeds and plants. Public gardens are also great resources for learning about native plants, allowing visitors to see them planted in designs, take classes, and take part in periodic plant sales/swaps. Some of these sources also sell plants mail-order.

ALPLAINS Seed Catalog. Huge spread of unique offerings from across the West. Sold in small packets. alplains.com

High Country Gardens. Bulk seed by species and in mixes, packets. highcountrygardens.com

Native American Seed. Variety of offerings from the southern Great Plains. seedsource.com

North American Rock Garden Society. Membership includes access to a massively diverse, cross-country seed exchange with other members. nargs.org

Pawnee Buttes Seed Inc. Seeds of prairie plants in both small and large quantities. pawneebuttesseed.com

Plants of the Southwest. One of the first to offer a wide variety of natives, this nursery is still among the best for native seeds. plantsofthesouthwest.com

Prairie Legacy, Inc. Seeds of many prairie and western plants in small and large quantities. prairielegacyinc.com

Prairie Moon Nursery. Seeds of many prairie plants in small and large quantities. prairiemoon.com

Prairie Nursery. Seeds of many prairie plants in small and large quantities. prairienursery.com

Western Native Seed. Diverse offerings of many western natives. westernnativeseed.com

Wild Ones. Local and regional seed swaps and information-sharing focused on regionally native plants. wildones.org

Acknowledgments

We would like to thank the following friends, collaborators, colleagues, and partners for helping make this book possible.

Bryan would first like to thank Derek von Drehle, who gave thoughtful daily support as partner and counsel through the writing process and regularly helped find plants that needed photographs, even on picnic dates.. Bryan would also like to thank Amanda Sammartino, who provided valuable feedback and superb editing for Bryan during early parts of his writing process.

Lauren thanks her partner Michael Hoffman for his cheerful, humorous support during the slog that is book writing. She also wants to call out her friends Kelly Grummons and the late Dave Salman, with whom she spent many happy times botanizing in the wild over the past thirty-five years.

Bryan and Lauren would both like to thank plantsman Mike Kintgen, who served as a much-valued resource for our plant profiles and allowed photography in his home gardens; Sherry Fuller and Scott Skogerboe, two of our region's finest propagators, who contributed their knowledge to our plant profiles, with Sherry also allowing photographs in her home garden; native plant propagator Stephen Hornbeck, who opened his home garden for photographs; and nurserymen and plant breeders Nich Boynton-Steele and Robb Smith, who provided valued counsel for our work. We also want to thank our talented and extremely patient copy editor Ellen Foreman for going above and beyond in beautifully parsing our enthusiastic, overly verbose verbiage to fit into this tome, and Timber Press staff, including Ryan Harrington, Senior Acquisitions Editor, and Matt Burnett, Senior Production Editor, for their strong and steady support and ideas for the project.

Photo Credits

All photos are by the authors except for those on page 8, thanks to Mike Kintgen, and page 302, thanks to Derek von Drehle.

Index

Page numbers in **bold** indicate plant profile on the corresponding page.

© Derek von Drehle

Bryan Fischer has been a gardener since he could hold a shovel. Now he is the Curator of Plant Collections for the Gardens on Spring Creek in Fort Collins, where he designed a half-acre Prairie Garden that has garnered national and international attention. Outside of the public garden realm, Bryan breeds and selects especially garden-worthy forms of native plants that retain their wildlife value, botanizes in wild spaces, and writes, speaks, and teaches regionally and nationally. Bryan is a regular contributor to *Fine Gardening*. He keeps a personal garden where he trials both design concepts and his new plant introductions. Bryan was a 2025 recipient of the Individual Partner Award from the non-profit Plant Select, recognizing his work forwarding sustainable gardening in the Rocky Mountain region.

Lauren Springer jumpstarted her career with the book *The Undaunted Garden*, her waterwise hellstrips, and the WaterSmart Garden she designed at Denver Botanic Gardens. She recently received the 2025 American Horticultural Society Landscape Design award. Other designs of note are at Denver Botanic Gardens' Chatfield Farms, Santa Fe Botanical Garden, and the Gardens on Spring Creek in Fort Collins. Also a propagator, she holds a master's degree in horticulture and has introduced numerous plants to the nursery trade. Her work is featured regularly in national and international books, programs, newspapers, and magazines. Through her plantings, writing, speaking, and plant introductions, Lauren continues to help move the Rocky Mountain region toward a more plant-rich, creature-supportive, beautiful and resilient future.